JONATHAN EDWARDS AND THE METAPHYSICS OF SIN

The great New England philosopher and theologian would not fail to have been impressed by Oliver Crisp's philosophical engagement with a central theme of his thought. Crisp's sympathetic treatment of Edwards' concept of sin is thorough, insightful and scrupulously fair. A book of the highest standard which will be of great interest to any philosophical theologian.
—Paul Helm, Professor Emeritus of the History and Philosophy of Religion, King's College, London and J.I. Packer Professor of Philosophy and Theology, Regent College, Vancouver, Canada

Jonathan Edwards (1703–1758) is widely regarded as America's greatest philosopher-theologian. In the last half century there has been a resurgence of interest in Edwards' work from historians, theologians and philosophers, aided by the publication of the Yale edition of Edwards' *Works*.

Edwards' thinking on sin has long been a mystery to scholars trying to fit his thought into the traditional categories of Reformed theology. What this study shows is that Edwards' theory of sin was an original contribution to philosophical theology, which can only be understood when read on its own terms as a philosophical theory about the nature of sin, its origin and transmission. This constitutes a substantial contribution to the literature on Edwards and, more broadly, to philosophical theology in general.

For my beloved

Jonathan Edwards and the Metaphysics of Sin

OLIVER D. CRISP
University of Notre Dame, Indiana, USA

LONDON AND NEW YORK

First published 2005 by Ashgate Publishing

2 Park Square, Milton Park, Abingdon, Oxon OX14 4RN
711 Third Avenue, New York, NY 10017, USA

Routledge is an imprint of the Taylor & Francis Group, an informa business

First issued in paperback 2017

Copyright © 2005 Oliver D. Crisp

Oliver D. Crisp has asserted his moral right under the Copyright, Designs and Patents Act, 1988, to be identified as the author of this work.

All rights reserved. No part of this book may be reprinted or reproduced or utilised in any form or by any electronic, mechanical, or other means, now known or hereafter invented, including photocopying and recording, or in any information storage or retrieval system, without permission in writing from the publishers.

Notice:
Product or corporate names may be trademarks or registered trademarks, and are used only for identification and explanation without intent to infringe.

British Library Cataloguing in Publication Data
Crisp, Oliver
  Jonathan Edwards and the metaphysics of sin
  1. Edwards, Jonathan, 1703–1758 – Contributions in
  hamartiology 2. Sin
  I. Title
  230.5'8'092

Library of Congress Cataloging-in-Publication Data
Crisp, Oliver.
  Jonathan Edwards and the metaphysics of sin / Oliver D. Crisp.
    p. cm.
  Includes bibliographical references and index.
  ISBN 0-7546-3896-0 (alk. paper)
  1. Edwards, Jonathan, 1703–1758. 2. Sin. I. Title.

  BX7260.E3C667 2004
  233'.14'092—dc22

2004007850

ISBN 978-0-7546-3896-4 (hbk)
ISBN 978-1-138-25174-8 (pbk)

Typeset in Times by J.L. & G.A. Wheatley Design, Aldershot, Hampshire.

Contents

Acknowledgements	vii
Abbreviations	ix

Introduction		1
	The Task of the Present Work	2
1	**The Divine Decrees**	5
	Distinguishing Supra- and Infralapsarianism	5
	Edwards on Election and Reprobation	7
	Appraising Edwards' Argument	16
	A Fatally Flawed Argument?	18
	Supralapsarian After All?	20
	Conclusion	22
2	**Adam's Fall**	25
	The Problem of Primal Sin	25
	Moral Agency and Original Righteousness	26
	Edwards' Two Accounts of the Fall	28
	Excursus: The Preference, Desire and Determination of the Will	33
	Summary of Edwards' Argument	40
	Adam's Self-deception	43
	Is Edwards' Account of the Fall Coherent?	45
3	**The Authorship of Sin**	54
	The Authorship Problem	54
	The Edwardsian Axis	55
	Tu Quoque	57
	Three Problems for the Edwardsian AP	61
	Comments on the Proxy Problem	66
4	**The Secret and Revealed Will of God**	79
	The Secret and Revealed Will of God	79
	Divine Commands and Insincerity	80
	Edwardsian Counter-arguments	81
	Conclusion: Does Edwards Solve the AP?	91

vi   *Jonathan Edwards and the Metaphysics of Sin*

5	**Temporal Parts and Imputed Sin**	96
	Chisholm on Edwards	96
	The 'Federal' Aspect to Edwards' Doctrine	101
	Temporal Parts and Perdurantism	104
6	**Inherited Guilt**	113
	The Defensibility of Inherited Guilt	113
	The Legal and Moral Bond Involved in Inherited Guilt	114
	The Perdurantist Element to Edwardsian Inherited Guilt	116
	Assessing Wainwright's Argument	119
7	**The Problem with Occasionalism**	130
	Occasionalism: The Fatal Flaw	130
	A Chastened Edwardsian Metaphysics	133

Appendix: The Imputation of Christ's Righteousness	137
Bibliography	141
Index	145

Acknowledgements

The following people have made this book possible: Paul Helm, my doctoral supervisor, whose guidance and friendship along the way has been invaluable; Profs William Wainwright, Peter Byrne, Martin Stone and the late Colin Gunton for their encouragement of the work, and, in the case of William Wainwright in particular, reading through and commenting on parts of the book in draft to my considerable benefit; Drs Daniel Hill, Steve Guthrie, Steve Holmes, John Bombaro, Anthony Garrood, Mark Nelson and Richard Fermer, all of whom have read, commented on, or helped with various points of argument. Prof. Kenneth Minkema of Yale University was most helpful at several points in chasing up references to unpublished *Miscellanies*, and offering his advice on matters Edwardsian. Miss Rosemary Smith was an invaluable help at early stages of the project with secretarial assistance. The publishers were also very patient with my various delays.

I should also like to record my thanks to several institutions for their support: The Whitefield Institute, Oxford; the Royal Grammar School, Guildford, and Chertsey Street Baptist Church, Guildford. None of the above mentioned persons or institutions are responsible for any errors that remain. An earlier temporal part of me is.

Abbreviations

The Yale edition of the works of Jonathan Edwards is still in process. Where works in this edition are cited in the endnotes, they are given as *YE*, followed by volume number, colon, and page reference, for example, *YE1*: 21. Two of these volumes, *YE1* and *YE3*, are cited in the body of the text as *FOW* (*Freedom of the Will*) and *OS* (*Original Sin*), respectively. A list of the Yale edition volumes cited in the text is given in the bibliography.

Introduction

In the past few decades there has been a renaissance in philosophical theology. In particular, there has been an increasing interest from analytic philosophers in the analysis of theological doctrines.[1] Alongside this, there has been a renewed interest from philosophers in classical theologians of the past, who have often wrestled with the philosophical issues that their theological commitments raise, with a greater rigour and sophistication than some modern theology does.[2] These thinkers have become dialogue partners, and resources for addressing contemporary philosophical concerns. This concatenation of philosophical and historical interests means that the study of Jonathan Edwards from the perspective of philosophical theology may draw on an increasing body of specialized literature which tackles many of the issues Edwards was interested in, with a technical rigour that Edwards would have wholeheartedly approved of.

This book is an attempt to assess Edwards' theological contribution on the concept of sin, or hamartiology, an area of his work that he thought through with considerable care, from the perspective of this particular philosophical literature. What he had to say on the metaphysics of the fall, original sin, guilt and the imputation of sin were highly original contributions to philosophical theology that are far from being facile or merely antique. In each of these areas of sin he sought to rethink traditional Reformed doctrines in light of early Enlightenment philosophy in ways that took him beyond the boundaries of his own theological tradition in important respects.

However, this should not be taken to suggest that Edwards' hamartiology was a break with that tradition. What is presented herein is not a 'strange new Edwards'.[3] He strove to make the puritanical doctrinal legacy relevant in the very different conditions in which he found himself. That meant reformulation and development, but not, as far as he was concerned, departure from that tradition. Nevertheless, the developments he instituted were important, and were linked with central tenets of the whole of his philosophical and theological vision, such as his occasionalism and idealism.[4]

What emerges from this study is a picture of sustained and careful thought about a central and defining cluster of philosophical issues pertaining to Christian theology. Edwards was not able, in the final analysis, to reconcile different aspects of his view of sin into one coherent whole. Nor was he able to resolve to his own satisfaction, problems that remained with respect to the content of the doctrines themselves. But what he did do was raise the standard of discussion about this cluster of issues to a new level of limpidity and philosophical acuity. In doing so, he clarified what the central problems are that philosophical theologians need to attend to in their analyses of sin. And this, I submit, is no small contribution to the ongoing discussion.

2 *Jonathan Edwards and the Metaphysics of Sin*

Philosophers and theologians would do well to take the Edwardsian doctrine of sin a great deal more seriously.

The Task of the Present Work

This is not the first exploration of Edwards' doctrine of sin in the literature.[5] But prior to this study, there has not been a comprehensive account of the metaphysics that Edwards used to underpin his doctrine of sin. The present volume sets out to remedy this lacuna. However, this is not simply a critical exposition of Edwards' hamartiology. There are other places that the reader may find such an account.[6] Instead, this is an analysis of the central structures of the metaphysics of sin in Edwards' philosophical theology. These central structures comprise (a) the doctrine of the divine decrees, (b) the problem of accounting for the first (human) sin, (c) the question of the authorship of sin, (d) the problem of the imputation of sin and (e) the question of original guilt.

Axiomatic to Edwards' discussion of sin are several issues that are now hotly contested. For instance, he believed in the Calvinistic notion of the depravity of humanity. That is, he believed that all human agents are born with a vitiated moral nature that prevents them from ever turning to God without divine grace enabling them so to do. The whole force of his treatise *Original Sin* (hereinafter *OS*) was to defend this notion against what he saw as 'Arminian' intrusions into the common, Reformed opinion in these matters.[7] We shall not be assessing whether Edwards' doctrine of depravity is defensible, but whether central structures in his doctrine of sin that rely upon this notion that all human agents are inherently sinful, yield a coherent whole or not. It seems to me that if these structures can be made to work together, then Edwards will have gone some considerable way towards demonstrating that his intuition about depravity was at least plausible.

A second contentious issue that Edwards assumed to be true in his discussions of sin was a pre-critical view of the inspiration and authority of Scripture. This means that, when he discusses the fall of Adam and Eve, he assumes that this is a historic event, and that the narrative of the primeval prologue of Genesis 1–3 is a historically accurate account of how Adam and Eve fell. It might be thought that the very fact that Edwards believed this means that his doctrine of original sin can no longer have a constructive use in current theological discussions on the nature of sin. However, this is an overhasty conclusion. Whether one takes the view that the fall is historic or not, the questions Edwards raises about the coherence of traditional problems in hamartiology, such as the fall, still require an answer from contemporary theologians. And it does not appear that one has to assent to Edwards' assumptions on the inspiration and authority of Scripture to find his arguments useful tools in contemporary reflection upon these issues, any more than one need believe that the ontological argument is a coherent, independent argument for the existence of God, to think that Anselm's perfect being theology has important and ongoing insights for contemporary philosophical

Introduction 3

theologians. Edwards' thinking on sin still has much of value for contemporary philosophical theologians.

The present work falls into several parts. To begin with, we shall examine Edwards' doctrine of the divine decrees that lie behind what he has to say about the nature of sin. We shall see that what he has to say about the divine decrees has important implications for the rest of his discussion of sin in the created order. Then, we shall turn to the analysis of the doctrine of the fall and the origin of sin. This involves considering related issues pertaining to the fall, the authorship of sin and the secret and revealed will of God. We then proceed to outline his theology of imputation, before assessing the coherence of his doctrines of original sin, original guilt and its imputation. In so doing, we shall have to take a tour of the doctrine of temporal parts and recent philosophical reflection on this, as well as touching on issues of personal identity and identity through time. Finally, there is an assessment of Edwards' contribution to philosophical theology on the doctrine of sin, with particular reference to Edwards' doctrine of occasionalism.

Oliver D. Crisp,
Center for the Philosophy of Religion,
University of Notre Dame, Indiana

Notes

1 Examples abound. Here are a sample of three recent authors: Swinburne's *Responsibility and Atonement*, Jonathan L. Kvanvig's *The Problem of Hell* and Thomas Morris' *The Logic of God Incarnate*.

2 Once again, there are a plethora of examples. Here is a small sample: Marilyn McCord Adams' work on Ockham and Anselm; the renewed interest in Molina from those concerned with issues surrounding Middle Knowledge, such as Alfred Freddoso and Thomas Flint; the theological appropriation of Leibniz by Robert Adams; the interest in Augustine across a wide range of fields. See, in this regard, *The Augustinian Tradition*, ed. Gareth B. Matthews, and the use of Edwards in particular by Roderick Chisholm, Philip Quinn, William Wainwright, Jonathan Kvanvig, Hugh McCann, Alvin Plantinga and Paul Helm.

3 At least one recent monograph has sought to demonstrate just this with respect to Edwards' views on the unregenerate and their eternal destiny. See Gerald McDermott, *Jonathan Edwards Confronts the Gods* and the review of this by Oliver D. Crisp in *International Journal of Systematic Theology*.

4 Occasionalism is the doctrine that God re-creates everything that exists out of nothing, at each moment, coupled with a causal thesis, that God alone is the sole causal agent of all things. For present purposes, idealism is the view that the world consists of ideas and minds perceiving these ideas. There is no material substance to speak of.

5 The most important previous study is C. Samuel Storms, *Tragedy in Eden: Original Sin in the Theology of Jonathan Edwards*. However, Storms' treatment is almost exclusively historical and theological in content. His work is concerned to trace the difference between Edwards' work in *Original Sin* and that of Edwards' opponent, John Taylor. They are, according to Storms, typical of the debate between New England Calvinistic Protestantism and Enlightenment deistic and Arminian thought respectively. The present study is not concerned with the historical detail of Edwards' milieu. It is a philosophical treatment of a family of theological doctrines that Edwards spent a considerable amount of his time in defending in his later treatises.

6   See, for example, John H. Gerstner, *The Rational Biblical Theology of Jonathan Edwards, Volume II*, chapters XX–XIV.

7   It is not clear that Edwards set himself against classical Arminianism, which, as Paul Ramsey explains, maintained that 'the Divine decrees were conditional, or dependent on God's foreknowledge of the faith in believers, and that Christ's atonement made possible, although not actual, the salvation of everyone'. It seems that by the eighteenth century, '"Arminianism" became but a loose term for all forms of the complaint of the aggrieved moral nature against the hard tenets of Calvinism', Ramsey, Editor's Introduction, *YE1*: 3.

CHAPTER 1

The Divine Decrees

The doctrine of the divine decrees can often appear to be more than a little arcane to contemporary students of theology. What do we mean by a 'divine decree'? What has God decreed? Does he ordain all things that come to pass, and if he does, in what order does he ordain them?

These are just some of the questions that a doctrine of the divine decrees raises. What Edwards has to say on this matter is far from being *merely* abstract. His views on what God decrees had an important impact on what he believed about other aspects of the doctrine of sin. As is often the case in theology, what is said in one place about one theological issue affects what is said about another topic in another area of theology. And Edwards was certainly a thinker who sought to bring together his reflections on theological *loci* into an integrated whole. Hence, what he says about what God decrees to come to pass will affect what he has to say about what actually does come to pass in the creation, with respect to the doctrine of sin.

There has been some debate about whether Edwards endorsed a *supra-*, or *infra*lapsarian position with respect to the doctrine of predestination. This chapter seeks to ascertain which of these two positions Edwards actually opted for. We shall see that this is particularly important as it bears upon two related problems that we shall encounter in the course of later discussion on sin: *how Adam sinned* and *the origin of sin*, the subjects of Chapters 2 and 3 respectively.

We shall proceed through four stages to a conclusion. The first sets out the problem at issue. The second offers a reading of Edwards' views on the matter. The third section seeks to analyse whether Edwards' solution is viable, in light of two recent accounts of Edwards' position on the divine decrees and election. The fourth section sets out Edwards' argument and shows that, as it stands, Edwards' argument is fatally flawed. In its place, I suggest that Edwards would have been more consistent if he had defended a purely supralapsarian position.

Distinguishing Supra- and Infralapsarianism

Let us begin by clarifying some key terms. I take it that a divine decree is a product of God's ordaining that such-and-such a thing will, or will not come to pass. If God decrees that a thing will or will not be, it will or will not be. There is no possibility that God might ordain and decree that a particular thing comes to pass, and that thing not come to pass. Thus, once God ordains a particular thing will happen, it must happen. For God's will, according to theologians like Edwards, cannot be frustrated by the interference of created beings. Such a view of a divine decree might well be controversial today, but it has been relatively uncontroversial in the Reformed tradition of which Edwards was a representative. For the sake of brevity, I shall simply assume henceforth that this concept of a divine decree is coherent, though it may be controversial.

We come next to supra- and infralapsarianism. For the purposes of the present argument, supralapsarianism is the view that the decree to redeem the elect and damn the reprobate is followed by the decree to permit the fall. By contrast, infralapsarianism is the notion that God decrees creation, the permission of the fall and election and reprobation in that order. Both these notions involve problems about the ordering of the divine decrees. Both are concerned with the priority of certain decrees in the election and reprobation of humanity over others. But whether one decree is antecedent to another involves a *logical*, not *temporal* discrimination. This is an important distinction for what follows, so it is worth pausing to note what these two notions involve.

A logical distinction seeks to tease out the different logical connections there are in a particular issue, and allots priority to those aspects of a problem that are antecedent to those which arise as a result of, or are consequent upon them. So, for example, an argument printed in a philosophy textbook has premises that lead to a conclusion. The order of the argument is logical (the premises are antecedent to the conclusion, from which the conclusion arises). Nevertheless the whole argument exists all at once, temporally speaking. If I read it in a textbook, the premises and conclusion are all present before my eyes, because they do not exist as discrete *temporal events*. By contrast, if I were to utter the premises and conclusion of a particular argument in, say, a debate with a friend in defence of my views, I should be expressing the parts of the argument in a way that had a chronological (that is, temporal), as well as logical order. For my uttering the first premise (whatever it might be), and the second and subsequent premises and conclusion takes time, each being a temporal event that follows in a chronological sequence. The first premise is uttered at a first moment, the second premise at a second moment and the conclusion at a third moment in time.

With respect to the divine decrees, it is the *logical* sequence and priority of the decrees with respect to election and reprobation that are the subject of what follows. The question of whether one decree follows another *chronologically* as a temporal event is a secondary issue.

The logical sequence of God's predestinating decrees is itself a fascinating and important question, particularly as it bears upon the issue of sin. The question before us is this: *did God ordain the election of the redeemed and the reprobation of the damned before the fall, or after the fall?*[1] If before, then this raises several significant problems for a concept of God. It seems to mean that God ordains evil, raising the question of the authorship of sin, the subject of Chapter 3. It also calls into question the character of the God who ordains this sin, for whom the fall is merely the consequence of his logically prior decree. But if God ordains reprobation post-fall, other, equally grave questions are raised about the divine nature: does God have to somehow 'react' to the sins of his free creatures, putting the incarnation and passion

The Divine Decrees 7

of Christ in place as a kind of fall-back measure because of the fall? If so, what does this say about divine omniscience and wisdom?[2]

The logical structure of the traditional supralapsarian view of the divine decrees proceeds on the basis of the maxim (taken up by Edwards), '*what is first in design is last in accomplishment*'. This means that the first proposition in the divine decrees with respect to his creation/creatures is the end in view, to which all other decrees are the means. This yields the following logical sequence of decrees:[3]

(1)   The decree of divine self-glorification in
    (a)   the salvation of the elect as a manifestation of divine grace and mercy,
    (b)   the reprobation of the damned as a manifestation of divine justice and wrath.

The constituents of (1a) and (1b) exist potentially, as ideas in the divine mind, not actually in the real world (although for Edwards, the real world is an ideal world).[4]

(2)   The decree to elect (1a) and reprobate (1b).
(3)   The decree to permit the elect and reprobate to fall.
(4)   The decree to justify the elect and condemn the non-elect.

By contrast, infralapsarians have traditionally suggested the following order that, as they see it, better fit a biblical chronology:

(1')   The decree to create man holy and complete.
(2')   The decree to permit man to fall by the self-determination of his own will.
(3')   The decree to save a certain number of humanity.
(4')   The decree to pass over the remainder of humanity for the purposes of salvation, punishing them for their sin instead.

The difference between these two conceptions of the divine decrees should now be clear. With this in mind, we can turn to a consideration of Edwards' views on the matter.

Edwards on Election and Reprobation

Edwards does not set out a systematic presentation of his arguments on this issue. What he does say has to be gleaned from several *Miscellany* entries, specifically numbers *292*, *700* and *704*, and related work in his dissertation, *End of Creation*.[5] It is to these sources that we now turn in order to ascertain Edwards' position on this matter.

Edwards on Miscellany 292[6]

As Edwards sees it, the dispute about the divine decrees and the fall concerns (a) whether the creation and fall of humanity are appointed for the salvation of some and

8 *Jonathan Edwards and the Metaphysics of Sin*

damnation of others respectively; (b) whether salvation and damnation are the end for which the creation and fall of humanity are the means; and (c) whether creation and fall are *appointed* as means to that end.

According to Edwards, the '*what is first in design is last in accomplishment*' principle is true with respect to the end and means to that end in God's decrees, but not with respect to every prerequisite condition for that end.[7] This sounds as though Edwards is trying to avoid the fallacy of division. This fallacy can be expressed in the following way: if the constituents A, B, C, D are together the means to the end of E, it does not follow from this that each individual constituent of the group A, B, C, D is by itself the means to E. So A is not by itself the means to E, nor B, to E, nor C to E and so on. What needs to be distinguished is

> . . . that man's creation and fall were intended last with respect to his last end, but not with respect to his subordinate ends; because they are proper means of the last end, but not [of] his third or fourth or fifth end – for at this rate, man was created for this end, that he might repent! But we are to conceive of things in this order; that that is first in execution is last in intention with respect to the ultimate end; that that is second in execution is last in intention with respect to the next end, etc.[8]

There seem to be three 'ends' in view here: the last, the subordinate and the ultimate. We can express this as three principles:

(i)   *The ultimate end of a thing* – an end valued for its own sake, such as God's self-glorification.
(ii) *The last end of a thing* – what is aimed at throughout a sequence of events, such as the redemption of the elect.
(iii) *Subordinate ends of a thing* – stages towards that last end. These are the proper means of that last end, but not of the other subordinate ends, such as regeneration.

Edwards does not clearly define (i) in the text of *Miscellany 292*, but he does do so in *End of Creation*, to which we shall come in a moment, and from which the working definition (above) is drawn.[9] Nor, in the text of *Miscellany 292*, does he clearly distinguish between (i) and (ii). He seems to use them interchangeably. Once again, it is in *End of Creation* that he differentiates these two ends with more care.

Nevertheless, we can apply these three principles to God's purposes for his creatures, in the context of *Miscellany 292*. Regarding humanity, creation is for the ultimate end of God's glory, for which creation is the means. All subordinate things decreed of man, including conversion, are towards this goal, because all such subordinate ends are the means to that last end. So the fall is a subordinate end to the glorification of God, the last end of all things. To illustrate this point, consider Trevor (an everyman). If his creation is the means to the greater glory of God (the last and ultimate end), then the intermediate end of Trevor's conversion along the way to this last end is a subordinate end. As a subordinate end it is the proper means of the last end (God's

The Divine Decrees　　　9

glory), but not of other intermediate, or subordinate ends, such as being born, or dying, or whatever. Nor, from what we have seen of Edwards' tacit appeal to the fallacy of division, is a subordinate end a separate means to an ultimate end, but only one of a coordinate set of means to that end (as A, B, C, D are the coordinate set of means to the end of E, but not individually separate means to E). This means that Trevor's creation, birth, development, conversion and so on, are *together* the means to the end of God's greater glory. But it is not the case that each of these constituents is *by themselves* the means to this end. Trevor's development is the means to his understanding the Gospel, which is the means to his conversion and so on. It is only taken together that they are the means to the end of God's glory. So, God does not intend Trevor's conversion prior to intending his creation, although his conversion is later in execution, and, on a permissive application of the *'what is first in design is last in accomplishment'* principle, would appear to mean this. In fact, creation is not the proper means of the conversion of Trevor, nor did God create Trevor to be converted. He created Trevor for his own greater glory. Hence, the *'what is first in design is last in accomplishment'* principle, has a restricted, rather than permissive application, as per (i), Edwards' definition of an ultimate end, and, if he is using (i) interchangeably with (ii), (ii), the last end of a thing, but not (iii), the subordinate end of a thing. As Edwards has it, 'that that is first in execution is last in intention with respect to the ultimate end; that that is second in execution is last in intention with respect to the next end, etc'.[10]

Edwards and End of Creation

We turn now, for clarification about the 'ends' to which Edwards refers in *Miscellany 292*, to Edwards' discussion of 'ends' in his dissertation on the end of creation.[11] What he has to say in *End of Creation* about different kinds of 'ends' that inform particular tasks, and God's work in creation in particular, considerably augments the previous discussion of *Miscellany 292*. So, Edwards says:

> A distinction should be observed between the *chief* end for which an agent or efficient exerts any act and performs any work, and the *ultimate* end. These two phrases are not always precisely of the same signification; and though the chief end be always an ultimate end, yet every ultimate end is not always a chief end. A chief end is opposite to an inferior end; an ultimate end is opposite to a subordinate end.[12]

From this, and the passage that follows it in *End of Creation*, we can set out a taxonomy of different sorts of 'ends'. There are *chief* ends and *ultimate* ends. Chief ends are always ultimate ends, the opposite of which are *inferior* ends. But ultimate ends are not always chief ends. The opposite of an ultimate end is a *subordinate* end. On clarifying what he means by chief and ultimate ends, Edwards says that chief ends are what are *most valued*, whilst ultimate ends are that end most valued *for its own sake*. This initial characterization can be developed in two ways in particular. First, *two different ends may both be ultimate ends, but not chief ends.* This could occur where two different ends are both valued for their own sakes (that is, are not subordinated to each other, or one to another, in some way), but one is more valued than another.

Edwards gives the example of a man going on a journey that has two ends in view: to see a new-fangled telescope, and to acquire a bride. Both of these 'ends' are ultimate according to the principles he has set out; neither is subordinate to the other, and both are distinct ends in view of which he sets out on his journey in the first place. But the chief end of the trip is to get his bride, whilst the inferior end is the visit to the telescope (though, of course, some dedicated bachelor-astronomers might dispute this ordering of ends).

A second amplification of his distinction between chief ends and ultimate ends, is that *an ultimate end is not always a chief end because some subordinate ends may be more sought after than some ultimate ends.* Here, the example given is of a man going on another visit with two distinct, non-subordinated purposes. The first is to visit some friends. The second is to claim an inheritance. The claiming of the inheritance is a subordinate end only. This is because the money this man stands to gain out of the inheritance is not sought after in and of itself, as an end in itself, but only as a means to the end of a more plutocratic lifestyle. It is this lifestyle that the inheritance promises to facilitate, that is the ultimate end in view in this instance. Yet getting the money from the inheritance may be a higher, more sought after 'end', than seeing the man's friends, even though visiting them is valued by the man on its own account, and not on account of something else, thereby fulfilling the criteria for being an ultimate end. So in this second amplification, the subordinate end of getting the inheritance is more sought after than the ultimate end of seeing the friends.[13]

However, Edwards immediately qualifies this by saying, somewhat paradoxically, that *a subordinate end is not more valued than the ultimate end(s) to which it is subordinate.*[14] What he seems to mean is this: though a subordinate end may be more sought after than an ultimate end, that ultimate end is what gives the subordinate end value, since it is subordinated to the ultimate end that it is directed towards. So though a subordinate end may be more sought after than an ultimate end, it is still subordinated to that ultimate end, such that that ultimate end is the end to which the subordinate end is directed.

He concludes the final chapter of *End of Creation*, by showing that God's chief (most valued) end is the sum of his ultimate ends in creating, and these ultimate ends (valued for their own sakes) are jointly his one chief end. In other words, the apparently different ultimate ends that are mentioned in Scripture that God has in view in creating (divine self-communication in revelation of truth and of grace, for example), differ in *sense*, but not *reference*. They all *refer* to the same chief end. This end is, of course, God's self-glorification: 'Thus we see that the great and last end of God's works which is so variously expressed in Scripture, is indeed but one; and this one end is most properly and comprehensively called, "the glory of God"; by which name it is most commonly called in Scripture.'[15] From this, it seems that Edwards' use of ultimate/ last and subordinate ends in *Miscellany 292* has matured by the time he comes to

The Divine Decrees

write *End of Creation*. In *End of Creation*, the term 'last end', as the end that is aimed at throughout a particular sequence of events still has a place as a kind of generic term for a supreme end in view.[16] But it is the chief end of all God's works, and the ultimate end(s) that culminate in this chief end that are the particular focus of the work: 'To avoid all confusion in our inquiries and reasonings concerning the end for which God created the world, a distinction should be observed between the chief end . . . and the ultimate end. These two phrases are not always precisely of the same signification.'[17]

Taking into account his use of chief and inferior ends in *End of Creation*, and Edwards' conclusion regarding the chief (ultimate) end of all God's works, we may apply this to the supra-infralapsarian problem in the following manner. The decree to elect some of humanity to salvation is a subordinate means to the ultimate end of redemption. The decree to redeem is ultimate inasmuch as it involves the end (valued for its own sake), of displaying divine grace and mercy (to which end election is directed as a subordinate means). This can be seen from what Edwards says in *Miscellany 993*: 'The work of redemption the greatest work of God and the end of all other works, and all God's decrees [are] contained in the Covenant of redemption.'[18] By contrast, the decree to reprobate the rest of humanity is a means to the ultimate end of glorifying his holiness and greatness. This can be clearly seen in *Miscellany 704*: 'God's glorifying his justice, or rather his glorifying his holiness and greatness, has the place of a mere and ultimate end. But his glorifying his justice in punishing sin (or exercising vindictive justice, which is the same) or by any other particular means, is not to be considered as a mere end, but a certain way or means of obtaining an end.'[19]

The decree to glorify divine holiness is ultimate in so far as it involves the end (valued for its own sake), of displaying a central divine attribute: holiness. It is for this very reason that divine justice is, according to Edwards, emphatically not an ultimate end. It is not an attribute, but a means to the display, or expression of an attribute of God:

> Vindictive justice is not to be considered as a certain distinct attribute to be glorified, but as a certain way and means for the glorifying an attribute . . . The considering the glorifying [of] vindictive justice as a mere end, had led to great misrepresentations and undue and unhappy expressions about the decree of reprobation. Hence, the glorifying of God's vindictive justice on such particular persons as has been considered as altogether prior in the decree to their sinfulness; yea [to] their very beings. Whereby it being only a means to an end, those things that are necessarily presupposed in order to the fitness and possibility of this means obtaining the end, must be conceived as prior to it.[20]

Both of these ultimate ends stand under the chief end of all God's acts, his own self-glorification. Redemption is the means by which God is glorified in his grace and mercy, whilst reprobation is the means by which God is glorified in his holiness. Both ultimate ends serve the chief end of God's self-glorification through glorifying different aspects of his divine character.

12   *Jonathan Edwards and the Metaphysics of Sin*

Much in Edwards' account of these different ends depends on the asymmetry of the decrees in election and reprobation as Edwards understands them. This is made clear in two further *Miscellany* entries, *700* and *704*, which we shall consider next.

Edwards on Miscellany 700

Here, Edwards takes up the general outline of *Miscellany 292*, and develops it in line with the asymmetry we have just referred to. He begins by showing that the decree of election, unlike the decree of reprobation, is ordained before any foresight God might have of an individual's works: 'God, in the decree of election, is justly to be considered as decreeing the creature's eternal happiness antecedent to any foresight of good works.'[21]

This means that in election the following proposition is true:

(E1) God decrees creaturely eternal happiness antecedent to, and independently of, any foresight of good works pertaining to those creatures.

This forms part of the traditional Reformed understanding of election. God elects according to his inscrutable will, not according to the good works that any concrete individual will commit at some point in the future. Thus, salvation is according to divine grace via the decree of election, not according to what an individual is able to contribute to their salvation (which, on the Reformed scheme of salvation, is zero).

But the same structure does not apply to propositions which capture the decree of reprobation, as Edwards goes on to point out in the same passage: 'he [God] does not, in reprobation, decree the creature's eternal misery antecedent to any foresight of sin: because the being of sin is supposed in the first things in order in the decree of reprobation, which is that God will glorify his vindictive justice; but the very notion of revenging justice simply considered supposes a fault to be revenged'.[22]

From this, it seems the following is true:

(E2) it is *not* the case that God decrees creaturely eternal misery antecedent to, and independently of, any foresight of sinful works pertaining to those creatures.

For clearly, in reprobation, what a particular concrete individual has done is the crucial factor in their being damned. This, says Edwards, is because the existence and being of sin is assumed in the decree of damnation. God will glorify his vindictive justice in damning some, but this very notion of such justice and its exercise presumes a fault that needs to be punished. The same is not the case with the decree of election. This is because God's glory is the sole consideration in his decree of election, not the works of any particular individuals. Otherwise, his election is not dependent upon his grace alone. Nor, says Edwards, does the exercise of divine grace *require* faith and works. Grace is the communication of divine happiness, not of faith and works. It just so happens, as a contingent matter of fact, that God has ordained this happiness to be communicated via faith and works.[23]

The Divine Decrees

So, it seems that according to Edwards in *Miscellany 700*, (E1) is ordained *supra lapsus*, without regard to the faith and works of the persons concerned, but presumably, with regard to the evil works of these persons, because *qua* elect, they are the objects of divine redemption. But (E2) is ordained *infra lapsus*, taking account of the sin and evil acts of those to whom it is directed.

Edwards is aware of the problems this poses for his Calvinism. If God decrees reprobation *infra lapsus*, then it seems as if this decree is dependent upon what creatures will do, in a way that his decree to elect is not. So, if Trevor is elect, but Wayne is reprobate, Trevor's election is *supra lapsus*, without regard to anything that he might do in the future, but purely because of God's arbitrary choice to redeem him. But Wayne's reprobation does take account of his future sin, and he is reprobated on the basis of his being a sinner in future. However, Edwards is at pains to point out that the (E2) decree does not *depend* on the sinful acts of creatures in the same way as the Arminians claim is the case:

> But yet God is far from having decreed damnation from a foresight of evil works in the sense of the Arminians: as if God in this decree did properly depend on the creature's sinful act, as an event the coming to pass of which primarily depends on the creature's determination; so that the creature's determination in this decree is properly to be looked upon as antecedent to God's determination, and [that] on which his determination is consequent and dependent.[24]

The Arminian position involves this kind of reasoning: God decrees the reprobation of some of fallen humanity. God foresees the sin of this number. This sin is libertarian in nature (that is, his foresight is of contra-causally free decisions, over which God has no control). Therefore, God's decree is dependent upon the contra-causally free decisions of this reprobate number. The problem with this is that if God creates libertarian creatures, how can he foreknow what they will actually choose until they have chosen it? (For if their choices are contra-causal, then it is difficult to see how God can foreknow them with certainty. A person may do one thing rather than another; but they may not. There is no compulsion involved, no sense in which they must do one thing rather than another. It seems that all the Arminian God can know is the probability that a person will opt for one thing rather than another, up to the point at which that person makes the choice they actually do.)

Edwards' Calvinism, which involves a version of theological determinism (the view that God determines all human actions, but that all humans are free to the extent that they are not prevented from or coerced into some action), means he cannot accept this Arminian conclusion. So, although Edwards endorses an (E2) decree *infra lapsus*, it is not to be taken with the libertarian thesis that is part of the Arminian solution to the dilemma of human freedom and divine foreknowledge.

What then does the divine decree of (E2) depend upon? Edwards does not say. But presumably, his point is that, unlike the Arminians who believe that 'God in this decree did properly depend on the creature's sinful act, as an event the coming to pass of which primarily depends on the creature's determination',[25] he believes that (E2)

14   *Jonathan Edwards and the Metaphysics of Sin*

depends upon the sovereign ordination of God alone. If this is the case, then it cannot be contingent upon the foresight of the libertarian sinful acts of those who are reprobate, since God would then be ordaining his decree on the basis of the libertarian actions of his creatures that he foresees, but over which he has no control. Instead, their damnation is according to the inscrutable will of God, which ordains reprobation for all those not elect according to (E1), that is, before the actualization of the creation. But what is more, God also ordains their sin. Their damnation is ordained in light of the foresight of their sin, as (E2) assumes, but this should be understood in a compatibilist sense. That is, God's 'foresight' of sin, is, strictly speaking, no foresight at all, since it is not simply that God sees what the sinner will do and punishes them accordingly with reprobation. He permits the sin they will commit. The Arminian appeal to contra-causal freedom in the decree to reprobate simply cannot obtain on Edwards' determinism. God foresees sin, but this sin is 'permitted' by God's ordination.

The point at issue is whether, in foreseeing damnation and ordaining reprobation on this basis as per (E2), God's decree is dependent on the choices of his creatures, which he has no power over, or whether his decree is merely dependent on sinful choices foreseen, but permitted (here read 'ordained') according to his hidden will. Edwards' opts for the latter of these two options. As we shall see in Chapter 3, this does not enable Edwards to avoid the problem of the authorship of sin (the motivation behind this manoeuvre). For it appears that God is ultimately still the one who ordains the sins that his creatures commit, and whom he then damns for his own greater glory.

Edwards on Miscellany 704

On the matter of the eternal decrees, Edwards writes in this *Miscellany* that

> . . . both the sin of the reprobate, and also the glory of divine justice, may properly be said to be before the decree of damning the reprobate. The decree of damnation may properly be said, in different respects, to be because of both these; and that God would not have decreed the damnation of the sinner, had [it] not been for [the] respect he had both to the one and the other. Both may properly be considered as the ground of the decree of damnation.[26]

He goes on in the same passage to make his views regarding the asymmetry of the divine decrees, and his own mediating position on the matter, absolutely clear: 'Hence God's decree of the eternal damnation of the reprobate is not to be conceived of as prior to the fall, yea, and to the very being of the person; as the decree of the eternal glory of the elect is.' This is because, as Edwards goes on to say, unlike the decree to reprobate, the decree to elect is prior to the very being of the subjects in question. God's desire to glorify himself is his chief end in all his works, and is therefore more than a mere ultimate end (where, as we saw in *End of Creation*, there could be more than one such ultimate end). His decree to elect is based in the desire of God to

The Divine Decrees 15

communicate his glory by his love and goodness. And this divine goodness supplies the being of the elect creature, as well as its happiness. So election is prior to reprobation because election is part of the chief end of God, reprobation being (by implication) an ultimate end only: 'For God's glorifying his love and communicating his goodness stands in the place of a mere or ultimate end, and therefore is prior in the mind of the eternal disposer to the very being of the subject, and to everything but mere possibility. The goodness of God gives the being as well as the happiness of the creature, and don't presuppose it.'[27]

Edwards saw the decree of election as devolving upon the following sequence of divine ordination. Prior to all other decrees is the decree to divine self-glorification, God's 'chief end', as *End of Creation* puts it. Then there is the decree to communicate the fullness of divine goodness and love to the creature. This stands in the place of an ultimate end, and divine goodness and love are the vehicles by which God delivers being and happiness to his creatures, as we have just seen. But divine goodness and love are expressed in terms of God's grace and mercy only *after the fall*. This has to be the case, since grace and mercy presuppose a sinful object requiring the exercise of these two divine attributes (otherwise there would be no need for their exercise). This grace and mercy is delivered to the elect, who are redeemed from the state of misery into which they have fallen *infra lapsus*: 'A decree of glorifying God's mercy and grace considers man as being created and fallen, because the very notion of such a decree supposes a great sin and misery.'[28]

Moreover:

> God's decree to glorify his love and communicate his goodness, and to glorify his greatness and holiness, is to be considered as prior to the creation and fall of man ... the designing to communicate and glorify his goodness and love eternally to a certain number, is to be considered as prior in both those mentioned respects – to their being and fall – for such a design in the notion of it presupposes neither. But nothing in the decree of reprobation is to be looked upon as antecedent in one of those respects to man's being and fall,[29] but only that general decree that God will glorify his justice, or rather his holiness and greatness, which supposes neither their being nor sinfulness.[30]

From these citations, it is clear that, on Edwards' scheme, there is an asymmetry involved in the way the decrees to elect and reprobate particular individuals work out.

In light of what Edwards has to say on the matter, and taking into consideration the prior supra- and infralapsarian arguments of (1)–(4) and (1')–(4') at the beginning of this chapter, we can sum up Edwards' argument as follows.

The decree of election is supralapsarian in the sense laid out in (1)–(2) and (E1), but not according to (1')–(4'), the infralapsarian position. By contrast, the damned are reprobated *infra lapsus*, according to that aspect of (1')–(4'), pertaining to (E2), which excludes (1)–(4). Thus, our analysis has shown that Edwards takes up the supralapsarian view regarding election, and the infralapsarian view regarding reprobation, in an attempt to forge a middle way between these two positions. However, it should

16 *Jonathan Edwards and the Metaphysics of Sin*

already be apparent that this *via media* is fatally flawed. But before analysing how it is flawed, a few words about other recent understandings of Edwards' position.

Appraising Edwards' Argument

There have been several recent attempts at classifying Edwards' argument into one of supra- or infralapsarianism. John Gerstner makes the case for Edwards' being an infralapsarian. He does this principally because he thinks this fits best with Edwards' concerns over the authorship of sin problem: 'One incidental proof that Edwards did not believe God to be the author of sin is his infralapsarianism. According to the supralapsarian view, God rejects the reprobate when considered as unfallen, *homo creabilis*. Edwards will have none of this, as it seems to make God the author of sin in a sinless creature.'[31]

However, from the foregoing assessment of Edwards' argument it should be clear that this is a misunderstanding on Gerstner's part.[32] Edwards' views on this matter are part of a debate in the tradition, where equally prestigious thinkers have taken quite opposite sides. Edwards himself cites two of these in this regard: Turretin and Mastricht.[33] As we have seen, Edwards is better understood as taking a mediating position, where God's decree of election is seen *supra lapsus*, whilst his decree of reprobation is *infra lapsus*. Thus, Gerstner's view is wide of the mark.

However, there have been those in the literature who have discerned the subtlety of Edwards' position. Stephen Holmes, in his recent monograph on Edwards,[34] recognizes that Edwards is engaged in forging a middle way between the two traditional approaches to this question of supra- and infralapsarianism. And he sees that Edwards advocates an asymmetrical relation in the decrees of election and reprobation.

However, whether Edwards answers the question of why, if redemption is God's first thought (logically speaking), the decrees of election and reprobation are asymmetrical in this fashion, is another matter. Holmes seems to think that he does address this problem. He says, 'there is a sense in which Edwards must be described as uncompromisingly supralapsarian after all. Regardless of the place of the decree of reprobation, God's first thought is emphatically that he will redeem, not that he will create.'[35]

I am inclined to think that Edwards' thoughts on the asymmetry of election and reprobation depend upon the kind of argument found in his published views on the matter, in *End of Creation*. There, as we have seen, God's chief and ultimate end in all things is his own self-glorification. This, it seems to me, must stand first in the logical order of the divine decrees for Edwards' position to work. It is only in this context that God can both elect some *supra lapsus*, and reprobate others *infra lapsus*. The reason being that only on this basis can Edwards say that God ordains the decrees in the logical sequence he does for his own glory. If redemption is God's first thought, before his thought of self-glorification, as Holmes suggests on the basis of *Miscellanies* like 993, then this will not work. The (logical) sequence of divine ordination means that redemption is logically consequent on one of (a) God thinks of the world he intends to create, (fore)seeing the need for creaturely redemption in that world (*supra lapsus*), or (b) God creates the world he intends to create, (fore)seeing the need for redemption at the point of the fall (*in lapsu*), or (c) God creates the world he intends to create and ordains the fall, and ordains the redemption of his elect creatures on the basis of the fall (*infra lapsus*). It cannot be God's first thought, as Holmes suggests, since then it would have to be before all three of these options, which does not make any sense.

Moreover, if, logically speaking, redemption was God's first thought, then, on the principle that '*what is first in design is last in accomplishment*', Edwards would be committed to the view that redemption was the chief and ultimate end to which God directed all his decrees. But, according to *End of Creation*, this is simply not the case. (Nor, I might add, does it make much sense eschatologically speaking. Surely the glory of God comes before redemption, since it is the need to safeguard the perfection of the divine glory that gives rise to the impetus to redeem, and the object of everlasting contemplation and praise in heaven, and everlasting horror and revulsion in hell.)

However, this is not what *Miscellany 993* actually says (and here, Holmes' reading of Edwards seems to be at fault too). The text, as Holmes has it, reads: 'the greatest work of God & the end of all other works, and all God's DECREES [are] contained in the Covenant of REDEMPTION'.[36] But this does not entail Holmes' view, that God's desire to redeem is logically first in order of decrees. What it entails is that God's greatest work, greatest in the sense of being the chief and ultimate end of God's works, is *contained* in the covenant of redemption. But this is not a radically new insight at all. Edwards is simply reiterating a standard Reformed doctrine.

Holmes seems to have equivocated on the difference between the *doctrine and act* of redemption (in the cross of Christ), and the *covenant* of redemption. In classical Reformed theology this covenant concerns the agreement, on the part of the second person of the Trinity with the first person of the Trinity, to undergo the humiliation of the incarnation and death on the cross, in order to bring about the salvation of the elect. But this does not mean that redemption was logically the first of God's decrees.

For although this covenant, in Edwardsian language, is the means to the ultimate end of (E1), it is not the chief end of God's decrees. It merely facilitates this chief end, which is the glorification of God. And this chief end is, as the text of *Miscellany 993* suggests, *contained* in the covenant of redemption. It is contained in it, in that it is the *raison d'être* of the covenant of redemption. Redemption is a means to the greater glory of God and this is entailed by the covenant of redemption. Consequently, this important aspect of Holmes' understanding of Edwards' resolution to the supra/infralapsarian problem is at fault. *Miscellany 993* does not say anything different from *End of Creation* on the matter of the logical order of the divine decrees: God's self-glorification is logically prior to all other decrees.

A Fatally Flawed Argument?

We have just seen that Gerstner's reading of Edwards is flawed (Edwards was not a traditional infralapsarian). And Holmes' reading of Edwards is flawed (God's chief end is self-glorification; redemption is the ultimate end to that chief end, it is not the chief end, or the logically first decree). But is Edwards' argument flawed? The answer is that it is, and fatally flawed.

Let us lay out Edwards' argument as we have seen it thus far:

(1") God decrees his self-glorification (chief end) in all his works.
(2") God decrees the outworking of his self-glorification in the redemption of the elect (an ultimate end).

The conjunction of (2") and our earlier principle, (E1), entails:

(3") God decrees the redemption of the elect, without reference to the faith and good works of the elect.

This proposition has an implication that Edwards does not appear to be aware of, but which, we shall see, is a significant problem in his argument. It is this: for a person to be the object of God's redemptive purposes, that person must require redemption. For instance, I cannot decide to buy an item back from a pawnbroker – redeem it – if I have not already pawned it. Perhaps I might foresee a situation in which I will pawn my watch and later redeem it. But the same condition applies, inasmuch as my watch can only be the object of my 'redemptive purpose' if I have pawned it. If I am considering pawning it, knowing I shall later redeem it, I am still only in a position to consider the notion of redeeming it as a consequence of the notion of having pawned it. So, the decree to redeem the elect in (3") requires that:

(4") sinful works are a necessary condition of redemption.

This, we shall see in a moment, is problematic for Edwards. In addition, Edwards maintains that:

(5") God decrees *to permit* the fall and sin of humanity.

Edwards' use of 'to permit' here appears problematic, since, given his theological determinism, he has to say something like:

(6") God decrees the fall and sin of humanity.

However, in order to assess the moral worth of an action, one needs a clear and appropriate understanding of the 'description under which' that action falls. Edwards'

The Divine Decrees 19

use of 'permit' is designed to guide the reader into adopting an appropriate description of God's ordering of the fall and away from other, potential descriptions, such as (6''), and weaker readings, compatible with, say, an Arminian notion of freedom. So, in (5'') Edwards' use of 'permit' flags up the fact that the fall is not something God could have ordained in isolation from the concatenation of events with which it is coordinated. Taken in this circumscribed sense, the use of 'permit' in (5'') stands. In what follows, we shall assume (5''), not (6''), obtains. We may proceed to:

(7'')   God decrees the reprobation of the non-elect.

The conjunction of (7'') and our earlier principle, (E2), entails:

(8'')   God decrees the reprobation of the non-elect taking full account of their sinful works.
(9'')   The decree to reprobate the non-elect is the means to the ultimate end of displaying the greatness of divine holiness (and thereby the outworking of (1'')).
(10'')   Thus, the redemption of the elect and the reprobation of the damned to display divine holiness are both ultimate ends in God's decrees (from (2'') and (9'')).
(11'')   But both these ultimate ends are subordinate to the chief end of divine self-glorification (from (1''), (2''), (9'') and (10'')).

The problems with this argument should now be obvious. We shall take them sequentially, in order of strength. First, the implication of (4''), regarding the condition of redemption, or the notion of the condition of redemption, vitiates (3''). For (4'') follows from (3'') and is implied by (3''). Moreover, if (4'') obtains, which it surely must for Edwards, since election is a means to the ultimate end of redemption (on (2'')), then (3'') cannot be logically prior to (5''). The reason for this is that the concept of redemption requires an object of redemption; something that needs to be redeemed. But there can be no redemption where there is no object that requires redemption. (3'') is logically prior in the divine decrees, on Edwards' scheme, to the fall, expressed in (5''). But if so, then how can Edwards explain the presence of the concept of redemption expressed in (3'')? It is not enough for Edwards to claim that God foresees sin and decrees (3'') on this basis, since the decree of (3'') implies (4''), as a necessary condition of (3''). This means that Edwards does not seem to be supralapsarian in his decree of election if this decree is logically dependent upon the notion of redemption.

Secondly, Edwards might be able to stabilize his supposed *via media*, by driving a wedge between election and redemption, such that the decree to elect entails an election to glory, with redemption as the merely contingent means to that end. On such a picture, Edwards could argue something like the following: the elect would have gone to glory even if there were no fall. And if there were no fall, presumably, there would have been no impediment to the elect being taken immediately to glory, since there would have been no need for redemption. Hence, there is a possible world in which (a) the elect exist, (b) the decree of election is a decree to glorification, and (c) there is no fall, and no sin (presumably, for Edwards, no decree to fall and sin). If this world is logically possible, then redemption need only be a contingent means by which God brings about the glorification of the elect, as per (b). However, Edwards cannot endorse such a construal of the decrees on the basis of the argument we have just set out. In fact, this means by which to make redemption contingent upon the world in which election takes place, is quite the opposite of Edwards' view. We have already seen that Edwards explicitly states that election is a means to the ultimate end of redemption, not an end in itself (as per (2")), above). According to Edwards, election is one aspect of the covenant of redemption. Redemption is not a matter that is contingent upon the way in which God construes the decree of election. Rather, election is dependent upon the way in which God construes the covenant of redemption.

The net result of this is that Edwards cannot make a coherent case for his *via media* approach to the decrees. His commitment to (3") implies (4") which is fatal to his bid for a supralapsarian decree of election and redemption. But, if he were to attempt to restabilize the supralapsarian component of his decree to elect, he would have to relegate redemption to the means, rather than the end in view of which election is ordained. Thus, his argument is compromised on two counts.

Supralapsarian After All?

There is one last issue to address in this chapter. Edwards appears to believe that one important reason for endorsing an infralapsarian view of reprobation is that the decree to reprobate presupposes that there are sinful persons who are in a position that requires the exercise of God's vindictive justice in reprobation in the first place.[37] He is right to point out that the decree of (E2) presupposes that there is a group of people who are already sinners, in need of redemption. In this sense, his infralapsarian position with respect to reprobation is consistent with his endorsement of a supralapsarian view of election. But, there is another, *consistently supralapsarian* way to understand the decree to reprobation, which takes into account Edwards' central contention about reprobation presupposing sin, whilst remaining within a supralapsarian scheme. Furthermore, on the basis of Edwards' theological determinism, it seems to me that this consistently supralapsarian position would better represent the general thrust of Edwards' thinking on the doctrine of sin, than his attempt at a *via media* does. Let us examine what such a position would involve.

It could be, along supralapsarian lines, that God decrees his self-glorification in the salvation of the elect as a manifestation of divine grace and mercy, and the reprobation of the damned as a manifestation of divine justice and wrath. This need only mean that God conceptualizes a possible world, in which he conceives all those parts, persons,

The Divine Decrees

properties and other metaphysical paraphernalia that will exist in that world if he creates it. This includes conceiving the fact that, if he creates this world, he will create persons with the property of 'moral depravity' that will be separated into two groups: those he elects to life, and those he damns to hell. Now, all this supralapsarian picture presumes is that God can conceptualize such a possible world prior to actualizing it and, on that basis, makes the decrees he does, ordaining that such a world be actualized as per (1). It does not presume that there are *actual* persons suffering from moral depravity as God conceives of such a world. God may conjure up the thought of a world populated with such people, elect and reprobate, and conceive of how he would allocate their eternal destinies, before ordaining the decree(s) that will bring about this thought. And this view is still able to incorporate Edwards' contention about reprobation presupposing sin, without the need for Edwards' infralapsarian view of reprobation. Edwards, in other words, appears to conflate the possible with the actual. It is perfectly possible for an imaginative person to conceive of a possible world in which he thinks of placing various persons, with various problems, in various situations and states of affairs. That is all that needs to be granted to the supralapsarian for their position to overcome the Edwardsian objection that the reprobate must exist prior to the decree to damn them (since such a decree presumes that there are persons who are guilty of sin, and stand condemned already for this decree to have currency). The distinction can be formalized thus:

(5)   God (fore)sees the sin of the reprobate.
(6)   God ordains the sin of the reprobate (according to Edwards, is the permitter of that sin).
(7)   God decrees the damnation of the reprobate.

Edwards claims that this demonstrates that for sin to be condemned it must be already in existence. But this does not follow. (5) makes no claim about whether the reprobate under consideration are potential or actual beings. That is, God could foresee the sin of the reprobate in a possible world, where the reprobate are only potential, rather than actual beings, and (5)–(7) still obtain. Therefore, Edwards' central argument in preference of an infralapsarian decree of reprobation does not provide the grounds he thinks it does for his asymmetrical account of the divine decrees.

This has two implications. First, since this claim is a central plank of Edwards' argument for his asymmetrical position on the divine decrees, it does not, as it stands, offer any more promising grounds for a stable *via media*. Taken together with the previous criticisms of Edwards' position, it is clear that Edwards' position is fatally flawed. Secondly, Edwards does not give a sufficient reason to abandon a completely supralapsarian position. In fact, his contention about the logical priority of the glory of God in the divine decrees in *End of Creation*, and his strong deterministic thesis outlined in his treatise *Freedom of the Will*, suggest that a purely supralapsarian position is more consistent with the central structures of his metaphysics.

Conclusion

Edwards' doctrine of the order of the divine decrees in predestination has been misunderstood. We have seen that two recent readings of Edwards' views, those of Gerstner and Holmes, both fail to adequately account for aspects of Edwards' argument. Gerstner tries to fit Edwards into a purely infralapsarian position, believing this will help him in his theodicy. We shall see in Chapters 2 and 3 that this is a vain hope. More importantly as far as the present discussion is concerned, this is simply not an adequate account of the carefully nuanced position that Edwards' attempts to formulate with respect to the predestinarian decrees.

Holmes' reading of Edwards is more adequate. He sees the central thrust of Edwards' position lies in his attempted asymmetrical account of a supralapsarian doctrine of election, with an infralapsarian doctrine of reprobation. However, his reading of Edwards fails to recognize that redemption is an ultimate, but not chief end in the divine decrees. This means that he privileges redemption over God's self-glorification, as the chief end of God's works. As a result he misunderstands the logical sequence of the divine decrees in Edwards' thought.

We have also assessed the success of Edwards' asymmetrical argument for the predestinarian decrees. A careful analysis of his argument shows that the asymmetrical position he defends is fatally flawed on two counts. First, his supralapsarian decree of election carries a material implication that vitiates the supra/infralapsarian distinction that Edwards trades on. For his position implies that a necessary condition of supralapsarian election is sin. This means that Edwards' supralapsarian decree looks distinctly like an infralapsarian decree after all. But secondly, if Edwards is to make his *via media* work, he has to distinguish between election and redemption in a way that undoes a central aspect of his doctrine of the supralapsarian decree, making redemption contingent upon election, rather than, as Edwards sees it, election as a means to redemption, an ultimate end.

Finally, I have suggested that the force of Edwards' argument, seen in the wider context of his theological determinism, would have been more consistent, and, perhaps, more coherent, if he had opted for a purely supralapsarian position on the divine decrees. It may well be that Edwards deliberately avoided such a doctrine because he saw the unpleasant consequences that would have had for his theodicy: God would be entirely responsible for sin. But as a consequence of this, Edwards' attempted middle way between supra and infralapsarianism fails.

Notes

1   As Turretin points out, these are not the only options available. It could be that God ordains reprobation, *in lapsu*, that is, in the fall, 'and maintain that man as fallen was considered by God predestinating', *Institutes of Elenctic Theology* I: IV: IX, p. 341. However, this is not a position that Edwards favours, so we shall pursue it no further here.

The Divine Decrees

2   It may well be that such a view entails a version of Molinism. However, nothing in the argument of what follows depends on this.

3   This, and the infralapsarian sequence are adapted from Berkhof, *Systematic Theology*, p. 120.

4   It is not clear what position Edwards took with respect to property attribution. Whether he would have understood potential ideas according to a substratum theory, with the divine mind, and other minds as the substrata, and ideas as clusters of properties attached to such substrates, or whether he would have endorsed a bundle theory of sorts, where there are no bare particulars, only bundles of properties, or, indeed, some other theory, is an open question.

5   The *Miscellanies* can be found in *YE13* (numbers a–500) and *YE18* (numbers 501–832). *End of Creation* can be found in *YE8*. There is a section in the 1834 two-volume edition of Edwards' works reprinted in *The Works of Jonathan Edwards Vol. II*, chapter X, *Remarks on Important Theological Controversies*, entitled *Concerning the Divine Decrees*. This is a fair, but not entirely accurate conglomeration of Edwards' *Miscellanies* on the subject, transcribed (and 'improved upon') by his son, Dr Jonathan Edwards Jr. Since the Yale edition of these *Miscellanies* is available, I have ignored these earlier transcriptions, since they are inaccurate in points of detail.

6   What follows is taken from the text of *Miscellany 292* in *YE13*: 383–4.

7   ''Tis said that that which is last in execution is first in intention; which is true with respect to the end and all the proper means, but not with respect to every prerequisite condition', *YE13*: 383.

8   *YE13*: 383.

9   See *End of Creation* in *YE8*: 407, for Edwards' understanding of what an ultimate end is.

10   *Miscellany 292* in *YE13*: 383.

11   In *YE8*.

12   *YE8*: 405, author's emphasis. What follows is taken from this introductory section to the dissertation, pp. 405–15.

13   Edwards goes on to claim that there are two kinds of ultimate end: the original end of a thing, and the consequential end of a thing. But this need not detain us here.

14   *YE8*: 408.

15   *YE8*: 530.

16   *YE8*: 410, 'if any being has but one ultimate end in all that he does, and there be a great variety of operations, his last end may justly be looked upon as his *supreme* end', author's emphasis.

17   *YE8*: 405.

18   *Miscellany 993* in *YE20*: 323, in upper-case letters in the text.

19   *Miscellany 704* in *YE18*: 316.

20   Ibid.

21   *YE18*: 282–3.

22   *YE18*: 283.

23   'It don't necessarily follow from the very nature of grace, or God's communicativeness of his own happiness, that there must be good works. This is only a certain way of the arbitrary appointment of God's wisdom, wherein he will bring men to partake of his grace', *YE18*: 283.

24   *YE18*: 283.

25   Ibid.

26   *YE18*: 315.

27   Ibid., p. 317.

28   Ibid., p. 317.

29   It is clear that when Edwards refers here to the fall, he intends the reader to understand the *decree to permit the fall*. Elsewhere in the same passage, he writes, 'those decrees ben't to be considered as prior to *the decree of the being and permission of the fall of the subject*, and the decree of election, as it implies', *YE18*: 317, emphasis added.

30   *YE18*: 317.

31   *Rational Biblical Theology, Vol. II*, p. 152.

32   Stephen Holmes has recently pointed this out in *God of Grace and God of Glory*, pp. 126–31.

24 *Jonathan Edwards and the Metaphysics of Sin*

33 In *Miscellany 292* in *YE13*: 384. Interestingly, Turretin advocates an infralapsarian position, whilst Mastricht attempts to steer a middle course between supra- and infralapsarians. He 'places predestination before creation and fall but makes its object merely the two classes of elect and reprobate, whereas election and reprobation proper are of individuals and presuppose man as fallen', ibid.

34 *God of Grace and God of Glory.*

35 *God of Grace and God of Glory*, p. 131. He goes on to cite *Miscellany 993* as his proof text for this view. A similar thought is expressed by Jenson: 'The end of God's moral government, as we have seen, is redemption. This doctrine determines Edwards' understanding both of the nature of God's historical agency and the general pattern of God's historical plotting', *America's Theologian*, p. 45.

36 Cited above, in *YE20*: 323. Holmes has it from the manuscript in *God Of Grace and God of Glory*, p. 131, n. 21. This is not the only place that Edwards makes reference to this idea: cf. *Miscellany 702*, Corol. 1, in *YE18*: 298, 'Hence [it] is a great confirmation that God's communicating happiness to the creature stands in the place of a supreme end, because we see that that work, even the making the creature happy by redemption, is the end of all God's other works.' See also *Miscellany 762*, Corol. 2, in *YE18*: 408: 'this wicked act of crucifying Christ [is] . . . the greatest of all decreed events, and that on which all other decreed events depend on as their main foundation, being the main thing in that greatest work of God, the work of redemption, that [which] is the end of all other works'.

37 'The being of sin is supposed in the first things in order in the decree of reprobation, which is that God will glorify his vindictive justice; but the very notion of revenging justice simply considered supposes a fault to be revenged', *Miscellany 700* in *YE18*: 283.

CHAPTER 2

Adam's Fall

The doctrine of the fall is notoriously troublesome. Yet the traditional doctrine of the fall has not been given the attention in the contemporary philosophical literature that other aspects of traditional theodicy have.[1] In this chapter we shall restrict ourselves to Edwards' defence of one central aspect of the traditional doctrine of the fall. That is, his attempt to show how it is possible that a morally unfallen individual like Adam could commit a sin. We shall ignore the wider issues raised for the doctrine of the fall by developments in the natural sciences and cognate disciplines, since the focus of this chapter is the coherence of this one particular aspect of Edwards' account of the fall, not the commensurability of the doctrine with related subject areas.

It might be claimed that, in light of work in the biological sciences and biblical studies, such an undertaking is naïve and implausible. How can one discuss the fall without reference to these areas of recent discussion? But this thinking is confused. Problems raised for the traditional doctrine of the fall by current theories of human development in the biological sciences, or the results of biblical studies with respect to the so-called primeval prologue of Genesis 1–3, are distinct from the traditional *theological* problem of the fall. This theological problem involves how the first human (whoever that was) possessed of a complete, unfallen moral nature could have chosen evil over the good, leading to the consequences of the fall. If this conundrum cannot be solved, then the traditional doctrine of the fall cannot get off the ground. In which case, the deliverances of biblical studies and the biological sciences with respect to the historicity of the first three chapters of Genesis are beside the point, because the traditional doctrine of the fall is unworkable. Of course, if Edwards' doctrine of the fall turns out to be internally coherent with respect to the traditional theological problem of the fall, this does not address the problems posed for the traditional doctrine of the fall by contemporary biblical studies and biology. But it would show that there is a way of construing the traditional theological problem of the fall that is coherent. And this is no small achievement; many theologians have tried, and failed to give an adequate account of this problem.[2] Thus, it is worth assessing the coherence of this traditional version of the problem of the fall, since without a resolution to this aspect of theodicy, other parts of a traditional doctrine of sin appear to be in jeopardy.[3]

The Problem of Primal Sin

Let us begin by clarifying the traditional theological problem of the fall under consideration. Following Scott MacDonald, we shall distinguish between *primal sin* and *original sin*. Primal sin is that first sin, by which evil entered the created order.[4]

26 *Jonathan Edwards and the Metaphysics of Sin*

MacDonald, like Augustine, takes the paradigm case of this first sin from a putative angelic fall. But the human fall is also an instance of primal sin. Thus, human primal sin pertains to the free choice of a rational human creature prior to the fall that gave rise to the first instance of human sin, whereas original sin pertains to the fallen state of humanity in its bondage to sin subsequent to the moment of primal sin (as traditionally understood). Edwards' focus is on human primal sin, and its consequences in original sin and imputation. He has much less to say about the angelic fall.[5] Nor, like Augustine, does he appear to have taken the angelic fall as his paradigm case of primal sin. Therefore, it is human primal sin that is the subject of this chapter. We shall leave the question of an angelic primal sin to one side. Let us call this aspect of the traditional doctrine of the fall, *the problem of primal sin*.

Edwards' account of the fall offers a potential solution to this theological problem, via an understanding of the fall as an instance of self-deception. In a nutshell, Edwards maintains that Adam and Eve fell because they deceived themselves into thinking that eating of the fruit was in their own best interests, when it was not. Having provided an Edwardsian solution to the problem of primal sin, we shall examine whether this solution is coherent. In keeping with one recent commentator (John Kearney), and contrary to the weight of previous scholarly opinion, Edwards' account is, I shall argue, *internally coherent*. But I shall show that, though Edwards' account does work on its own terms, it is not *externally consistent*. That is, it is not consistent with other aspects of Edwards' metaphysics.

Moral Agency and Original Righteousness

Edwards' articulation of the doctrine of the fall depends upon several related metaphysical commitments that it is important to grasp, in order to do justice to Edwards' case. The first involves his conception of moral agency. The second deals with what he understands by original righteousness. The substance of Edwards' account of how Adam sinned develops out of a distinction between *sufficient* and *confirming* grace. This leads into the question of how Adam's will was perverted. We shall look at each of these aspects to the problem in turn.

Moral Agency

Edwards developed this notion in his treatise, *Freedom of the Will* (hereinafter *FOW*), to the effect that moral acts are acts that are caused by a person's dispositions and desires, over and against the libertarian view of the 'Arminians', that moral acts are uncaused, or contra-causal acts.[6] However, the virtue or vice of a person's dispositions or acts of will do not, according to Edwards, lie in the *cause* of those dispositions or actions, but in their *nature*:

> Thus for instance, ingratitude is hateful and worthy of dispraise, according to common sense; not because something as bad, or worse than ingratitude, was the

cause that produced it; but because it is hateful in itself, by its own inherent deformity. So the love of virtue is amiable, and worthy of praise, not merely because something else went before this love of virtue in our minds, which caused it to take place there . . . but because of the amiableness and condecency of such a disposition and inclination of the heart.[7]

Crucial to this aspect of Edwards' thesis about the compatibility of free will and determinism, is the notion that moral actions are actions that have a cause. Actions which are said to be contra-causal are not thereby *more* moral because they are 'free' in accordance with liberty of indifference. They are *non-moral*, because they have no cause. In fact, Edwards goes beyond this to show, time and again, that the contra-causal account of moral agency and volition taken up by the 'Arminians' ends up in contradiction or absurdity.[8]

Edwards was convinced that moral agency consists in both a moral faculty, such that a person can distinguish right courses of action from wrong ones, and a capacity to reason whereby the agent is subject to the influence of moral inducements (such as exhortations to do a particular thing, or warnings to refrain from so doing):

To moral agency belongs a moral faculty, or sense of moral good and evil, or of such a thing as desert or worthiness or praise or blame, reward or punishment; and a capacity which an agent has of being influenced in his actions by moral inducements or motives, exhibited to the view of understanding and reason, to engage to a conduct agreeable to the moral faculty.[9]

So it is the agent, not the will, which is free to choose one course of action over another. And only an agent who has a moral faculty can be described as making 'free' choices, according to Edwards.

Whether this aspect of his compatibility thesis is convincing or not, what is important with respect to his doctrine of the fall is that Edwards believed that the actions of moral agents are caused by desires and motives, the very nature of which ensure that the actions they give rise to are praise or blameworthy. We may take these notions about moral agency and virtuous action, and apply them to Edwards' discussion of original righteousness in *Original Sin* (hereinafter *OS*), as a prerequisite to his doctrine of the fall proper.

Original Righteousness

In *OS* II: I: I, Edwards sets out what he means by original righteousness against his opponent, Dr John Taylor. Taylor's criticism of this doctrine appears to have been that it is inconsistent with the nature of virtue that it be concreated with a person. For an act to be virtuous, a person must desire or choose it over other, less virtuous or vicious alternatives. Edwards takes this to mean that 'its being essential to all virtue that it should follow choice and proceed from it'.[10] That is, virtue does not consist in a concreated disposition that gives rise to acts of a virtuous nature. Instead, it consists in the (presumably contra-causal) choice of virtue over vice when a person is presented

28 *Jonathan Edwards and the Metaphysics of Sin*

with such alternatives. Edwards *qua* theological determinist wants to say that virtue is concreated with Adam, and that this concreation constitutes the endowment of original righteousness, 'the creation of our first parents with holy principles and dispositions'.[11] The problems with this account of original righteousness according to libertarians like Taylor is that if virtue is concreated, then virtuous choices are not about making a 'free' decision that is morally virtuous or vicious. Rather, they are about acting in accordance with one's given moral nature or acting against that nature. The general principle Edwards draws out from this is 'Not that principles derive their goodness from actions, but that actions derive their goodness from the principles whence they proceed.'[12]

So, an act is virtuous only in so far as it proceeds from good principles and a virtuous disposition. Virtue is not to be had in the acts a person performs, but in the dispositions that give rise to those acts, as Edwards maintained with respect to moral agency: 'a virtuous temper of mind may be before a good act of choice, as a tree may be before the fruit, and the fountain before the stream which proceeds from it.'[13] With these notions of moral agency and original righteousness in mind, we may consider the substantive issue in Edwards' articulation of the fall.

Edwards' Two Accounts of the Fall

Edwards actually offers two accounts of the fall in his *corpus*. In *OS* IV: II, Edwards sets out the first of these, in the context of his discussion of the authorship of sin problem. He offers a second account in his *Miscellanies*, to which we shall come presently.

Sufficient and Confirming Grace in OS

In the *OS* version, Edwards begins by arguing that the corruption of Adam's human nature does not require the infusion of some 'positive influence'.[14] Rather, it involves the withholding of that special divine influence which enables Adam to continue in original righteousness, such that Adam gives himself over to his natural appetites, leading to the corruption of his moral nature. Since this foundation of his doctrine is so crucial to what follows, I cite it in full:

> I think, a little attention to the nature of things will be sufficient to satisfy any impartial considerate inquirer, that the absence of positive good principles, and so the withholding of a special divine influence to impart and maintain those good principles, leaving the common natural principles of self-love, natural appetite, etc. (which were in man in innocence) leaving these, I say, to themselves, without the government of superior divine principles, will certainly be followed with corruption, yea, the total corruption of the heart, without occasion for any positive influence at all: and that it was thus indeed that corruption of nature came on Adam, immediately on his fall, and comes on all his posterity, as sinning in him and falling with him.[15]

By way of explaining how this state of affairs came about, Edwards distinguishes between two kinds of principles, *inferior* or natural principles, and *superior* or supernatural principles. Inferior principles are the natural principles of human nature, including such things as self-love, natural appetites and passions, 'which belong to the nature of man, in which his love to his own liberty, honor and pleasure, were exercised'.[16] Superior principles are concreated supernatural endowments of God, contained in the 'divine nature', meaning, 'the spiritual image of God, and man's righteousness and true holiness'.[17]

Edwards seems to envisage a situation in which Adam was created with both inferior and superior principles, with the superior principles ordering and controlling the inferior principles of human nature. Thus, Adam was possessed of a desire in the state of original righteousness, to love and serve God, and to order his human nature in such a way as to serve this end rather than other, lesser ends, such as that of self-love. But when Adam sinned, this concreated ordering of human nature by superior, and divinely constituted principles was overturned. The immediate result was that the inferior principles of human nature became the ruling principles of Adam's human nature, and instead of a God-ward orientation in all his actions (as per the superior principles), Adam set up the 'objects of his private affections and appetites, as supreme'.[18]

So, the depraved disposition of the human heart arises, according to Edwards, from a privation of certain supernatural principles, not from the infusion of an evil principle. This same privative state obtains in Adam's posterity. The superior principles withdrawn from Adam at the point of primal sin are also withheld from the rest of humanity, so that they are all born enslaved to the natural principles of human nature.[19] This connection between Adam and his posterity over their sinful state post-fall is established not only via a federalist view of imputation,[20] but also to the notion of an 'established course of nature': 'For Adam's posterity are from him, and as it were in him, and belonging to him, according to an established course of nature, as much as the branches of a tree are, according to a course of nature, from the tree, in the tree, and belonging to the tree; or . . . "just as the acorn is derived from the oak".'[21]

Edwards means that God has established that the effects of Adam's primal sin be applied in the natures of all his descendents according to a divinely ordered state of affairs. He does not mean by this that God ordains a course of nature to take effect from the point of Adam's first sin, as if this course of nature were some law or principle that obtains independently of his will once instituted. Nor does he mean that this course of nature is like a physical law, which describes a physical constant of the universe, such as, say, the law of gravity. Instead, he means that God institutes this course of nature as the occasion of his acting in a particular way towards that hunk of matter that constitutes Adam and his posterity: 'Where the name "nature" is allowed without dispute, no more is meant than an established method and order of events, settled and limited by divine wisdom.'[22]

At this point a question arises: why is it that if a lack of original righteousness is transmitted to Adam's posterity in this manner, principles of holiness are not likewise transmitted? For instance, if Gary becomes a Christian, why is it that the principles of

30 *Jonathan Edwards and the Metaphysics of Sin*

holiness that are imputed, or infused into Gary at the moment of his conversion are not carried over to his children by an 'established course of nature'? Edwards' reply is simply that that is the way God orders things according to his will and wisdom. Indeed:

> Grace is introduced among the race of mankind by a *new establishment*; not on the foot of the original establishment of God, as the Head of the natural world, and Author of the first creation; but by a constitution of a vastly higher kind; wherein Christ is made the root of the tree, whose branches are his spiritual seed and he is the head of the new creation.[23]

There is a similar federal argument applied to the related question of why Adam's first transgression alone was imputed to his posterity. Edwards' response to this is that it was a condition of the covenant of works that the first transgression of the covenant would be the reason for judgement, not subsequent transgressions thereafter: 'But of the tree of the knowledge of good and evil you shall not eat, for in the day that you eat of it you shall surely die' (Genesis 2:17).[24]

More will be said about this topic in later chapters (including the forensic aspects of this arrangement). For now, all we need is the notion that the federal nature of imputed sin does not appear to be transmitted as simply a corrupt disposition in all Adam's posterity. Rather, it is transmitted as a divinely established principle, whereby the withholding of superior and supernatural properties present in Adam before the primal sin were withdrawn after it, and continue to be withheld from all his posterity at all times subsequent to his primal sin.

Sufficient and Confirming Grace in the Miscellanies

Edwards' explanation of how Adam fell in *OS* is developed and augmented in important respects by his discussion of the subject in his *Miscellanies*. The first significant entry on this topic is *Miscellany 290*. Here a quite different account is given of how Adam sinned. Instead of a distinction between the withholding of superior principles, and resulting reign of inferior principles post-fall, Edwards explains that Adam sinned because God did not give him a deposit of confirming grace, to enable him to withstand the temptation of the serpent:

> If it be inquired how man came to sin, seeing he had no sinful inclinations in him, except God took away his grace from him that he had been wont to give him and so let him fall, I answer, there was no need of that; there was no need of taking away any that had been give him, but he sinned under that temptation because God did not give him more . . . [Moreover] . . . He did not take away that grace from him while he was perfectly innocent, which grace was his original righteousness; but he only withheld his confirming grace, that grace which is given now in heaven, such grace as shall fit the soul to surmount every temptation.[25]

Here, Edwards says Adam was created in original righteousness. This state did not include a deposit of confirming grace. Confirming grace is that grace which enables

Its possessor to withstand any and all temptations, corresponding (one presumes) to the scholastic category of *non posse peccare* (not able to sin). Adam was not in possession of this species of grace in his state of original righteousness. Instead he possessed the species *posse non peccare* (able not to sin). So, the withholding of confirming grace (what we might call *non posse peccare* grace) does not mean Adam was in the extremely weak moral state of *non posse non peccare* (not able not to sin). Rather, he was in a moderately weak state of *posse non peccare*. In such a state, Adam could withstand temptation to sin (it was *possible* for him to do so; he was *able* to do so). But, as a matter of fact, he did not withstand temptation; he sinned. This view is confirmed by *Miscellany 290*: 'This was the grace [*non posse peccare*?] Adam was to have had if he had stood, when he came to receive his reward.'[26] Adam could only have stood if it was possible for him to have stood, to be able to have received confirming grace. So, Edwards' understanding of these matters depends upon issues that pertain to his discussion of free will. The question of *how* Adam sinned depends upon a prior problem: in what sense was Adam free from sin pre-fall?

Clarification comes from two further miscellany entries. First, in *Miscellany 291*, Edwards suggests that man pre-fall was more free than he is now, because he was able to make moral choices where reason and judgement were paramount, and subordinated the desires of the 'inferior principles'. So, pre-fall, Adam's moral nature was orderly and coherent, whereas post-fall it has been vitiated and is therefore disordered. The rational judgement no longer holds sway in moral choices.[27]

Then, in *Miscellany 436*, Edwards says:

> And this must be what is meant when we say, that God gave our first parents sufficient grace, though he withheld an efficacious grace, or a grace that would certainly uphold him in all temptations he could meet with. I say, this must be meant by his having sufficient grace, viz. that he had grace sufficient to render him a free agent, not only with respect to [his] whole will, but with respect to his rational [will], or the will that arose from a rational judgement of what was indeed best for himself.[28]

Edwards defines the rational will as a 'will arising merely from the rational judgement of what is best for him'.[29] There is also another aspect to inclination, namely the 'appetite'. This arises, 'from the liveliness and intenseness of the idea, or sensibleness of the good of the object presented to the mind . . . which is against the other, rational, will, and in fallen man in his natural state overcomes it, and keeps it in subjection'.[30] He suggests that although both the appetite and rational will are two components in the whole will (that is, the inferior principles of the will, not the superior, supernatural principles); yet the rational will is not free, but is the 'servant of sin'. It is this vitiation of the rational judgement that is absent from moral choice pre-fall. What took place at the fall was a deception of this rational will, so that Adam was deceived into thinking that something was best for himself which was not the best, but rebellion against God. This point is amplified in *Miscellany 437*:

The case must be thus, therefore, with our first parents, when tempted: their sense of their duty to God and their love to it must be above their inferior appetite, so that that inferior appetite of itself was not sufficient to master the holy principle; yet the rational will, being perverted by a deceived judgement and setting in with the inferior appetite, overcame and overthrew the gracious inclination.[31]

The Bigger Picture on Sufficient and Confirming Grace

We seem to have the following picture from the *Miscellanies*. Adam is concreated with a deposit of sufficient grace, which enables him to act without sinning (*posse non peccare*), in accordance with an ordered moral nature where his rational judgement orders his natural appetites. Adam's primal sin occurred because he was somehow deceived. Perhaps this deception occurred because he was led to believe that he did not need to use this sufficient grace, and could trust to his own appetites. Edwards is not entirely clear. Nevertheless, Adam was somehow deceived and the result was a disordering of human capacities, so that natural appetites took over the ordering of Adam's moral nature from his rational judgement. But, all this amounts to is a description of a model of Adam's state prior to the fall, and his state post-fall. It offers no real explanation of *how* he was deceived into sinning, nor does it explain how his moral nature was vitiated in this way. So, the central question raised by the fall remains unanswered in the *Miscellanies*.

What is more, the account Edwards gives in the *Miscellanies* differs in important respects from the account we have seen him lay out in *OS*. In *OS* Adam is concreated with both inferior and superior principles. The inferior principles correspond to Adam's natural appetites, the superior principles to his true holiness and the presence of the Holy Spirit. But on sinning, the superior principles are withheld. In the *Miscellanies*, the emphasis is on the inferior principles. It is because Adam allowed his natural appetites to take precedence over his rational will, that he succumbs to temptation and sin.

Edwards does not seem to reconcile the differences between these accounts anywhere in his *corpus*. However, I suggest the following reconstruction. Adam's inferior principles incorporate both his natural appetites and his rational judgement. In addition to these two aspects of the nature of Adam, there is the supernatural deposit of God's presence, enabling him to live and act in a consistently holy manner. Taken together, these constitute a sufficient grace. That is, a grace sufficient to withstand temptation, and remain sinless (*posse non peccare*). Had Adam withstood temptation, he would have been given a confirming grace in addition to this initial deposit of sufficient grace, whereby he would have been elevated to a state of impeccability (*non posse peccare*). This would have confirmed the presence of the superior principles in his moral nature, and somehow prevented the possibility of Adam ever sinning from that moment onwards. However, he was deceived, and sinned. At this point, the superior/supernatural principles that made up part of Adam's pre-fallen nature (that is, were properties essential to his sinless state) were withdrawn. Adam and his posterity thereafter are not able not to sin (*non posse non peccare*), since God's superior grace is withdrawn from them.

However, this reconciliation of Edwards' two accounts still does not answer the central question of how Adam was deceived into sinning. If anything, this version of Edwards' position makes it even harder to see how such a deception could have taken place. For if, as part of his moral condition pre-fall, Adam was supplied with superior principles to enable him to live in a way pleasing to God, then how could he have been deceived?

At this point, further clarification of Edwards' views in an *excursus* on three key concepts in his account of free will may help understand how Adam could be deceived. The three areas are will and preference, will and desire, and the determination of the will. These three issues occur in his initial discussion and definition of terms at the beginning of *FOW*, where he lays out his own position over and against that of John Locke. Edwards' concern to delineate his own position on these aspects of the will in *FOW* has considerable bearing upon our question about how Adam sinned. If he was deceived into sinning, then he must have preferred (or part of him must have preferred), desired and been determined to act in this way, rather than in accordance with those superior principles and rational will that governed his moral nature pre-fall.

Excursus: The Preference, Desire and Determination of the Will

Before plunging into the *excursus*, a word about Edwards' use of John Locke's *Essay Concerning Human Understanding* in *FOW*. The opening sections of *FOW* deal with the explanation of the terms Edwards goes on to use in the rest of the treatise. In much of what he has to say there, he is setting out his own position against that of Locke's chapter, 'On Power', whose work acted as a foil to Edwards' own thinking on the question of free will (and was a state-of-the-art text at the time Edwards was writing). Throughout his discussion of these issues, Edwards is concerned to show that, contrary to Locke's mature views, will and preference and will and desire mean the same thing.[32] Hence, in what follows, I shall contrast what Edwards has to say on the matters of preference, desire and determination of the will with that of Locke, as Edwards himself does.

Will and Preference

As far as Edwards was concerned, 'the will (without any metaphysical refining) is plainly, that by which the mind chooses anything'.[33] Yet Locke in his *Essay* defines the will as preferring or choosing where preference can be taken to mean a desire to do something that may actually be outside the agent's volitional capacity, such as a preference for flying rather than walking.[34] For Edwards, such a distinction between choice and preference was erroneous because what the mind communicates to the body necessarily follows. So although a man may vaguely wish to fly, he cannot choose to do so, nor can he prefer to do so if preference is concomitant to choice because it is physically impossible.[35] Thus, a person may choose only those actions that they are capable of performing. (I may wish to do impossible things, but I cannot choose to do them, since they are beyond my powers to do, like flying.) Preference for one over another potential action is, in this regard, preference for one or other action that a person is able to perform.

Let us apply this to Edwards' account of Adam's primal sin. According to Edwards in *FOW*, what a person chooses is what he prefers. So what Adam chooses, is what he prefers. And what he prefers falls within his volitional capacities. So Adam prefers one action to another, and chooses on that basis to do that action. From this it is clear that, in a particular volition, he chooses on the basis of preference. And in the instance of primal sin, he prefers sin to obedience. But this raises a further problem for Edwards' account of the fall: how could Adam prefer sin, when his desire, according to Edwards, was for God supremely in all his choices in his pre-fallen state?

Will and Desire

We turn to Edwards' second distinction between will and desire for an answer to this problem. Locke asserted that the will of a person might be contrary to their desires. A person could will to choose that which he did not desire, because it was expedient in a particular state of affairs:

> The will is perfectly distinguished from desire, which in the very same action may have a quite contrary tendency from that which our wills sets us upon. A man, whom I cannot deny, may oblige me to use persuasions to another, which at the same time I am speaking, I may wish not to prevail on him. In this case, 'tis clear the will and desire run counter. I will the action, that tends one way, whilst my desire tends another, and that the direct contrary.[36]

So a person B could desire that his words do not persuade a second person C, though he phrases his speech in such a way that he will persuade C, because he is obliged to do so on the basis of a previous obligation to a third person, A, who wishes C to be persuaded by B. But for Edwards this is not possible, since, contrary to Locke, will and desire are a single unit. According to Edwards, to desire a thing is to want it, and to want it provides the motivation requisite to will that thing in volition.[37] To will is to desire, since without a preference for one choice above another there can be only equilibrium and, therefore, no volition. In fact, Edwards maintains that will and preference are, for all practical purposes, the same as will and desire.[38] Yet in this discussion of the unity of will, desire and preference Edwards says nothing about the problems associated with competing desires, or the relative strength of different desires, or how the mind decides upon one desire over another in a particular instance. His concern is rather to see off Locke's notion that will and desire may run counter to one another by affirming the unity of will, preference and desire. When he moves on to discuss the motivation of the will (in *FOW* I: 2), he allows that there are motives of various strengths, some of which are weaker than others. Volition depends upon the strongest motive, which results in choice. But his emphasis on the unity of the will and preference/desire means he does not deal with the question of competing desires in anything like enough detail, which, as Paul Ramsey points out, 'reveals in him, a too extreme conception of the unity of human powers or a too monolithic view of the motivations to action'.[39] It also leaves his own position looking rather mechanistic and wooden.

The net result of this with respect to Edwards' attack on Locke's view of will and preference is that Edwards is faced with a dilemma. On the one hand, he wishes to maintain that will and desire are a unit in volition, *contra* Locke. But on the other hand, he must contend with Locke's belief that there can be circumstances in which I might take a choice contrary to my desires. We can represent this as follows:

(1)   Will and desire are united in volition.
(2)   There may be instances where one is faced with a conflict of interest between desire and will in volition.

This appears, *prima facie*, contradictory, for it seems to involve being able to will what one does not will and desire what one does not desire. We shall designate this a second-order conflict, since it is not that the will and desire in *a particular volition* are contrary, but that the agent is willing what they do not will or desiring what they do not desire.[40] This can be expressed in the following manner:

(3)   A dilemma may arise where an agent is presented with a second-order conflict in which they will what they do not will and desire what they do not desire.

Worse still, there may be instances where an agent may be faced with a conflict of interests where the will and desire in a particular volition appear to be at odds. This is where the real problem lies, so we shall designate it a first-order conflict. We can show this as follows:

(4)   It is conceivable that an agent may be presented with a particular choice where each option would entail a first-order conflict between their will and desire.

However, Edwards can respond with the following argument:

(5)   (1) can be shown to be inconsistent with (2) where the conflict in (4) is only apparent. Providing a sufficient reason can be given to demonstrate this, then (4) folds, and so, by implication, does (3), since (3) is parasitic on (4).

This sufficient reason is predicated on a hidden bifurcation in Locke's example. Locke asserts that the will and desire are in first-order conflict because B desires that he does not persuade C whilst at the same time carrying out an action willed because of an obligation to A that will lead to the opposite effect. However, Edwards maintains that in this Locke is obscuring the fact that in each volition B is willing according to desire. There are in fact two volitional procedures going on in tandem, rather than a single, conflicting one. B's desire masks a suppressed, or intentional *willing*, whilst B's action masks an expressed, or formal *desire*. To extrapolate: B desires that C remains unpersuaded by his conversation. This desire masks a suppressed will; were this desire genuine, then B would act upon it leading to a choice consistent with his desire. Instead, that will is suppressed in the face of a previous (greater) claim upon B made by A. As a result, B's volition on the basis of his expressed desire is withheld.

This leads into an analysis of B's actual volition. Here B secretly desires to acquiesce to A's prompting, leading to B's actual volition (for if he did not, then no volition would result, since B is able to make a morally responsible choice free from coercion, and A is not violating this condition). And, according to Edwards, this has to be the case, otherwise B would be acting on the basis of no desire. Were B acting from no desire, then he would be acting without an inclination to choose the action he has chosen, which is patently nonsensical. So, with regard to his volition, B is acting in accordance with a second desire whose expression is masked by the desire that is expressed. Far from there being a formal contradiction between B's expressed desire and will leading to volition, we are faced with a suppressed will (resulting in volition being withheld) and a second masked desire, that is expressed in the will that leads to the formal volition. Therefore there is a bifurcation of desire and volition at work in Locke's example. Consequently, Edwards' initial premise, that one must desire to act upon a choice, which is willed in volition, is reinstated. Otherwise, claims Edwards, we are committed to the view that B is acting out of a volitional equilibrium, which would result in no choice, rather than a choice contrary to desire. Therefore, Edwards' appeal to (5), on the argument just offered, neutralizes the apparent conflict between (4) and (3).

This applies to unfallen Adam in the following way. Even if Adam is deceived into taking the fruit of the tree and eating it, he has to *desire* to act in accordance with the deception, and his desire must be to *prefer* what is offered by the primal sin to continuing in his state of original righteousness. On this basis, what Adam willed in the case of his primal sin, he desired to do, preferring that sin to not sinning and therefore acted upon that desire. There is no sense in which Adam could have willed the primal sin without desiring it. Nor did he will it because he was constrained to do so by the serpent, when he secretly wanted not to desire it, in accordance with God's will. For Edwards, will and desire are one on the basis of preference, in volition. What then, of the deception that Edwards speaks of? Up until now, it might be thought that Edwards is offering something like the following model of deception to explain the fall. Where A and B are moral agents, T is a proposition which captures a non-trivial moral truth and D is a proposition which expresses the truth of T ambiguously:[41]

(1)   A comprehends T.
(2)   A comprehends D.
(3)   A withholds T and explains D to B.
(4)   B believes D to be T (and believes T to express an important moral truth).

(5) B believes D.
(6) B acts on the basis of D (that is, in accordance with his belief in D *qua* T).
(7) B thereby sins.

In this scenario, B is not in full possession of the facts. He has been deceived into thinking that D is T by A, when in fact the whole truth of T has been withheld from him. As a result his culpability is surely diminished. In fact, from what we have now seen of Edwards' views on preference, desire and will, the correct analysis of Adam's deception is more like this:

(1') A comprehends T.
(2') A comprehends D.
(3') A withholds T and explains D to B.
(4') B comprehends the truth of T, but
(5') B prefers (that which is expressed in) D to (that which is expressed in) T.
(6') B desires (that which is expressed in) D over (that which is expressed in) T.
(7') B acts on the basis of his preference and desire in accordance with D, not T.
(8') B thereby sins.

Here, B is culpable. On Edwards' account, this occurs because the inferior principles of his moral nature (specifically, his natural appetite) take precedence in the order of his desires over that of his rational judgement. The result is sin and the vitiation of his moral nature. But this raises a further query. If Adam desired and preferred primal sin (for whatever reason), what determined his willing that outcome, rather than another, which would have preserved him in original righteousness?

The Determination of the Will

Thus, we come to the third question of what motivates, or determines, the will. In contrast to Thomas Chubb (one of the opponents Edwards has in view in *FOW*), Edwards contends that the will determines upon the strongest motivation in any act of volition: 'It is sufficient to my present purpose to say, it is that motive, which, as it stands in the view of the mind, is the strongest, that determines the will.'[42] These motives are graded on the basis of which option best suits the mind at the time of choice, with the proviso that no one willingly chooses evil or disagreeable options. According to Edwards, there are immediate and remote motives that affect the will. The strongest of these at the time of choice will prevail upon the mind, resulting in the desire that the will acts upon in volition. Edwards gives an example of a drunk and his bottle.[43]

The drunk has a variety of potential motivations between which he has to choose. The immediate motivation is to feed his addiction, but there may also be more remote motivations, for example, considerations about the long-term effects the alcohol will have upon his body. The strongest motivation in his deliberations will lead to choice.

But the object proposed to the mind may affect the outcome of a decision in one of two ways. First, by the nature and circumstances of the object and, second, by the manner and view of an object. An object that is beautiful and pleasant, and the amount of pleasure or discomfort associated with an object, will affect a choice, as will the view the mind has of that pleasure; whether it is remote, uncertain or future. Therefore an agent chooses on the basis of what seems best to him and his well-being at the time.

Naturally, a stated motivation can be disingenuous. For example, the drunk may say that he wants to give up his addiction because he is concerned about the effects upon his health, but go on drinking anyway. In this instance, according to Edwards, the motivation to give up has been overridden by the more immediate need of his addiction. His stated motive was not his intended motive, since his desire for the bottle overcame all other desires, leading to a choice based on an immediate gratification, rather than the long-term gains of withholding the immediate motive and acting upon the long-term desire he initially stated.

Here, too, Edwards is working out his position in conscious awareness of Locke's arguments. Locke's *Essay* had originally described a position on motivation of will that was the impetus behind what Edwards went on to say. The idea was that the will determines upon the greatest good and acts upon this, on the understanding that no one willingly acts towards an evil, or perverse end. But in revising his *Essay* in later editions, Locke (as is well known) altered his position. He withdrew his earlier view, and insisted that the will determined its actions on the basis of uneasiness:

> The motive, for continuing in the same state of action is only the present satisfaction in it; the motive to change is always some uneasiness: nothing setting us upon the change of state, or upon any new action, but some uneasiness. This is the great motive that works on the mind to put it upon action, which for shortness sake we shall call determining of the will . . . I am forced to conclude, that good, the greater good, though apprehended and acknowledged to be so, does not determine the will, until our desire, raised proportionably to it, makes us uneasy in the want of it.[44]

Edwards retained Locke's original view regarding the greater good, declaring that Locke's revised view was an unnecessary refinement that could be subsumed under the greater good view anyway. This could be done by showing that it is better and more agreeable to remove that which is disagreeable or causes uneasiness, so that the end or aim of a particular choice involving unease must be to remove that unease, and the means to that end is the search for that which is more agreeable, that is, the greater good.[45] Edwards discussed this point in *The Mind*, where he pointed out that even in the case of a voluntary refusal to act, the will of the agent was making a choice commensurate with his position and not Locke's:

> That it is not uneasiness, in our present circumstances, that always determines the will, as Mr. Locke supposes, is evident by this, that there may be an act of the Will, in choosing and determining to forbear to act, or move, when some action is

proposed to a man; as well as in choosing to act. Thus if a man be put upon rising from his seat, and going to a certain place; his voluntary refusal is an act of the Will, which does not arise from any uneasiness in his present circumstances certainly. An act of voluntary refusal is as truly an act of the Will, as an act of choice; and indeed there is an act of choice in the act of refusal. The Will chooses to neglect: it prefers the opposite of that which is refused.[46]

So, Edwards' objection to Locke's revised view is that Locke's distinction is an unnecessary artifice. But according to John E. Smith, Edwards' motivation was not explicitly to combine 'the motivations to voluntary action with the appearance of good to the mind'. Instead, 'Edwards claimed to be speaking only of "the direct and immediate object of the act of volition", which is to say that he brought together what Locke had distinguished'.[47] Locke's later position was that there was a difference between the greatest apparent good, which may be remote and therefore unappealing, and the good that makes itself felt in uneasiness. Edwards' conflation of these two things was one of his original contributions to the debate. Smith again: 'it is the greatest apprehension of the good that determines the will, by which Edwards means that good is apprehended not only by a judgment, but by "having a clear and sensible idea of any good".'[48]

This can be seen in Edwards' earlier work in *The Mind*, where he says something very similar: 'It is not that which appears the greatest good, or the greatest apparent good, that determines the Will. It is not the greatest good apprehended, or that which is apprehended to be the greatest good; but the greatest apprehension of the good.'[49]

What Edwards meant by this is that the good is apprehended not only by a *judgement* of the understanding, but also by having a clear and sensible *idea* (*qua* Locke) about any good. And it is only when these are combined, and the agent considers that a particular choice will result in what they apprehend (through a judgement of understanding based upon a clear, sensible idea of the end in view) to be the greatest good, that the will determines upon that choice. But, these are all activities of the agent, not different faculties working in concert.

The Fall in Miscellany 436

Let us apply this last aspect of our discussion to the question of Adam and the fall with the help of *Miscellany 436*, where Edwards takes up some of these themes and applies them to Adam. We have already seen that, according to Edwards, 'sufficient grace' means that Adam had grace sufficient to render him a free agent viz. his whole will, including that rational will arising from his rational judgement of what is best for himself. But a rational judgement of what is 'best for himself' is not what is best *absolutely considered*, but what the mind's sense of what is 'best for itself' is. This, like Edwards' notion of the drunk and his bottle, concerns the apprehension of what is perceived to be lovely in itself being best for the agent. Edwards' argument in explanation of the deception of the fall in *Miscellany 436* works in this way. The mind's sense of the absolute loveliness of a particular thing (call it x), directly influences only the will of appetite. By 'will of appetite', Edwards means, 'if the soul wills it merely because it appears lovely in itself, it will be because the loveliness draws the appetite of the soul'.[50] It may indirectly influence the rational will in convincing the person's (call him P) rational judgement that that which is lovely in itself is best for P and P's happiness. P could have a rational judgement of x in this way (that is, could regard x as lovely in itself and best for P's own good), but without a sense of the beauty and pleasantness of x, it will not influence the will in volition. So, if P has only a rational judgement of the beauty of x, but has no sensibility of the beauty of x and doesn't think x is best for himself, then the will (of P) will never choose x. Or again, it could be that P is strongly sensible of the beauty of x, and wills x, even though P thinks x is not the best for himself. For example, P might will a particular sensual pleasure. P may be sensible of the pleasantness of sensual 'judgements' (to borrow Edwards' language), and will the sensual pleasure on that basis, though P is convinced that such pleasure is not that which is best for himself (it may be immoral, for instance). Hence, P may be free regarding his rational will and yet refuse that which he judges to be in itself most lovely and will instead that which he rationally knows to be evil.

It is on the basis of this argument that Edwards believes that deception is a crucial element in explaining how Adam fell:

> Therefore man, having sufficient grace as to render him quite free with respect to his rational will (or his will arising from mere judgment of what was best for himself), could not fall without having that judgment deceived, and being made to think that to be best for himself which was not so, and so having his rational will perverted: though he might sin without being deceived in his rational judgment of what was most lovely in itself, or (which is the same thing) without having his conscience deceived and blinded, might rationally know at the same time, that what he was about to do was hateful, unworthy, etc.; or in other words, though he might know that it was what he ought not to do.[51]

The rational judgement of Adam was perverted by being deceived into thinking that x was best for himself, when it was not. This is not to suggest that Adam's rational judgement was impaired at the time of his choice for primal sin, but that Adam chose that which was in itself hateful, over that which was absolutely lovely. So, Adam allowed his inferior appetites to overthrow his rational judgement, including his sense of duty and love towards God, by choosing that which was hateful, but which he had been deceived into thinking was best for himself. His rational judgement remains unimpaired post-fall, but no longer reigns over his inferior appetites.

Summary of Edwards' Argument

We are now in a position to sum up the content of Edwards' argument. Previously, we saw that:

(1') A comprehends T.
(2') A comprehends D.
(3') A withholds T and explains D to B.
(4') B comprehends the truth of T, but
(5') B prefers (that which is expressed in) D to (that which is expressed in) T.
(6') B desires (that which is expressed in) D over (that which is expressed in) T.
(7') B acts on the basis of his preference and desire in accordance with D, not T.
(8') B thereby sins.

Add to this what we have just seen regarding the determination of the will:

(9') B determines upon 'the greatest apprehension of the good' in choice.
(10') The 'greatest apprehension of the good' involves,

    (a) The natural appetites in,

        (i) a sensibility of the absolute beauty of a particular choice ('what is best absolutely and most lovely in itself' (*YE13*: 485)) and,

        (ii) an apprehension that the particular choice is the best for B himself as well as,

    (b) a rational judgement that a particular choice is the best.

These conditions, taken together, yield the motivation for volition. Moreover, according to Edwards and *contra* Locke's revised position, volition is determined by the strongest motivation, resulting in choice. Hence,

(11') These conditions, taken together, yield the strongest motivation for B to choose T, rather than D.

However, as we have seen, B chooses the alternative expressed in D not T. The problem here is that, in choosing D over T, B is choosing in accordance with his natural appetites, but against his rational judgement. So, although pre-fall Adam did make choices in accordance with (9')–(11'), in the case of primal sin, he was determined to act in the way he did by a disordered moral nature, in this way (replacing 'B' with 'Adam'):

(8'') Adam determines upon what *seems to his natural appetites* to be 'the greatest apprehension of the good' in primal sin.
(9'') This 'greatest apprehension of the good' involves,

    (a) The natural appetites in,

        (ii) an apprehension that the particular choice is the best for Adam himself,

over and against,

> (i) a sensibility of the absolute beauty of a particular choice ('what is best absolutely and most lovely in itself' (*YE13*: 485)).

That is, Adam chooses what seems best to him over and against what is best absolutely considered. This takes place where Adam's rational will perceives the sinfulness of the choice proposed, but he allows his natural appetites to override his rational judgement, such that:

> (b) Adam's rational judgement that the particular choice for primal sin is not the best

is ignored.[52]

The motivation that arises for the primal sin is still sufficient for volition, but it arises from a disordered moral nature. This needs to be carefully distinguished from a vitiated moral nature. Adam's moral nature may be disordered and not vitiated, but it cannot be vitiated without being disordered. That is, the notion of a disordered moral nature as I am using the term, is applicable to the self-deception that leads to Adam's primal sin. Thereafter, his nature is vitiated, and Adam is no longer in a state of grace.

This should not be taken to mean that post-fall no human being can ever make choices that are in accordance with their rational judgement. What Edwards is saying is that post-fall there is a disposition to sin that was not present pre-fall. A fallen human being may still make choices that are reasonable, in accordance with the rational judgement. So, for example, a drug addict may make a decision to refrain from taking any more drugs, since he recognizes that, according to his rational judgement, continued substance abuse will result in his premature death. And he may make this decision against his natural appetites (his physical and psychological addiction to the drug).

But whereas before the fall, choice was always according to an ordered 'whole will' of reason and appetite, in accordance with the concreated superior principles, post-fall, there is a disposition to sin, now that humanity is no longer in a state of (sufficient) grace. So, whereas the drug addict may make a particular choice according to his rational judgement, over and against his natural appetites, it does not follow that this will occur on every occasion. And according to Edwards' account of the fall, it cannot occur on every occasion of choice, since the drug addict (or whoever) has a disposition to sin post-fall. Indeed, it is this very disposition to sin that has led the addict to become dependent upon the drugs he uses in the first place. So it is not the case that post-fall human beings can choose according to their rational judgement on every occasion. This is because the introduction of a disposition to sin as a result of a vitiated moral nature means that the preponderance of moral choices will be in accordance with the disposition to sin, and the vitiated moral nature humanity inherits from Adam.

Adam's Self-deception

We have seen that a crucial constituent of Edwards' account is his understanding of Adam's fall as a species of self-deception, leading to the vitiation of Adam's moral nature. This presents a way of solving the problem of primal sin, with which we began the chapter. But before turning to consider whether Edwards' account of Adam's self-deception can act as a solution to the problem of primal sin, we need to consider the paradoxical nature of self-deception itself.

Let us begin with the concept of deception, drawing on an article by Samuel Guttenplan in the process.[53] Deception would appear to involve something like the following scenario. Trevor knows that the Kempton races begin at 3:30 p.m., but he manages to get Gary to believe that they begin at 4:30 p.m., thus deceiving Gary. Now, what is important in this example for the present purpose is that Trevor deliberately sets out to provide Gary with a false belief. It will not work if Trevor sincerely believes that the Kempton races do start at 4:30 p.m. If he were to believe this, though it were a false belief, and though he passes on this false information so that Gary also comes to hold a false belief about the time of the races, he does not intend to deceive or pass on misinformation. Crucial in the deception of others and oneself, as Guttenplan points out, is the connection between how one acts and what one believes. Self-deception is not a case of acting paradoxically, such that a person believes both proposition p and proposition ~p at one and the same time. Instead, it is a case of acting as if one believed that p whilst also acting as if p was false. The problem with this is that acting as if p was or was not false is not the same as believing that p, or ~p. An example: Trevor's wife is having an affair with Gary. Trevor suspects that this is going on from the furtive telephone conversations and his wife's sudden and unexplained interest in Bingo four times a week, as well as other, incidental and anecdotal evidence. However, he loves his wife, and does not want to believe that their relationship is a sham or that it is over. So he takes no steps to confirm his suspicions. He continues to behave as if nothing is amiss. However, his wife confronts him with the truth one evening and Trevor is shocked and appalled by what his wife reveals to him, though, in fact, this is not news to him at all.

Here Trevor acts as if he believes that his wife is not having an affair, whilst at the same time believing that she is having an affair. But he does not believe both contradictory propositions at the same time, though he acts as if he does. So, how can this peculiar state of affairs be explained? One solution is that Trevor holds one belief unconsciously, such that he is not consciously aware that his beliefs conflict, or does not want to bring himself to believe that his beliefs conflict. Alternatively, it could be that Trevor has compartmentalized his beliefs, so that he acts in certain situations as if one belief is not true and the other is. We would need to flesh out these two options with far more detail were they to stand on their own as explanations of the paradoxical nature of self-deception.

However, Edwards' account is akin to both these options without being exactly parallel to either. It is similar to the suppression of one belief unconsciously, whilst holding its opposite consciously (the rational will and natural appetites serving in these respective capacities). But it is not exactly like the psychoanalytic solution since Edwards does not claim that Adam holds one belief consciously, whilst denying any conscious knowledge of the other. (Nor would this be a particularly plausible solution to the problem of primal sin. Adam has to be aware that the primal sin is wrong at more than an unconscious level, for the breaking of the covenant in eating the forbidden fruit to have any real force as an explanation of the curse and original sin.) Edwards' account is much more like the compartmentalization solution. Adam holds the belief of his rational will and the desire of his natural appetites in tandem. But he is able to choose to sin only because he ignores, or compartmentalizes, the part of his mind that involves his rational will and opts for the desire of his natural appetite instead. However, Edwards' account is more subtle than this. He wants to account for both Adam's sinful act and the complex nature of belief that went into Adam's fall in such a way that Adam is responsible for his sin, and that sin arises from a disordered, but not vitiated moral nature, thereby avoiding imputing Adam's sin to God. The question is, will this work as a solution to the problems with self-deception, and as a solution to the question of primal sin? Let us examine Edwards' attempted resolution in more detail.

Edwards believed that Adam had a moral nature before the fall, but that eating the fruit of the tree of the knowledge of good and evil actually brought about an increased knowledge of both good and evil:

> ... without doubt it was a tree of the knowledge of good properly, as much as evil. And the lively perception of good so much depends on the knowledge of its contrary, evil, that there was as much attained of new knowledge of good, as there was knowledge of evil; and this was the end of it principally, the knowledge of good.[54]

Thus, with respect to the primal sin, Adam seems to have been in a state of limited moral knowledge prior to the fall. However, God is not unjust in punishing Adam and Eve for their sins, since Adam had a sufficient grasp of the moral payload of the alternatives set before him to make an informed choice. And – according to Edwards at least –the net result of his choosing sin was an increase in his store of moral understanding, though at the significant cost of being disbarred from fellowship with God in Eden. Thus, the fact that he sinned because he deceived himself into thinking that rebellion against the divine command was better for himself means that God is not unjust in his punishment of Adam subsequent to the primal sin.

To illustrate this, consider the following example, in the style of Richard Swinburne's account of self-deception in *Responsibility and Atonement*.[55] Trevor is caught stealing a watch from an old lady. When he is asked to explain himself, he says, 'It is only luck that the woman had that watch. And anyway, no one really loses anything these days, because they are all insured against loss.' This means of self-deception concerning the moral nature of his action involves Trevor convincing himself that what he has done is not morally wrong. Instead he tries to convince himself that his action is morally indifferent, or good.

It is true that in the case of Adam there is a significant difference from the case of Trevor the thief. Trevor's moral nature is already, according to Edwards, morally vitiated, whereas, prior to his primal sin, Adam's is not. Nevertheless, compare Swinburne's explanation of the thief, utilizing Freud's analysis of self-deception: 'He [Freud] showed how self-deception was an intentional act of suppressing some belief from consciousness, which also involved the act of suppressing from consciousness the belief that you were performing that act or any other self-deceptive act.'[56] Edwards claims that Adam suppresses the rational judgement (conscience) that disobeying the command of God is wrong in the particular matter of the forbidden fruit, under the influence of the serpent. Notice that it is only in this particular instance that his rational judgement is ignored. Edwards' position does not require that Adam's conscience/ rational judgement be entirely impaired, only that it is ignored in this particular instance. Such instances are not hard to find in human nature. If I am tempted to commit adultery, and am fully aware of the fact that I am married whilst at the same time entertaining thoughts of illicit sexual encounters with another woman, and then act on those thoughts, I have suppressed my conscience in that one instance. It does not follow that my conscience is suppressed in every other area of morality.

So, like Swinburne's use of Freud, Edwards' account of Adam's fall need only presume that Adam suppresses the particular belief of his rational judgement with respect to the fruit of the tree. Edwards' view also means that Adam chooses the action he does because he believes it is best for him, and this motivation overrides his rational judgement. He does not suppress from consciousness the belief that he is performing that act or any other self-deceptive act. Instead, he convinces himself that what he is doing is for his own good, without recourse to what action would be the best course absolutely considered, thereby compartmentalizing his beliefs, and the decisions he takes on the basis of these beliefs. Thus, Edwards' account seems to be an interesting and plausible way of explaining how Adam acts against his own best interest (absolutely considered), and in accordance with what he presumes to be his best interest (in the particular case of the forbidden fruit).

Returning to the problem of primal sin, if Adam acts in a manner consistent with this picture of self-deception, then God does not act unworthily in punishing Adam. Adam knew that there was an alternative to obedience, though he may not have known the content of that alternative.[57] Nevertheless, he knew that the alternative was contrary to what God commanded. And he knew that he should have acted in accordance with the command. He acted as he did because he convinced himself that disobedience was in his own best interest when it was not (and he knew it was not). Hence, the fact that he sinned is due to an instance of self-deception, not to any character flaw in God.

Is Edwards' Account of the Fall Coherent?

We have seen that Edwards is able to resolve the problem of primal sin in his account of self-deception. But is this account coherent? The general consensus in the secondary

46 *Jonathan Edwards and the Metaphysics of Sin*

literature is that it is not. Thus, Clyde Holbrook writes: 'The sequence of events in Adam's fall leaves Edwards mired in a difficulty from which he never successfully freed himself. Once having established Adam's original righteousness, how could he explain the take-over of the lower faculties?'[58]

However, John Kearney has recently sought to rehabilitate Edwards.[59] His defence of Edwards' argument has several aspects. The first is that God was under no obligation to provide Adam with confirming grace. The second is that Edwards' account is not guilty of circular reasoning. The third is that an intrinsic property of creatureliness is having a mutable will. Although Kearney is able to defend the first two theses, we shall see that he is unable to defend the third, and this alone is fatal to Edwards' position.

Divine Obligation and Confirming Grace

In the first thesis, Kearney is responding to John Gerstner's claim that, 'if the grace is truly sufficient it must be efficacious; if it is not efficacious it is not sufficient'.[60] According to Gerstner, Edwards' use of the notions of sufficient and confirming grace amount to 'a distinction without a difference'. If the grace Edwards speaks about is supposed to be sufficient for Adam to withstand sin, then it is not only *sufficient* to the job, it should be *efficacious* in enabling Adam to resist temptation and remain in a state of grace. In other words, a grace that is truly sufficient is a grace that is efficacious. But this is simply muddled. We have already seen that Edwards' distinction between the two kinds of grace is concomitant with the scholastic notions of *posse non peccare* and *non posse peccare*. The distinction does differentiate two quite different moral states, pre- and post-fall.

Gerstner goes on to say that if sufficient grace amounts to a *posse non peccare* state, then Adam is not in a significantly better moral state than his progeny are, since his progeny are able to make decisions in accordance with their rational wills just as Adam himself did. All human beings have the ability to choose in accordance with their rational wills on at least some occasions. When, for instance, the drunk abstains from alcohol on the road to recovery, he is choosing in accordance with his rational will over and against his natural appetites. And if all humans can choose to act in accordance with their rational wills on some occasions, how is this significantly different from Adam pre-fall?

However, as previously mentioned, Edwards maintains that the problem lies not with natural *ability* to sin or refrain from sinning, but in *inclination* to sin. Adam pre-fall was not inclined to sin, yet he chose to sin. Humanity post-fall may choose not to sin on a particular occasion, but people are inclined to sin because they no longer possess the property of being in a state of (sufficient) grace. It is this distinction that Gerstner overlooks.[61] Nor is God under any obligation to keep Adam in a state of grace. In a sermon on *The Justice of God in the Damnation of Sinners*, Edwards makes this plain. In the same sermon he also states that it is unreasonable for God to be held accountable for not providing Adam with a deposit of grace that would prevent him from being able to break the conditions of the covenant of works:

> Such is God's sovereign power and right, that he is originally under no *obligation* to keep men from sinning; but may in his providence permit and leave them to sin. He was not obliged to keep either angels or men from falling. It is *unreasonable* to suppose, that God should be obliged, if he makes a reasonable creature capable of knowing his will, and receiving a law from him, and being subject to his moral government, at the same time to make it *impossible* for him to sin, or break his law.[62]

Let us examine the two claims of this passage in more detail. First, God is not obliged to give his creatures confirming grace. He is under no obligation because he has not bound himself over to provide them with this deposit of grace. In addition, the command forbidding the fruit of the tree of knowledge of good and evil was, 'given for the trial of Adam's obedience'.[63] Presumably, Edwards means that efficacious grace was a reward for obedience to the condition of the covenant of works, which Adam failed. Had he prevailed, he would have been rewarded for overcoming the temptation, with confirming grace, and the *non posse peccare* state. So, *contra* Gerstner, God is not culpable for withholding the deposit of confirming grace, since he is under no obligation to his creatures where he has not bound himself over to provide such a deposit. And, since the deposit was conditional upon successful completion of a period of probation provided for under the covenant of works, there is no reason why God might not withhold this grace when Adam failed to comply with the provisions of the covenant.[64]

But Edwards' second claim is that it is unreasonable for God to be held accountable for not providing Adam with a deposit of grace that would prevent him from being able to break the conditions of the covenant of works. For God is not bound in some way to give certain, as yet unmade creatures, particular properties. The claim that God should have created Adam with the property of confirming grace and that he is somehow culpable for not having done so, is false. It appeals to the following implausible principle:

> (P) It is wrong to bring into existence, knowingly, a being less excellent than one could have brought into existence.

Robert Adams has used this principle to show that God might not create the best possible world, a notion that Edwards would have found repugnant.[65] Be that as it may, all that is needed in the present circumstance is the notion that it is not incumbent upon God to create a creature with confirming, rather than sufficient grace, not that it is not incumbent upon God to create the best possible world.

P is implausible because there are numerous counter-examples to it. For instance, a person breeding peacocks is not thereby culpable for not having brought about the procreation of a more excellent form of life (primates, for example), though it was open to this person to breed either creature. Apply this reasoning to Adam. Where creating Adam with sufficient grace might be thought to be less excellent than creating him with confirming grace, should God create Adam with the latter, rather than the former property? We might answer this question with another: in what sense do creatures that have not yet been created exercise moral rights over their creator? God could create Adam with only sufficient grace, and this would be a perfectly moral act. Indeed, taking up Robert Adams' point, God's creation of a creature that was bound to fall might be seen as an instance of divine grace, a perfection rather than an imperfection.[66] So Kearney is right that there is a distinction to be made between the two kinds of grace that Edwards outlines, *contra* Gerstner. And God may supply sufficient, but not confirming grace without compromising his integrity.

Is Edwards' Reasoning (Viciously) Circular?

Second, Edwards in *OS* claims that, 'although there was no natural inclination in Adam, yet an inclination to that sin of eating the forbidden fruit, was begotten in him by the delusion and error he was led into; and this inclination to eat the forbidden fruit, must precede his actual eating'.[67] Clyde Holbrook, in his editorial introduction to *YE3*, says that this amounts to circular reasoning: 'How could a delusion be "begotten in him" or how could he be "led into" delusion without presupposing a sinful propensity to which the temptation could appeal?'[68] Much depends here on what is meant by 'sinful propensity'. Holbrook could mean either an inclination to sin in general, or an inclination to commit one particular sin.

But Edwards is clear that the second of these meanings for 'sinful propensity' need not entail the first (as we have already noted in regard to the problem of self-deception). That is, a person may be inclined to commit one particular sin on a particular occasion, without having a general inclination to sin on many different occasions. Indeed, a person might be inclined to sin on a particular occasion, and that be the first sin that establishes a general inclination to sin, or be the first instance of a sin that forms a habit to commit such sins again, on other occasions. Take, for example, Edwards' drunk and his bottle. There must be a first drink that leads to another, and from thence to eventual addiction. This is what happened in the case of Adam's primal sin:

> 'Tis true, as was observed before, there is no effect without some cause, occasion, ground or reason of that effect, and some cause answerable to that effect. But certainly it will not follow, from thence, that a transient effect requires a permanent cause, or a fixed influence and propensity. [Yet:] However great the sin of Adam, or of the angels, was, and however great means, motives and obligations they sinned against; whatever may be thence argued concerning the transient cause, occasion, or temptation, as being very subtle, remarkably tending to deceive or seduce, or otherwise great; yet it argues nothing of any settled disposition, or fixed cause at all, either great or small; the effect both in the angels and in our first parents, being in itself transient, and for aught appears, happening in each of them, under one system or coincidence or influential circumstances.[69]

So, Edwards is not guilty of circular reasoning in this respect. His position is consistent with Adam developing an *inclination* to sin from an initial, primal sin. So, here again, Kearney's defence of Edwards holds, whilst Holbrook's criticism folds.

Is Having a Mutable Will an Intrinsic Property of Creatureliness?

The third thesis that Kearney defends is that an intrinsic property of creatureliness is having a 'mutable' will (in fact, what he has in mind is more than a mutable will; it is a will that is able to *mutate* in the direction of sin):

> If Adam is created such that he is determined to hold his ground in the face of every temptation, then it is as if he has been programmed by God to be always inclined to do the right thing. In the abstract it is logically possible for God to create a being who is always so inclined, but in the context of Edwards' theology, where God is absolutely sovereign and human beings are utterly dependent upon him for their very existence, being a creature means having imperfections, one of which is a mutable will.[70]

Kearney maintains that if such a state of affairs did not obtain in Edwards' thinking, then there would be no need for a redeemer, and no need for God to demonstrate his justice and mercy, because Adam and his posterity would have remained morally pristine. But this is not an adequate justification of Edwards' position for several reasons. First, if it is logically possible for God to create a world with creatures that are always inclined to do the good *posse non peccare*, with sufficient grace, then why did God not actualize such a world? To respond, in effect, that this is just the way things are in Edwards' metaphysics is to concede that Edwards presents no compelling argument for his case.[71] In point of fact, as William Wainwright has shown elsewhere, Edwards believes that God must create a world, and must create this world, two extremely contentious claims that I do not intend to pursue here (though I find them a convincing account of Edwards' views).[72] But even if this point is ceded to Wainwright, so as to save Kearney further trouble, the fact that Edwards endorses a strong compatibility thesis (and, as we shall see in succeeding chapters of this thesis, rejects the notion that anything created persists through time, defending instead an occasionalism) does not entail that creatures are in some way bound to be imperfect. And it certainly does not entail that an intrinsic property of creatureliness is having a 'mutable will', if that means a will that is intrinsically liable to change.

But let us even grant this notion to Kearney. If God determines that Adam sins, and if, in the final analysis, Adam's primal sin obtains because God has ordained (or 'permitted') it to take place, then the responsibility for the fall, and the entrance of sin into the world lies not with Adam, but with God. After all, Adam is determined to act as he does by God himself, the ordainer and cause of all events that come to pass. However, for the question of culpability to have bite, Edwards needs to endorse the view that God is the proximate, not just ultimate cause of sin. (And we shall see in the next chapter that Edwards does endorse this view.) This distinction works as follows.

50 *Jonathan Edwards and the Metaphysics of Sin*

God could be the ultimate cause of all things inasmuch as he is the creator of all things. But this is not strong enough to demonstrate that he is culpable for Adam's sin; only that he is the ultimate cause for Adam existing and persisting long enough to sin, and the one who sustains Adam through his sin, and permits his sin to take place. But Edwards goes beyond this view of God's involvement in the created order to endorse occasionalism. This theory involves two distinct theses. A thesis about creation, specifically, the endorsement of a continuous creation thesis with the denial of a doctrine of conservation. And, secondly, a thesis about causation, to the effect that God causes all events to take place, coupled with the denial of secondary causation. This yields a view of the created order as radically and entirely contingent upon God's action at every moment of its existence. Thus, Edwards' endorsement of occasionalism means that God *is* the proximate, not just ultimate cause of sin, because no other being has causal power. God alone has causal power, and God alone is therefore the proximate cause of Adam's sin. [73]

Thus, Kearney's defence of Edwards is only partially successful. He has succeeded in showing that, contrary to previous opinion, Edwards does offer a carefully nuanced account of how Adam first sinned. This account is *internally* coherent. That is, it is coherent in terms of the argument Edwards sets out in its favour. But it is not *externally* coherent. That is, it is not coherent when set alongside other aspects of his metaphysics, particularly his commitment to absolute divine sovereignty, understood occasionalistically. Moreover, his theory raises questions that he does not satisfactorily resolve. For instance, on the question of self-deception, Edwards' account implies that the property of self-deception is intrinsic to human nature both pre- and post-fall. But if that is the case, then Adam had the property (perhaps a dispositional property) of self-deception prior to the fall, which calls his moral innocence into question. There is also a question as to whether Edwards' account has the consequence that human nature has an inevitable tendency to degenerate. And, perhaps most serious of all, it appears to make God the author of sin. But that is the subject of the next chapter.

Notes

1 Several contemporary philosophers have ventured to comment on the fall. Richard Swinburne reinterprets it in ways commensurate with an emerging species of hominoid in *Responsibility and Atonement*, p. 141. By contrast, Eleonore Stump has sought to work within the framework of the traditional doctrine of the fall. She claims that, although the doctrine of the fall seems false to many people, it is not 'demonstrably false' and may well be compatible with contemporary evolutionary theory. See 'The Problem of Evil' in *Faith and Philosophy* 2 (1985): 398–9 and her response to Michael P. Smith's criticisms of her position in the same journal.

2 See, for instance, the problems Augustine has in explaining primal human sin in *City of God*, Bk xiv: 10–14.

3 It is worth pointing out that a solution to the traditional theological problem does not necessarily commit the philosophical theologian to one particular understanding of the compatibility of the doctrine with evolutionary theory, or the findings of biblical studies. In a similar vein, Peter van Inwagen has argued that the Genesis creation and fall accounts are theological stories, not scientific accounts of

creation, and should be treated as such. See 'Genesis and Evolution' in *God, Knowledge and Mystery*.

4   See 'Primal Sin' in *The Augustinian Tradition*. MacDonald defines primal sin as 'a corruption of rational nature that gives evil its first foothold in God's creation', p. 115.

5   See, for example, *Miscellanies 320* and *438* in *YE13*, and *664b*, Sections 6–9 in *YE18*. Edwards' main contention seems to have been that those angels that rebelled did so because they thought that the prospect of Christ taking on human nature would mean that they would have to worship him as both human and divine, and this was beneath them.

6   Edwards defines a moral agent as 'a being that is capable of those actions that have a moral quality, and which can properly be denominated good or evil in a moral sense, virtuous or vicious, commendable or faulty', *YE1*: 165.

7   *YE1*: 340.

8   *YE1*: 225.

9   *YE1*: 165. Edwards believed that this moral agency was what made up the natural endowment of the *imago dei*. The spiritual endowment of moral excellency was lost at the fall. That, according to Edwards, is the means by which the natural endowment was exercised effectively according to divine order. After the fall, the spiritual endowment was lost, or corrupted. See *YE2*: 256.

10 *YE3*: 225. In fact, according to Edwards, Taylor 'most confidently affirms, that thought, reflection and choice must go before virtue, and that all virtue or righteousness must be the fruit of preceding choice. This', Edwards observes, 'brings his scheme to an evident contradiction', *YE3*: 226.

11 *YE3*: 223.

12 *YE3*: 224. Edwards' view is in sharp contrast to that of Aristotle in this respect. Aristotle's virtue theory as traditionally understood, claims that actions develop character. A person becomes good by doing good. See *The Ethics*, I: I, p. 25ff.

13 *YE3*: 224.

14 'he [Taylor] supposes the doctrine of original sin to imply, that nature must be corrupted by some *positive influence* . . . Whereas truly our doctrine neither implies nor infers any such thing', *YE3*: 380, author's emphasis.

15 *YE3*: 381.

16 Ibid.

17 Ibid.

18 *YE3*: 382.

19 *YE3*: 383.

20 This is the view, to which we shall return in a later chapter, that Adam acts as the federal representative, or head, of humanity, such that his sin as the head of the race is imputed to his posterity. It is a position championed by theologians in the Reformed tradition.

21 *YE3*: 385.

22 *YE3*: 386.

23 *YE3*: 386, author's emphasis. For more on the imputation of Christ's righteousness, see the Appendix.

24 'So that the very establishment, or covenant itself, as God revealed and stated it, implied that the first, overt, explicit violation should be the abolishing of the covenant as to future proceedings, because that was in the establishment, that on the first violation God would immediately proceed to judgment', *Miscellany 717*, in *YE18*: 349.

25 *YE13*: 382.

26 Ibid.

27 *YE13*: 383.

28 *YE13*: 485.

29 *YE13*: 484.

30 Ibid.

31 *YE13*: 486. Unfortunately, in this instance, greater reflection on these issues does not yield greater insight on Edwards' part. See, *Miscellany 501* in this regard, *YE18*: 51.

32 See Ramsey's comment to this effect in his introduction to *YE1*: 51.

33 *YE1*: 137.

34 See *An Essay concerning Human Understanding*, Bk. II; chapter XXI; sect. 17.

35 *YE1*: 138.

36 *Essay* II: XXI: 30, p. 250.

37 *YE1*: 139.

38 *YE1*: 139, cf. Editor's Introduction, pp. 51–2: 'Edwards argues that on closer inspection it will be found that (1) "will" and "prefer" and (2) "will" and "desire" mean the same thing.'

39 *YE1*: 52.

40 In what follows I have adapted the concepts of first- and second-order conflict from Harry Frankfurt's discussion of first- and second-order desires in 'Freedom of the will and the concept of a person' in *The Importance of What We Care About*.

41 I am assuming here that deception often trades on linguistic ambiguity. Example: if my wife asks me whether I studied at Aberdeen, she might have in mind the ancient university in that city. If I reply 'yes', in the knowledge that my wife intends the ancient university, when I have actually studied at Robert Gordon University, then I am not lying, but I am not telling the whole truth. My response trades on the linguistic ambiguity involved in her question, leaving her with a false belief about where I have studied.

42 *YE1*: 141. Edwards goes on to explain that there may be many different things which together act to motivate the will. So 'the strongest motive' is not an empty tautology: 'when I speak of the "strongest motive", I have respect to the strength of the whole that operates to induce to a particular act of volition, whether that be the strength of one thing alone, or of many together'.

43 *YE1*: 143.

44 *Essay*, II: XXI: 29, p. 249.

45 See *YE1*: 143, and the Editor's Introduction, Part 4: Nos. 3 and 4. In *Locke on the Human Understanding*, p. 135, E.J. Lowe asks whether there is really any merit in speaking of greater goods when it is in danger of becoming a vacuous tautology: *I willed what was the strongest desire* collapses into *I willed what I willed*. 'For it is hard to see how one is to identify one desire as being stronger or more urgent than others . . . save in terms of its being the desire that was acted upon.' According to Lowe, comparisons between different strengths of desire have an appearance of solving the problem whilst denying the substance of it. However, when I am faced with a dilemma, do I not choose on the basis of alternatives? And do I not choose that alternative which appears the best option at the time of choice? And is this not something akin to what the early Locke and Edwards are trying to advocate? There are other reasons why Locke's revised account is less than satisfactory. Lowe points out that Locke seems guilty of allowing second-order volitions in by the back door. Previously, Locke had disavowed the iterability of volitions: we cannot will to will a thing. This was used as a countermeasure to ward off possible infinite regressions of iteration. But here Locke appears to be introducing just this conception: we can withhold acting upon immediate desires for the long-term good, on the basis of unease. In other words, we can will not to will an action because by forbearing long term benefits accrue.

46 *The Mind*, in *The Works of Jonathan Edwards, Volume I*, p. ccxxvii.

47 Smith, *Jonathan Edwards, Puritan, Preacher, Philosopher*, p. 16.

48 Ibid.

49 *The Mind*, in *The Works of Jonathan Edwards, Volume I*, p. ccxxvii.

50 *YE13*: 485.

51 *YE13*: 486.

52 Kearney, also points this out in 'Jonathan Edwards' Account of Adam's First Sin'.

53 See Guttenplan, *A Companion to Philosophy of Mind*, pp. 558–60.

54 *Miscellany 172*, in *YE13*: 324.

55 See *Responsibility and Atonement*, pp. 174–5.

56 *Responsibility and Atonement*, p. 174.

Adam's Fall 53

57 A person may know that there is an alternative to the course of action they are contemplating, without knowing the content of that action. Consider the case of a child whose mother says, 'Don't touch that trifle or there will be trouble.' The child is in no doubt that there is an alternative to the parental imperative, though they may not be clear what that alternative entails.

58 Clyde A. Holbrook, Editor's Introduction, *YE3*: 51. A similar point is made by James Hoopes in 'Calvinism and Consciousness from Edwards to Beecher', in Hatch and Stout (eds), *Jonathan Edwards and The American Experience*, pp. 213–14.

59 In 'Jonathan Edwards' Account of Adam's First Sin', Kearney's account of Edwards' argument is certainly the best, and clearest in the literature to date. It has superseded earlier, faulty accounts by John Gerstner in *Rational Biblical Theology, Vol. II*, ch. XXII, and Clyde Holbrook's Editor's Introduction to *YE3*.

60 *Rational Biblical Theology, Vol. II*, p. 306.

61 See *Rational Biblical Theology, Vol. II*, pp. 304–306 and 'Jonathan Edwards' Account of Adam's First Sin', p. 132.

62 'The Justice of God in the Damnation of Sinners', in *The Works of Jonathan Edwards, Vol. I*, p. 670, author's emphasis.

63 *Miscellany 322*, in *YE13*: 403, cited in Kearney, 'Jonathan Edwards' Account of Adam's First Sin', p. 133.

64 Kearney cites *YE14* in this respect, from a sermon entitled, 'All God's Methods Are Most Reasonable', p. 168.

65 See Adams, 'Must God Create the Best?', in *The Concept of God*.

66 Ibid., pp. 105–106.

67 *YE3*: 228–9.

68 *YE3*: 51.

69 *YE3*: 191 and 193 respectively. Cited in Kearney, 'Jonathan Edwards' Account of Adam's First Sin', p. 137.

70 'Jonathan Edwards' Account of Adam's First Sin', p. 138.

71 This is not to say that there may not be an argument for this view, along some greater good theodicy line. It is just to say that Edwards does not seem to have such an argument.

72 See Wainwright, 'Jonathan Edwards, William Rowe, and the Necessity of Creation', in *Faith, Freedom and Rationality*.

73 Edwards' concept of occasionalism is the subject of Chapter 7.

CHAPTER 3

The Authorship of Sin

In the last chapter, we saw that Edwards made a valiant attempt at trying to cut the Gordian knot that the doctrine of the fall entails. We ended by pointing to the problem of the origin of sin, and the question of the authorship and responsibility for its origin. In a way characteristic of Edwards, he sought to provide a novel solution to this most difficult of theological problems. In so doing, he raises several interesting metaphysical questions which refer back to his characterization of the fall, and have implications for what he says regarding the imputation of Adam's sin (to which we shall turn in Chapter 5), and the metaphysics of persistence-through-time that accompany his defence of original sin.

This chapter outlines and assesses Edwards' resolution to the authorship of sin problem. I shall argue, against one recent exponent of Edwards' doctrine, but in concert with the majority of previous interpreters, that Edwards' attempted resolution to this issue fails to give an adequate account of the problem. However, Edwards rightly points out that the fact that he is unable to resolve this problem is common to both theological determinists like himself, and to theological libertarians, like the Arminians, whom he opposed.

To begin with, we shall set out the authorship problem in the context of the wider problem of evil. Then we shall focus in on the contours of Edwards' response to this problem. There have been several treatments of Edwards' response to this problem. We shall pay particular attention to two of the most recent and most thorough of these, those of William Wainwright and John Kearney.[1]

The Authorship Problem

Many, but not all, of the historic formulations of the problem of evil have been set out as *defeaters* to Christian belief.[2] In the logical problem of evil, this has characteristically taken the following form,

(1)   God exists.
(2)   God is omnipotent, omniscient and benevolent.
(3)   Evil exists.

However,

(4)   If evil exists, then where 'God' denotes a being who is omnipotent, omniscient and benevolent, such a being cannot obtain in any possible world.

The Authorship of Sin 55

This logical problem of evil, beloved of analytic philosophers of religion, is not an issue that detains Edwards (unlike his immediate contemporary, Hume). Instead, he deals with the more traditional theological problem of the entrance of evil into the world. Yet, having said this, one would expect that the problem of the origin of sin would admit of a similar kind of analysis to the logical problem of evil. Where (1), (2)&(3) obtain (and where a solution to the logical problem of (4) is proffered),

(5) God ordains that no event comes to pass without God willing that it should happen.
(6) If God does ordain that no event comes to pass without his willing it should happen, then God wills and ordains evil.

The resulting problem is,

(7) If God wills evil, then he cannot be essentially benevolent.

Now, clearly it is not a necessary truth that God ordains all events that come to pass. He may well place restrictions upon the exercise of his power for some perceived benefit that might result from this, as is argued by some theological libertarians with respect to creaturely volitional freedom. But such a picture need not detain us since our concern is with those who stand in the Augustinian tradition of theological compatibilism, and with Edwards as a representative of that tradition.

In this argument, as before with the logical problem of evil, there appears to be a logical component involved. But the question is not directed to the *prima facie* incompatibility of God and evil as the broader logical problem of evil is. The authorship-of-sin question presumes that God and evil coexist together. Instead of querying how this might logically be the case, the authorship question is: if (1)–(3) obtain, then whence evil? Or, to put it another way: the logical problem presumes the properties of (2) as an entailment of (1). It is from this conjunction that the problem with (3) arises. But the authorship question calls the properties of (2) into question where (3) and (1) are given. So the question here is: is (2) an entailment of (1) given (3)? If so, how can (3) arise? And if not, whence evil?

We shall designate this problem of the authorship of sin and evil, the AP.[3] From the foregoing it should be clear that, unlike the logical problem of evil, the AP is not a defeater to theism and therefore for Christian belief *per se*. One could still be a rational Christian theist and not have an answer to the question raised by the AP. If anything, it presents an aspect to the problem of evil that amounts to a *rebuttal* of one or more core beliefs within Christian theism associated with the nature of God (for example, benevolence).

The Edwardsian Axis

Edwards' theological determinism yields a particularly difficult version of the AP made more difficult by Edwards' thorough method of approaching the problem.

Edwards is a victim of his own relentless thoroughness in his dealings with the AP. He believed both that all creaturely volitions are necessary, and that God orders and determines all events that come to pass.[4] Put more formally, using the previous argument modified where necessary, Edwards adheres to the two following principles:

(P1)   All creaturely volitions are necessary.[5]
(P2)   God determines all events that come to pass.

His occasionalism yields an additional principle:

(P3)   God is the sole cause of all events; all mundane 'causes' are merely occasions (one mundane event has no power to cause another).[6]

From this the earlier argument can be adapted thus:

(1)   God is omnipotent, omniscient and benevolent.
(2)   Evil exists.
(3)   Given (1), (P1)&(P2), God ordains that no event comes to pass without his willing that it should happen.
(4)   But then, God must will evil.

Edwards' response to the AP falls into three parts.[7] The first is a *tu quoque* argument deployed against the Arminians, to the effect that whether his response to the AP is adequate or not, this is a problem common to theological libertarians as well as determinists.

The second and central issue pertains to whether God is causally and morally responsible for sin. This has several parts: the definition of 'author of sin', the distinction between permission and positive agency in sin, and the nature of moral responsibility. In addition, it opens up the question of divine justice in the following way. If person P's sin is ordained by God, then such a person cannot be held responsible for their sin, since they could not have done otherwise. However, according to Edwards, P is responsible and God justly judges P for his sin, despite it being theologically determined.

The third problem is the apparent insincerity of divine commands with respect to those who are unable to respond to them, that is, if God commands person P to do action x, but God has already ordained that P do action y instead, then his exhortations to do x are insincere. This relies on the distinction between the hidden and revealed will of God, found in Calvin, Aquinas and others, which we shall deal with in the next chapter.

Each of these areas of response has problems that Edwards is unable to overcome. But in addition to this, his concept of occasionalistic causation, particularly as it is developed in *OS*, means that though the three aspects to Edwards' argument may be individually problematic, they are jointly incoherent.

Tu Quoque

By its very nature, a *tu quoque* argument can only point out that the issue under consideration is a problem common to all the participants to the debate.[8] That is what Edwards seeks to do as he begins his discussion of the AP in *FOW* IV: 9: I. Nevertheless, whether it is true that those of a theologically libertarian persuasion have as great a burden of proof to overturn as theological determinists like Edwards do is separate from the question of whether Edwards can proffer a reasonable defence of his own position in the face of this potential rebuttal of his determinism. In other words, Edwards' *tu quoque* does not, and cannot, serve to alleviate the burden of proof that the AP presents his theological determinism with. All this tactic can hope to do is point out that theological libertarians are in the same boat as theological determinists, when it comes to solving the AP.

However, it is relevant to the related, but distinct, question of whether theological libertarians are any better off than theological determinists with respect to mounting a defence against the AP.[9] If theological libertarians can be shown to be better off than their determinist counterparts with respect to solving the AP, then Edwards is not simply faced with meeting the AP, he is placed at a significant disadvantage in presenting a solution to it. For if the Arminians (or whoever) are able to mount a simpler, more successful defence of their conception of God's responsibility for sin because of their libertarianism, then determinists like Edwards need to give good reasons for why their position is to be preferred to the libertarian alternative.

Therefore, although this is not actually part of a solution to Edwards' problem with the AP, it is worthwhile ascertaining whether he is disadvantaged by his adherence to theological determinism in comparison with the libertarian alternative. If he is, then it is incumbent upon him to show why, in addition to solving the AP, his determinism is to be preferred as a solution to the AP, to a potentially less complicated, more plausible libertarianism (assuming libertarianism is more plausible on balance). However, if he is not disadvantaged – if his *tu quoque* stands – then an Edwardsian defence of theological determinism in the face of the AP may proceed on a level playing field, so to speak.

Edwards' central contention here is that the AP 'is a difficulty which equally attends the doctrine of the Arminians themselves; at least, of whose of them who allow God's certain foreknowledge of all events'.[10] Hence, this touches upon that staple of contemporary philosophical discussion: the question of freedom, foreknowledge and subjunctive conditionals of freedom.

William Wainwright claims that Edwards' contention in the *tu quoque* is only partially successful. It fails to establish that the God of the Arminians is as equally the author of sin as the Calvinist God. Wainwright's argument turns on the difference between the two conceptions of free will and divine foreknowledge that underpin the Arminian (libertarian) and Calvinistic (determinist) approaches to this issue. That is, on a libertarian understanding of human free will, it makes no sense to claim that God can make true the acts of freely created agents. It does make sense to claim this for the determinist's God. So, when Edwards claims that God permits sin (as we shall see in a moment), he means something quite different from a similar, Arminian claim, where such Arminians allow 'God's foreknowledge of all events'.[11] Edwards means something like 'God's permission of action x is a causally sufficient condition for x taking place'. Whereas, the Arminian/libertarian means 'God's permission of action x is a sufficient, but not *causally* sufficient condition of x taking place'.

This is the case, Wainwright points out, because such libertarians believe that God does not 'produce' sin, nor does he 'bring it about', since sinful actions are actions which are free of divine interference. He does bring about the state of affairs in which free agents may exercise that freedom in sin. But he is not the causally sufficient condition of that sin.

The principle at issue is this:

(A)   If a person does action x or brings about x and knows that x is a sufficient condition of action y, then he does y or brings about y (is the 'author' of y).

Wainwright maintains that (A) is plausible for x, where x is a causally sufficient condition of y's obtaining (as with Edwardsian determinism). But it is less plausible where x is a causally necessary but not causally sufficient condition of y (as with Arminian libertarianism). And it is least plausible where y is a random or contra-causal decision (which Edwards claims is a constituent part of Arminian accounts of free will).

Here is the rub: because the God of the Arminians exercises significantly less control over human agents than the Calvinist God does (given the different readings of (A)), it is not clear that if the God of the Calvinists (and Edwards in particular) is responsible for sin, the Arminian God is also responsible.[12]

However, all is not lost for Edwards, even if this is granted, which, I think, it must be.[13] For Wainwright goes on to point out that the central contention behind Edwards' *tu quoque* argument is successful. This contention is that even if the Arminian God does not have the same problem with (A) that the Calvinist does, because of their libertarianism with respect to the counterfactuals of freedom, nevertheless, this does not mean that the Arminian God is *less* responsible for sin than the Calvinist's God. God could still be responsible for sin, though he is not its author. And if this can be demonstrated, then Edwards has gone a considerable way towards showing that he is not at a theological disadvantage in holding to a Calvinistic compatibility thesis with respect to creaturely freedom.

Wainwright examines the doctrine of double effect (DDE) as a means to drawing this out with respect to the Edwardsian *tu quoque*. According to the DDE, 'there is a morally relevant difference between the harmful consequences of our actions which we intend and those we merely foresee'.[14] This involves four notions:

(1)   The action itself is good.
(2)   Only a good, not an evil effect, is intended.

The Authorship of Sin

(3)   A good effect is not produced by an evil effect.
(4)   There is a proportional reason for permitting the evil effect.[15]

Some contemporary proponents of this principle even claim that harmful actions that are foreseen, are always to be preferred to intended harmful actions, even when such foreseen, but non-intended harmful actions result in more harm than intended ones (given similar circumstances).[16]

The application to the AP is as follows. Arminians typically suppose that the alternatives facing God with respect to the fall were:

(A1)   Respect Adam's autonomy, not interfere in his choices and allow the resulting sin to occur.
(A2)   Prevent Adam's sin, forestalling sin and its evil consequences for humanity.

Clearly, (A1) corresponds to a situation foreseen but not intended by God (intended, instead, by Adam's libertarian free choice). (A2) corresponds to an intentional situation, where God acts to prevent a certain outcome, violating Adam's freedom in the process. It is this kind of scenario that leads Arminians to believe their God is less blameworthy than the Calvinistic deity. However, this is a false belief, because it does not pick out the relevant choices. Those choices that are relevant in this regard pertain to creation rather than the fall, since in (A1)&(A2) at least one human moral agent, Adam, is presupposed. Instead, the choice is between something like the following:

(A1')   Not to create libertarianly free being(s).
(A2')   To create libertarianly free beings knowing that at least one of them will sin.
(A3)   To create libertarianly free beings every one of which will not sin.

(A3) depends upon there being an actualizable, not just logically possible world, where no beings suffer from moral depravity.[17] Arminians think that something like (A2') obtains. This is a scenario in which sin is foreseeable, but not intended by God, (though, of course, the libertarian human agents intend it). With respect to the principles behind the DDE,

(1')   The creation of libertarian beings is in itself a good action (*qua* (1)).
(2')   Only a good (creation), not an evil effect (sin), is intended (*qua* (2)).
(3')   A good effect (libertarian freedom) is not produced by an evil effect (sinful actions) (*qua* (3)).
(4')   There is a proportional reason for permitting the evil effect: the good effects of creation significantly outweigh harmful ones (*qua* (4)).

This might seem to demonstrate that the Arminian is better off than the Calvinist on DDE principles. But this is not the case. Closer analysis shows that the Arminian position has parity with the Calvinist in this aspect of the *tu quoque*.

First, according to the Arminian, God intends, rather than merely foresees, creaturely sin in this respect: he creates Adam and Eve in a weak moral condition knowing that they will not be able to resist temptation and will fall. The point is that Adam was created with a weak moral condition that God foreknows will *inevitably* lead to sin on at least one occasion. God could have created Adam in a stronger moral state where he was libertarianly free but not bound to sin. But God did not do so. The fact that God did create Adam in the former, weaker, moral state means that he creates him intending that he fall at some point.[18]

Moreover, if (A3) is a possible world (presuming transworld depravity is not an essential property of all world-indexed individuals for a moment, and that such a world is an actualizable, not merely logically possible world – a notion Plantinga rejects), then the Arminians have an even greater problem to overcome. Although such a world might be morally objectively less good than a world where evil is actualized for a greater good (as Edwards argues with respect to the doctrine of the atonement), it may still be such that no individual in that world ever sins, and no morally detrimental effects result from this.

So, on two counts, it is not clear that the Arminians are able to satisfy the qualifications of the DDE without cavil. If God creates an (A2') world, then he intends to create creatures who are bound to fall. The other options are not to create any libertarian world, as per (A1'), or to create a world of libertarian creatures none of whom will ever sin, as per (A3). But (A3) may be logically possible but not actualizable by God, as Plantinga has shown in his Free Will Defence. And even if it were actualizable (by free creatures, say), as we have seen, it would create even more problems for the Arminian to deal with. Finally, it might be noted in passing that the Arminian is no better off with respect to at least one construal of (3'). Like the Calvinist, if the Arminian believes that a good effect (salvation) is produced by the evil of sin, then, though as (3') stands the Arminian is correct, as applied to the soteriology of Arminianism, it is false.

The Calvinist option, in light of our four DDE principles fares similarly:

(1")   The action itself is good: the creation of compatibilist humanity is necessary for the actualization of the elect (*qua* (1)).[19]

(2")   A good and an evil effect are intended, since God is the cause of all volitions (denial of (2)).

(3")   A good effect (actualization of the elect) is not (directly) produced by an evil effect (sin).

Nevertheless, it is produced through the medium of an evil effect, which means that (3) as it stands is not met by the Calvinist:

(4")   There is a proportional reason for permitting the evil effect: the greater good (*qua* (4)).

The Authorship of Sin

So, on the Calvinistic picture, (2) and (3) cannot be endorsed unequivocally. But this means that in this crucial element of their argument, the Arminian is on something like a par with the Calvinist. Both parties are unable to satisfy (2) and (3) of the DDE. The fact that there are different reasons for this result is irrelevant. What matters is that both the Arminians and the Calvinists struggle to meet the same criteria of the DDE. So the DDE cannot be used to support the claim that the Arminian deity is less blameworthy than the Calvinist God, because he is not causally responsible for all events, due to libertarian freedom.

In sum, Edwards' initial claim that the Arminian God is on a moral par with the Calvinist's regarding responsibility for sin appears to be false. Arminian libertarianism yields a different state of affairs from the determinism of Calvinism, and this affects the level of culpability involved in permitting sin (the difference between whether an agent *will* or *must* sin). But this does not enable the Arminian to escape the force of Edwards' *tu quoque*. The notion that there is a significant moral difference between intended harm and foreseen harm which would feed into the Arminian (libertarian) idea that an agent will sin, but may not sin, actually leaves the Arminian in much the same situation as the Calvinist. Neither party can credibly claim to be able to show that their Deity intends only the good, and not the evil effect of his creating this world. Nor can they show that the good effect of creating this world was not produced by means of an evil effect, such as sin.

Thus, Edwards is wrong in one respect, but right in another. Wrong that there is a strict parity between his Calvinism and the Arminians, but right that the Arminian position does not insulate them from parallel problems for moral responsibility. By contrast the Arminians are right, but wrong. Right that there is no strict parity between themselves and Edwardsian Calvinism. But wrong in thinking that this entitles them to invoke a moral principle like the DDE in their defence. Thus, Edwards is not handicapped by his determinism. The Arminians are not, as Wainwright concludes, significantly better off than the Calvinists, with respect to the AP. With this result in place, we may address the substance of Edwards' defence against the AP.

Three Problems for the Edwardsian AP

Given Edwards' theological determinism, expressed in part in (P1)&(P2) (we shall come to (P3) in due course), the first part of Edwards' defence proper pertains to moral responsibility. In light of (P1)&(P2), God appears to be ultimately causally *and morally* responsible for Adam's sin. We shall focus on three aspects to this problem that have been drawn out by Edwards and his critics. These we shall call *the problem of defining 'author of sin'*, *the permission and positive agency problem*, and *the proxy problem* respectively.

On Defining 'Author of Sin'

In *FOW* IV: 9: II,[20] Edwards distinguishes between two ways in which the term 'author of sin' may be construed. The first, common use is 'the sinner, the agent, or actor of sin, or the doer of a wicked thing; so it would be a reproach or blasphemy, to suppose God to be the author of sin'. But a second use is 'the permitter, or not a hinderer of sin; and at the same time, a disposer of the state of events, in such a manner, for wise holy and most excellent ends and purposes, that sin, if it be permitted or not hindered, will most certainly and infallibly follow'.[21] Edwards endorses this second way of thinking about God as the author of sin over the former. Let us designate these two senses of 'author of sin' AS1 and AS2 respectively.

Wainwright points out that AS1 has two conditions, which Edwards seems to conflate. These are, AS1(a) that God must be the agent/actor/doer of action x, and AS1(b) that God's performance of x must be sinful.[22] It may be that God is the AS1(a) but not AS1(b) agent of action x. If he is, then God is not clearly the author of (all) sin. Edwards can argue that God is the actor in the sense of AS2 in a way compatible with AS1(a) without incurring AS1(b). And that is exactly what AS2 sets out to demonstrate: God can permit the sin of an agent for some greater, holier, good. In this way, God may be the author of sin (he permits it) but not the one who sins. An example Edwards uses is the crucifixion of Christ. God permits the sin of those who murder Christ, for the greater good of humanity in the salvation of the elect. But, although he is the author of the sin that leads to Christ's death (*qua* AS1(a)), he is not the one who sins in killing Christ (*qua* AS1(b)).

So, in summary, Edwards makes clear that God need not be the author of sin in the conventional sense of the word (that is, AS1). But he may be the author of sin in the AS2 sense he sets out, namely, as the permitter of sin (although there are considerable questions about some of the assumptions lurking behind these claims). However, this raises further questions with respect to the distinction that Edwards seems to be making between permission and positive agency in a particular action.

Permission and Positive Agency

With AS2 informing our notion of the divine authorship of sin, we turn to *FOW*: IV: 9: III:

> There is a great difference between God's being concerned thus, by his permission, in an event and act, which in the inherent subject and agent of it, is sin (though the event will certainly follow on his permission), and his being concerned in it by producing it and exerting the act of sin; or between his being the orderer of its certain existence, by not hindering it, under certain circumstances, and his being the proper actor or author of it, by a positive agency or efficiency.[23]

We shall designate the difference between these two kinds of act as *permitting* (as per AS2) and *positive agency*. *Permission* carries the meaning (for present purposes at least) of non-interference, or forbearance, as when Trevor does not interfere in Wayne's fight with Gary, though (perhaps) he could have done so.[24] In the case of God, such permission is, as Paul Helm has pointed out, for a particular purpose, rather than a

The Authorship of Sin   63

general permission. And this particular purpose is, according to Edwards, to the holy end(s) of the divine plan.[25] *Positive agency*, by contrast, means an agent's actual causal involvement in a particular act (whether as a partial or total cause we leave open at present). Thus, if Trevor were to punch Gary and Wayne in the face, he would be exercising a positive agency in bringing about physical damage to both Gary and Wayne.

Wainwright proceeds to use this distinction to demonstrate that Edwards' view entails that God exercises positive agency, not merely permission in the origination of sin.[26] The idea that underlies Edwards' notion is that *person A permits person B to do action x*. But this has consequences that Edwards cannot approve of. For if this is a correct description then,

(i)   A's non-interference is a causally necessary condition of B doing action x, but

(ii)   A's non-interference is not a causally sufficient condition of B doing action x,

since A permitting B to do x is not necessarily the only causal reason why B does x. To go back to our previous protagonists, if Trevor forbears from interfering in Wayne's fight with Gary, then it may be that his forbearance is a necessary condition of Wayne fighting Gary (perhaps Wayne has such a high regard for Trevor that if he told him not to fight Gary, he would certainly not fight Gary). But it is not clear that this non-interference on Trevor's part is a causally sufficient condition of Wayne fighting Gary. It is, after all, Wayne's decision to hit Gary, not Trevor's. The situation is perhaps different with a deity; a deity might be causally responsible inasmuch as he creates and conserves Wayne in being at all those times in which he is thinking about and acting upon his desire to fight Gary. But even this is not enough to ensure that a deity is a causally sufficient condition of Wayne's action. There may be mundane causation involved. For God to be the necessary and sufficient condition for the occurrence of sin, some other condition needs to be added to (i) and (ii); a condition like (P3) (though not necessarily as strong as (P3)).

Edwards claims that God's permitting x is both a necessary and sufficient condition for the occurrence of sin. But even if he can find an argument to substantiate this (using, say, (P3)), this only generates another problem. For if this is the case, then God does more than merely permit sin; he is a positive agent in bringing it about. But Edwards' point in all this appears to be something slightly different. What he seems to be getting at is this: A is the author of B's being (or doing) x only if A brings about B's being (or doing) x by acting on B, or bringing about some positive influence to bear upon B.[27] Edwards maintains that this means God is not *morally* responsible for the sin of moral agents, though he is *causally* responsible. That is, he causes the state of affairs and desires of the particular moral agent to obtain such that Wayne will necessarily hit Gary, and God is causally responsible for this. But given Edwards' endorsement of the compatibilist principle of liberty of spontaneity, God is not morally responsible for Wayne hitting Gary, since it is still Wayne who chooses to do the hitting. He is not forced to hit Gary, though, of course, he is constituted so that he will hit Gary given a certain state of affairs determined by God.

But will this work? Does it stay within the parameters Edwards sets himself, namely, permission rather than positive agency? Take the example Edwards uses of the sun (*FOW*: 403–404). The sun is the positive agency that brings about the heat and light that brightens our planet. But when it is withdrawn during the night, the darkness that results is not brought about by the positive agency of the sun. It occurs, as the sun's rays are withdrawn. Unfortunately, this analogy will not yield the result Edwards needs. For the sun, unlike God, is not a moral agent. If it were, then it *would* be the author of the resulting cold and dark, since it would be acting as a voluntary agent in bringing about the state of affairs where darkness obtains.

Or take another example, this time involving a moral agent: Judas' betrayal of Christ. According to Edwards' argument, Judas' betrayal depends entirely on God's ordination (given (P1)&(P2)). That he does this by permitting Judas to sin, rather than acting positively to bring this about, does not alter the fact that the moral responsibility for this action, given (P1)&(P2), is God's alone. So although Edwards may be able to find a way to preserve his distinction between permission and positive agency, this does not seem to be able to bear the weight of absolving God of the moral responsibility for sin that Edwards thinks it should. We shall return to this with respect to the proxy problem.

Matters are complicated by the fact that Edwards maintains more than a theological determinism, as has already been hinted at. He was an occasionalist, as per (P3). But his occasionalism means that any distinction between permission and positive agency is undermined. For if there are no real causes apart from God's causal agency, then God's permission of x cannot mean anything less than his bringing x to pass, since any agent other than God has no ability to act as a cause whatsoever. But if it means this, then there is little or no difference between permission, on an occasionalistic view of God's causal action in the world, and positive agency. For God is the only causal agent.

The Proxy Problem

The third aspect to this problem is drawn out by John Kearney in a recent article on Edwards and the AP.[28] Given (P1), (P2) and the permission and positive agency problem, God is clearly causally responsible for all events that come to pass. Moreover, all such events are necessary. But, as we have already seen, the question this raises with respect to the AP is whether God is also morally responsible for all events. If he is, then he is the author of sin. We left the permission and positive agency problem with this issue of divine moral responsibility regarding the AP unresolved, taken on (P1)&(P2) only. The addition of (P3) is, as we have seen, fatal to Edwards' argument. This is what the proxy problem addresses.

Kearney defends Edwards against the charge that his theological determinism entails that God is morally responsible in this respect. His argument relies upon a second Edwardsian distinction (or a second distinction within the same problem) between the expression of an agent's will (in an action), and the expression of an agent's will in another agent's (sinful) choices. Put more formally:

The Authorship of Sin 65

(PX) if A wills action y, (where A is also the necessary and sufficient causal condition of y obtaining) and y is brought about by agent B, is A still morally responsible for B's action?

We shall call (PX) *the proxy problem for moral responsibility*, or *proxy problem* for short, since it involves one person acting as the agent for another, in this case, B for A. This problem poses the following two interrelated questions:

(PX1) Can A be causally responsible and not morally responsible for y?
(PX2) Can A be morally responsible and not causally responsible for y?

Both of these are interesting questions, and both will be addressed in the course of the following argument, although it is (PX1) that is the principal object of our analysis. For (PX1) is the question before Edwards with respect to this aspect of the AP, in light of the findings of the permission and positive agency argument. If God can be shown to be causally but not morally responsible for sin, then there may be grounds for Edwards to build a defence against the AP from the perspective of the theological determinist.[29]

We come to the argument for the proxy problem. In Edwards' thought, moral responsibility is tied to the related notion of praise and blameworthiness. He expounds his views on this matter in *FOW*: IV: 13.[30] There, Edwards makes the claim that praise and blameworthiness lie in the *nature*, not the *cause* of volitions and dispositions.[31] That is, an action x may be the result of my causing x to come about, but it does not follow that I am morally responsible for x if I did not choose to do x.

This may seem obscure, but can be elucidated with the help of the following example. Imagine that Trevor is hypnotized by a master hypnotist, the Great Suprendo. Whilst in a hypnotic trance, the Great Suprendo suggests to Trevor that when he awakes, he should find his friend Wayne and throttle him. Trevor awakes from the trance, locates Wayne and promptly begins to throttle him, as the Great Suprendo suggested he should.[32] Now, as Trevor begins to throttle Wayne it is clear that he is causally responsible for closing off Wayne's trachea by choking him. (The hypnotist does not do it.) But it is not clear that he is also blameworthy for this action, since he does it under hypnotic suggestion. Thus he is causally, but not necessarily morally responsible for throttling Wayne.[33]

Edwards makes a similar distinction when he speaks about a person's will being in an action (and therefore blameworthy), and not in an action (and therefore not blameworthy). In so far as the nature of the act derives from the choice of the moral action, that agent is culpable. But in so far as the voluntary nature of that choice is diminished (as with the hypnotism), just so far is that person not culpable for their action. So the question of whether an act is committed by a person is secondary, with respect to blame, to the question of whether choice was involved in the performance of it. It is 'not so much because they are from some property of ours, as because they are our properties'.[34] So external, 'overt' actions are not a reliable guide to moral responsibility. Only choice is.

The application of this to Edwards' solution to the AP is as follows. If God is responsible for my sinful volitions, this is because they are the expression of his will. But, of course, on Edwards' compatibilist thesis, my choices are mine and therefore blameworthy. After all, God does not choke Wayne; Trevor does. So it is not God who is culpable for throttling Wayne; Trevor is. (But this – as we shall see in a moment – involves a sleight of hand on Edwards' part that cannot work.)

Edwards adduces further grounds for his argument from the Calvinian distinction between the hidden and revealed will of God. With respect to the divine hidden will, God cannot be morally responsible for my actions because his hidden will determines all things for a greater good, not for some other, evil outcome. Yet my actions – where they are actions of my choosing, not constrained by things outside myself – are orientated towards an evil end, such as Trevor choking Wayne, or whatever.[35] So God is not morally responsible for my choice here, though (via his hidden will), he is causally responsible for my choice. His causation of my action is motivated by a greater good, an end that presumably outweighs or balances off the evil of my act for some greater good. And since he does not commit the act itself, he cannot be morally responsible for it.[36]

A similar case is made for God's revealed will. But here God expressly forbids evil in what he has revealed (in Scripture, for example). The problem with this is that it makes God's revealed will seem disingenuous, in light of his hidden will (more on that presently). Edwards claims that his revealed will is not disingenuous because, once more, the choice is mine, not God's. Thus God may expressly forbid murder, whilst being the necessary and sufficient cause of my murdering Wayne, and no contradiction result because the choice to murder Wayne is mine, not God's.

Comments on the Proxy Problem

So much for Edwards' defence against the proxy problem. Does it work? Here Antony Flew's classic essay, 'Divine Omnipotence and Human Freedom',[37] offers several helpful pointers by way of assessing Edwards' proposal.

Volitions, Praise and Blame

First, some comments on Edwards' distinction between the nature and cause of volitions with respect to praise and blame. His distinction does not necessarily remove all moral responsibility from the actor(s) involved. In the case of the hypnotist, for example, if a person is discovered to have been acting under hypnotic suggestion, as in the case of Trevor throttling Wayne, we would normally want to reconsider Trevor's culpability in light of this fact. Nevertheless, he would not necessarily be *without blame* for such an action. For Trevor had submitted to the hypnotism in the first place. The same goes, *mutatis mutandis*, for similar thought experiments where mind-altering drugs or other stimulants take the place of hypnotism (alcohol, for instance). In these cases

The Authorship of Sin 67

too, the person involved is not blame*less* for actions committed whilst 'under the influence' of some particular stimulant. Quite the opposite. If a man who is intoxicated smashes a shop window in an uncharacteristic display of violence, his moral responsibility may be diminished by the fact that he acted under the influence of alcohol, but it is not negligible. Although he may have not been able to make a rational decision in those circumstances, such that his action whilst drunk was not *clearly* voluntary,[38] this does not mean that he bears no responsibility. In fact, he was irresponsible in his use of alcohol and is therefore culpable, whatever his state of mind may have been whilst he was inebriated (even if he cannot recall his action afterwards).

But what about situations where the influence a person is under is irresistible, like the hypnotism example? The same reasoning obtains. The point is that I have chosen to submit myself to the conditions that brought about the diminishment (or obliteration) of my moral responsibility for the particular act in question. In so far as my choice leading to that state was voluntary, just so far am I responsible for what comes after, where what comes after is dependent upon my initial, voluntary choice. But if I was force-fed alcohol or drugs, or strapped down to the hypnotist's chair, then my culpability is diminished, vis-à-vis, any actions I perform whilst under the influence of that particular thing. But that is not the point here. The point is that Edwards claims that the *nature* not the *cause* of a person's volitions affects their culpability in the choice of a particular action. What he does not take into account is the fact that choices leading up to that choice are crucial in determining the amount of culpability on the event itself.[39]

It may be that *I* make the choice, and that is what counts. But there are circumstances in which my moral responsibility diminishes or increases depending upon actions I take before my present action, as in the case of the hypnotist. So it is not clearly the case (*pace* Edwards), that I may be the cause of an action and not morally responsible for that action if, in choosing to place myself in the circumstances that lead to that particular choice, it is I who voluntarily take the choice that leads to the subsequent choice of the action in question. In short, Edwards' distinction does not take account of what action has gone before, that brings about the present state of affairs with respect to my present volition.

Causal and Moral Responsibility

The second comment on Edwards' argument is actually a comment about the case of the hypnotist (obviously, *not* a thought experiment used by Edwards). As Flew points out, this example does not adequately capture the relation between God and human moral agents. Unlike the analysis just presented, there are no prior choices that may affect the causal and moral responsibility I bear with respect to God. A person does not choose to come under the influence of God as one might the hypnotist, drugs or alcohol. This means that there is a significant dis-analogy between human choice and moral responsibility and God's choice and moral responsibility. However, far from vindicating Edwards' analysis of nature and cause, this means that the argument he presents in *FOW*: 427–8 relies on a false analogy between divine and human actions and volitions. But does it mean, in addition to this, that no one is completely morally responsible for their actions, whether they are *their* choices or not? Not necessarily. And here Edwards' argument may begin to make some headway.

Whether compatibilism is true on predestinarian grounds, or just because this is the way things are[40] does not alter the fact that if a species of compatibilism obtains, then Edwards is right to insist that moral responsibility only applies where a person has made a voluntary choice. The question of whether I acted in a certain way *is*, as Edwards claims, a secondary matter. Moreover, causal responsibility and moral responsibility *are* thereby distinct, but related matters. I may – on a compatibilist account – be causally but not morally responsible for a particular act as per (PX1). Indeed, the converse holds: I might be morally responsible for inciting a crowd to riot through my speech, for instance, but not causally responsible (at least, not in terms of Edwards' positive agency) for the individual actual acts of violence members of the crowd carry out after listening to my speech. And this, of course, is one example of how (PX2) might obtain.[41]

This means that the compatibilist core of Edwards' distinction between the nature and cause of voluntary acts regarding culpability remains intact. Whether the compatibilism in question is theologically motivated, or simply a form of atheological soft determinism, the nature and cause of an act are distinct issues with respect to volition and moral responsibility, as Edwards contends.

However, the fact that Edwards defends a *theological* determinism is not without significance. As has already been pointed out, there is an important dis-analogy between human and divine moral agents and their choices. This means that the position seems to be that 'While there is no "contradiction in speaking of God as so arranging things that all men always as a matter of fact freely choose to do the right"; the ideas of God arraigning and punishing anyone who freely chose the wrong, if he so arranges things that his victim does so act, "outrages . . . the most ordinary justice and humanity"'.[42]

In other words, Edwards may be right regarding theological determinism, but wrong regarding the justice of God's eternal decree. Put another way, God may not be morally responsible for my actions, though he is causally responsible for them. But the justice of condemning me for a sin he has ordained – though it is mine – seems skewed, to say the least. Ordinarily, if a person were to be causally, but not morally responsible for another person's crime, only to condemn that person for their crime having been causally responsible for it coming to pass, such a person would be considered unjust.[43]

Flew maintains that Calvin for one saw this implication and decided to bite the bullet: '[For Calvin] the damned were damned "by a just and irreprehensible, but incomprehensible judgment". In thus seeing and accepting the implications of omnipotence he showed himself to have both a clearer head and a stronger – shall we say? – stomach than most believers.'[44] Edwards, however, did not do so; he maintained that God's justice is inviolable. A thumbnail sketch of why Edwards believed this should make this point plain.

Edwards' argument for divine justice in the damnation of sinners is to the effect that God is just in so acting because the creation and reprobation of the damned are one aspect of the divine programme of self-glorification. As his dissertation on the *End of Creation* makes clear, God's 'great and last end' is but one, 'and this one end is most properly and comprehensively called, "the glory of God"'.[45] The damned glorify God through demonstrating God's inviolable justice: He will deal with sin and punish it infinitely in hell. But he manifests his grace and mercy to the elect who will enjoy the infinite pleasures of his presence in heaven eternally. Thus, on Edwards' picture, God's great and last end in creation is his self-glorification in the display of his righteous anger in the punishment of the wicked, and his grace and mercy in the saving of the saints.

The problem with this is that it begs the question. Divine justice is displayed in the damnation of the wicked, by the ordination and causation of the existence and persistence of the wicked through time. God is not morally responsible for the sins that they voluntarily choose, but he is the necessary and sufficient cause of their existence and persistence, through his direct action in creation and conservation. But this is to return to our initial problem: God causes the wicked to act wickedly but without moral culpability for their individual actions, only to blame them for actions he caused them to perform!

This brings us back to Wainwright's analysis of permission and positive agency. If Edwards is to use this as a means of evading the unpalatable consequences of this aspect of the AP in his determinism, he is left with the claim that God's permission (but not his positive agency) in sin is a necessary but not causally sufficient condition of sin, which is exactly what he denies with respect to praise and blame.

The Transitivity Principle

Third, there is an issue with respect to the transitivity principle that (PX) entails.[46] If A wills action y and y is brought about by B, then A wills y (via B). It is not just that A wills y and B wills y on behalf of A, therefore y obtains. (Example: Trevor wants to punish Gary for injuring him. Wayne wants to punish Gary on behalf of Trevor. So, Wayne punishes Gary on behalf of Trevor. Gary is thereby punished according to Trevor's wishes and at his instigation, though not by Trevor, but by Wayne.) With respect to divine volitions, Edwards surely means A wills y and (in order to bring about y) A wills that B wills that y. This much Edwards is willing to concede. God is causally responsible for all actions on the basis of (P1)&(P2). In fact, I take Edwards to mean by this that God is the necessary and sufficient cause of y obtaining or of ~y obtaining. The sticking point is his distinction between this causal determinism and moral responsibility. The sleight of hand at work here depends upon his view that God may will Trevor to hit Wayne, and be the cause of this act, but not the one morally responsible, since it is Trevor, not God, who hits Wayne. Whereas the transitivity principle obtains with respect to causal responsibility, it does not, according to Edwards, obtain for moral responsibility. Trevor is a moral agent, he acts on his

70 *Jonathan Edwards and the Metaphysics of Sin*

desire to hit Wayne; God does not force him to do so. But of course, it is God who has willed Trevor to have the desire to hit Wayne in the first place. Trevor's agency in the matter of hitting Wayne does not absolve God of blame, since God not only wills that Trevor hit Wayne. His causal responsibility means that he also supplies the desire to do so, and sustains Trevor at all those times at which he is engaged in the premeditation and action that result in the bringing about of Wayne's being struck by Trevor. Trevor may be the moral agent who makes the choice to hit Wayne, but all those desires, motives and dispositions that go into the choice and resulting act are supplied by God, such that Wayne is struck.

What this means is that God's causal responsibility appears to *entail* his moral responsibility. If God's causal responsibility is the necessary and sufficient causal explanation of Trevor's sin, what more is required for this to entail that God bears moral responsibility for that sin too?

The Principle of Alternate Possibilities

This brings us to the fourth comment on the proxy problem. Edwards' discussion of this matter has much in common with the contemporary debate about the principle of alternate possibilities, initiated by Harry Frankfurt.[47]

Contemporary compatibilists usually defend their compatibilism by using a conditional analysis of a particular action to explain what they mean by the notion, 'person x *could* have done otherwise than in fact he did'. This is particularly important for the question of moral responsibility. If x is determined by something (whatever that may be) to act in this way, rather than that, how can he be held morally responsible for the actions that follow from this? The question for present purposes has to do with the AP and moral responsibility for sin. We have already seen that there is one sense in which Trevor could not have done otherwise than in fact he did according to Edwards, since Trevor is constrained by his desires and motives to choose to hit Wayne rather than to refrain from doing so. Moreover, on (P1)&(P2) God supplies all these desires. This means that a conditional of the form, 'Trevor could have refrained from hitting Wayne' actually means, according to compatibilists who use conditional analysis in explaining responsibility, 'if Trevor had chosen to refrain from hitting Wayne, he would have refrained from hitting Wayne'.

What is crucial here is whether the first part of this conditional – that he *could* have so chosen – makes sense. That is, was Trevor in a position to choose such that he could have acted differently and would have done so had he so chosen? Laying aside complications, such as the possibility, in Lehrerian terms, that Trevor has a pathological fear of violence, or of blood, or of cutting his skin, or whatever that would mean he could not have so chosen,[48] the point here is that Trevor *could not* have chosen to do other than he did, *unless* God had ordained that Trevor did other than he did. Or, to return to our A's and B's, B could not choose ~y, unless A wills B to ~y and A ordains B to ~y, where A represents God, and B some other, human moral agent. This is because, on Edwardsian compatibilism, divine will and divine ordination are one and the same in effect: *necessarily, for any y, if A ordains y, then A wills y*. And, necessarily, *if A wills y, then A brings y about*. This is the case because, for Edwards, God's will is unimpedible: what he wills inevitably comes to pass, since there is nothing that can frustrate the divine will.

This presents problems for Edwards' concept of the liberty of spontaneity. Let us formulate this principle. Where, as before, *A* is a moral agent, *t* a particular time and *x* an action:

(LS)   A is free at t with respect to x if, and only if, either A brings it about at t that x because A wants at t to bring it about that x or A refrains from bringing it about at t that x because A wants at t to refrain from bringing it about that x.[49]

As Mann points out, this is attractive to compatibilists because (LS) presumes three things: that a person's wants are themselves causes; that a person's wants are caused, and to be free is to have a harmony between a person's wants and actions. The problem for a *theological* compatibilism like Edwards', especially with respect to our present concern, is that a person's wants are supplied by God (the causal responsibility thesis). And God not only wills, he ordains that at t A will x, as opposed to ~x (or either (x or ~x)).

So, an Edwardsian conditional analysis of actions like Trevor's actually turns not on what Trevor (or whoever) *might* have done if they had so desired it, in conformity to the principle of liberty of spontaneity. Instead, an analysis turns on what *God wills* and *ordains* Trevor to have done. Trevor himself would and could have chosen differently if and only if God willed and ordained that Trevor chose differently. This may seem a mundane implication of Edwards' position for those familiar with the structure of a theological LS and its philosophical implications. But it is crucial to his bid to absolve God of moral responsibility. Edwards' central claim here hinges on being able to distinguish causal from moral responsibility with respect to God permitting, but not positively acting as agent in the sin of Trevor (or whoever). But it is not clear how he can make this distinction work. For causal determination of the sort that Edwards endorses in (P1)&(P2) appear, even without the complications of (P3), to leave no room for Edwards to distinguish the two. Causal determination entails moral responsibility, for Edwards.

An Edwardsian might respond by saying something like the following: God may be causally but not morally responsible for sin because the sinner is the one who does the sinful act, not God. Just as, with the example of the hypnotist, hypnotized-Trevor is causally, but not morally responsible (or not altogether morally responsible) for throttling Wayne, so God may be the causal agent of an act, but not the one morally responsible for that act.

But, of course, this only underlines why Edwards' analysis will not work. For Edwards' view to be viable, he needs to distinguish between causal and moral responsibility, such that agent A is causally but not morally responsible for the act carried out by agent B. The problem is, *on what basis can Edwards make such a distinction*? This point can be illustrated with reference to the debate about the principle of alternate possibilities (PAP) in the contemporary literature. Frankfurt defines PAP:

> (PAP) a person is morally responsible for an act only if they could have done otherwise.

This principle has two elements: the conditional analysis, that is, '(s)he could have done otherwise', and the problem of moral responsibility. It is the latter notion that we are after, in connection with the former. Frankfurt's well-known and much debated thesis, is that the PAP is false. There may be circumstances that are a sufficient condition for an act to be performed by a person, which makes it impossible for that person to do otherwise, but do not impel that person to carry out that act, or in any way produce the persons' action. An example: Trevor wants Wayne to fight Gary. If Wayne does not fight Gary, Trevor will intervene and force Wayne to do so. However, it so happens that Wayne wants to fight Gary anyway. Although Trevor's intervention will inevitably intimidate Wayne into fighting Gary if need be, in point of fact, Wayne fights Gary because of his prior desire to do so, without knowing that Trevor will take steps to ensure this outcome anyway, if he does not decide to fight Gary. Here is an example of a situation in which Wayne could not do otherwise than fight Gary (presuming Trevor's intervention would be irresistible), but in point of fact, he does not act as he does *because* he cannot do otherwise. He acts as he does in ignorance of the fact that he cannot do otherwise, and from a desire to act as he does. Yet he is still morally responsible for the outcome (or so says Frankfurt).[50] So PAP does not work as it stands: 'To the extent that the principle of alternate possibilities derives its plausibility from association with the doctrine that coercion excludes moral responsibility, a clear understanding of the latter diminishes the appeal of the former.' Moreover, PAP is mistaken because:

> It asserts that a person bears no moral responsibility – that is, he is to be excused – for having performed an action, if there were circumstances that made it impossible for him to avoid performing it. But there may be circumstances that make it impossible for a person to avoid performing some action without those circumstances in any way bringing it about that he performs that action.[51]

In its place, Frankfurt proposes a revised version of PAP:

> (PAP') a person is not morally responsible for an action if that person did the action *only* because they could not have done otherwise.

The question with respect to Edwards then, is this: does Trevor (or whoever) act as they do *only* because they could not have done otherwise? If they do so act, then it appears that Trevor (or whoever) is absolved from moral responsibility, and God is morally culpable for Trevor's action, as well as being causally responsible.

To make the point that God is morally and causally responsible given Edwards' compatibilism, let us explore one more F-style counter-example to PAP.[52] This time,

Trevor wants Wayne to fight Gary and threatens Wayne with an irresistible threat to the effect that if he does not fight Gary there will be serious and violent consequences for him. However, unbeknown to Trevor, Wayne had already decided to fight Gary anyway, before Trevor issued his threat. Instead of acting on the basis of the threat offered him, Wayne acts on the basis of his own desire to fight Gary, a desire that predates the threat. Here, Wayne could not have done otherwise (because of the threat), but he acts as he does through a prior decision and desire to fight Gary anyway.

In this scenario Wayne *can* do otherwise than act on the basis of his desire, or Trevor's threat: he can suffer the consequences of Trevor's threat to his person. For this reason, this second scenario is not an effective counter-example to PAP. But moral agents are not in the same situation in the case of God's irresistible ordination. A moral agent in a parallel situation where A is a divine agent taking Trevor's place, and B a human moral agent taking the place of Wayne, cannot choose to take the consequences of divine decisions against him, the reason being that B has no power to resist the will and ordination of A. B would only be able to resist in this way if A ordained and willed that B resist. That is, for B, A's coercion does entail (unlike our Wayne and Trevor F-style counter-example) that B must act as (s)he does if God ordains it. In fact, the very ability to even conceive of acting contrary to a divine agent, on Edwards' scheme, is caused by the divine agent in question.

Nor is the situation more like our initial characterization of the Wayne–Trevor scenario, where A ordains that B does action x at t, but if B does not do x at t, then A will interfere to ensure that B does x coercively. Edwards' theological determinism precludes such a scenario. God cannot be reactive in this way, for B cannot do other than x where A ordains and wills x of B, since God is the necessary and sufficient cause of B doing x. But then, B is not morally responsible for doing x, and the distinction Edwards attempts to make between causal and moral responsibility will not work.

One further scenario, this time from van Inwagen. He presents his own F-style counter-example to Frankfurt's counter-examples to PAP (!). One of them, the *principle of possible action*, runs as follows:

> (PPA) a person is morally responsible for failing to perform an action only if they could have performed that action.[53]

Van Inwagen has the following kind of situation in mind: Trevor sees a crime committed, and goes to telephone the police to report it, but then decides not to. However, unbeknown to him, the telephone exchange is out of order, so even if he had tried to report the crime by telephone, he would not have been able to do so. In this situation, Trevor is not culpable for failing to report the crime, since he could not have done so, though he did not know at the time that he could not have done so. Once again, Trevor is causally responsible for withholding the action he was going to perform, but did not; but he is not morally responsible for having done so. The simple reason being, that he could not have done so, even if he had tried. So causal and moral responsibility are distinct issues in this scenario too.

However, this principle will not help Edwards either.[54] An action that an agent performs or withholds, is, on Edwards' scheme, due not to what Frankfurt calls *personal* reasons (I could have done x, but did not), but *impersonal* (I could have done x only if God ordained that I do x). For if God is the sole causal agent in all events, then an agent does (or does not do) what they do, solely because they are caused to do so by the action of God, not themselves. God acts *in* and *through* the moral agent, in their own desires, habits and choices, in the states of affairs and circumstances into which God places a particular agent, and in the events that he brings about. Whether this obtains because a particular moral agent withholds, or refrains from a particular action, or carries it out, makes no significant difference in terms of distinguishing God's moral and causal responsibility.[55] For in both instances, if God is causally responsible for every volition and event, then he is morally responsible too.

In summation: Edwards seeks to drive a wedge between casual and moral responsibility with respect to divine action in the world. But F-style counter-examples show that this can only obtain in states of affairs that involve non-divine agent(s). If one of the agents involved in a particular action is divine, and if a theological determinism such as Edwards' obtains, then the distinction between causal and moral responsibility cannot hold. God is the causal and moral agent responsible for that action, and therefore, for sinful actions.[56]

The Problem of (P3)

We come to the fifth and final comment on Edwards' argument against God's moral responsibility for sin. Up until now, we have assumed that on (P1)&(P2) Edwards has insurmountable problems with the AP. But he has even more serious problems than (P1)&(P2) yield for him, because he adheres to (P3) too. This means that there are two separate issues at work here. On the one hand, Edwards has a problem on (P1)&(P2) if God is the sole ordainer of all that comes to pass (which does not entail occasionalism). On the other hand, God is the sole cause of all things that come to pass, entailing (P3).

This means that even if Edwards is able to counteract those arguments brought against him thus far ((P1)&(P2)-style arguments), his adherence to the causal thesis of (P3) is fatal to his analysis of divine moral culpability. For on this thesis, God is the only real cause of all things. If God alone causes all things, then he is both causally and morally responsible for all events that come to pass, since he alone has directly caused all those events to come to pass. Edwards himself does not make this connection. Nevertheless, (P1)&(P2) present considerable difficulties to Edwards' analysis of God's moral responsibility for creaturely sinful actions. But together with (P3) they defeat Edwards' argument against the proxy problem, laid out in (PX).

Notes

1   The authorship problem in Edwards' thought has attracted interest from several sources in recent and not-so-recent literature. These include John H. Gerstner, *Rational Biblical Theology, Vol. II*, pp. 149 ff.; Clyde Holbrook's editorial introduction to *YE1*: 60–64; John Kearney, 'Jonathan Edwards and the "Author of Sin" Charge'; C. Samuel Storms, *Tragedy in Eden*, chapter 4; Rufus Suter, 'The Problem of Evil in the Philosophy of Jonathan Edwards'; and William Wainwright, 'Theological Determinism and the Problem of Evil: Are Arminians any better off?'. Although this issue is touched upon in other secondary literature on Edwards, when it is, it is only mentioned in passing. See, for example, Robert Jenson's comments in *America's Theologian*, p. 148.

2   A defeater is, roughly, a reason for giving up a belief that you hold – the reason proffered 'defeats' your belief. Such defeaters come in different varieties. For instance, there are rationality defeaters that mean one can only persist in believing the defeated proposition on pain of irrationality. There are also undercutting defeaters that undercut one's reason for believing a proposition. There are also warrant defeaters and rebutting defeaters. But I need not go into those here. Plantinga sets these versions of defeaters out in *Warranted Christian Belief*, p. 359.

3   It is worth noting that sin and evil are not synonyms. Sin is usually taken to be something like 'any want of conformity unto, or transgression of, the law of God' (*Westminster Shorter Catechism*, Question 14). That is, its principal orientation is towards moral evil. Moral evil may well have consequences for the natural world (as the biblical account claims is the case with the sin of Adam), but it need not. If I stab my grandmother, that has serious moral consequences not just for my grandmother, or myself but for a whole range of people, family, friends and authorities, whom it may involve. But natural evil does not result. However, if I drown a village of Africans by building a dam ten miles downstream from them, that probably will have moral and natural consequences for the environment surrounding the village that is flooded. By contrast, evil is a much broader term than sin, comprising all kinds of moral and natural evil. Nevertheless, the two are intertwined in our problem. For if God is the author of evil, there does seem to be an unwelcome moral consequence for the divine nature, namely that creating evil is a sinful act.

4   '[E]very event which is the consequence of anything whatsoever, or that is connected with any foregoing thing or circumstance, either positive or negative, as the ground or reason of its existence, must be ordered of God; either by a designed efficiency and interposition, or a designed forbearing to operate or interpose. But, as has been proved, all events whatsoever are necessarily connected with something foregoing, either positive or negative, which is the ground of its existence.' Moreover, 'as God designedly orders his own conduct, and its connected consequences, it must necessarily be, that he designedly orders all things', *YE1*: 432. See also *YE1*: 397.

5   In fact, for Edwards, all divine volitions are necessary too: 'How can we prove, that God certainly will in any one instance do that which is just and holy, seeing his will is determined in the matter by no necessity [as the Arminians claim]? We have no other way of proving that anything *certainly* will be but only by the necessity of the event. Where we can see no necessity, but that the thing may be, or may not be, there we are unavoidably left at a loss', *YE1*: 418, author's emphasis.

6   See *YE3*: IV: III. To be precise: one aspect of his occasionalism yields this principle (the other aspect having to do with a continuous creation thesis).

7   The two places where Edwards discusses these issues in detail are *YE1*: IV: 9: 397–412 and *YE3*: III: 2: 380–88.

8   However, in addition to this, Edwards believes that his *tu quoque* holds because foreknowledge entails the necessity of what is foreknown (as he argues in *FOW* II: 12). Therefore the Arminian position is unstable because it is as necessitarian as the Calvinists', whether they admit this or not.

9   This is the question that William Wainwright has recently set out to answer in 'Theological Determinism and The Problem of Evil'.

10   *YE1*: 398.

11   This caveat is important in light of current discussions of 'Openness of God' theism.

12 Wainwright goes one step further by claiming that 'the God of the Calvinists is the author of sin while the God of the Arminians is not', 'Theological Determinism and The Problem of Evil', p. 87.

13 Whether the libertarian thesis of such Arminians is more coherent than the compatibilism of Calvinists like Edwards is a separate question, and one that Edwards contests with great rigour in *FOW*.

14 Wainwright, 'Theological Determinism and The Problem of Evil', p. 87. However, as Wainwright admits, this is a notoriously difficult distinction to draw.

15 Adapted from Wainwright, ibid., p. 87.

16 Wainwright cites Phillipa Foot in this regard. See, for example, her 'The Problem of Abortion and the Doctrine of Double Effect' in *Virtues and Vices and Other Essays*.

17 For these distinctions, see Alvin Plantinga, *The Nature of Necessity*, pp. 184ff.

18 It is no response to this for Arminians to say that God creates all humans with free will, but without intending that they sin. If God creates Adam with a weak moral nature such that he will sin on at least one occasion when tempted then he must intend that Adam sin. For it is possible for God to create a human being with free will who is not bound to sin. Nor is it sufficient to claim that God intends the good of creating Adam for the end of redeeming him through Christ, and that his sin is a foreseen, but unintended by-product of this state of affairs. The reason being that it is built into the divine creative *intention* that Adam will inevitably sin, on this weak moral nature view.

19 The phrase 'actualization of the elect' refers to the bringing into existence of a number of humanity whom God has elected to eternal life according to his eternal decree, understood in terms of the theological framework of Calvinism.

20 *YE1*: 399.

21 Ibid.

22 See 'Theological Determinism and The Problem of Evil', p. 83.

23 *YE1*: 403.

24 The point here is to do with non-interference, not with the principle of alternate possibilities, that this example invokes, and which we shall return to in due course.

25 See Paul Helm, *The Providence of God*, p. 173. There Helm sets out several models of God's action in the world, including one similar to that outlined here. On the question of God's end in creation in Edwards' thought, see *YE8*: 526 ff.

26 Wainwright, 'Theological Determinism and The Problem of Evil', pp. 82–3.

27 Adapted from ibid., p. 82.

28 Kearney, 'Jonathan Edwards and the "Author of Sin" Charge'.

29 This crucial distinction is overlooked by C. Samuel Storms in *Tragedy in Eden*. There he claims that for Edwards to avoid the force of the AP, he must construe the divine permission of sin as having no causal influence in the inception of an evil disposition (p. 216.) Otherwise, God is the immediate cause of all sin, and therefore the author of sin in the sense of AS1. But this is only the case if God is both causally and morally responsible for sin. If he is causally but not morally responsible – which is exactly what Edwards claims is the case – then Storms' criticism has no force.

30 *YE1*: 427–8.

31 '[N]atural sense don't place the moral evil of volitions and dispositions in the cause of them, but the nature of them', *YE1*: 427.

32 The fact that hypnotism does not necessarily work in this irresistible fashion need not concern us; a popular picture of hypnotic arts will suffice for the purposes of the thought experiment.

33 Mark Nelson has suggested to me that this scenario is not to the point since it is about the cause, not the nature, of Trevor's volition. If the Great Suprendo hypnotically induces Trevor to have a desire to kill Wayne, then Trevor seems morally responsible on Edwards' account of the importance of the nature of the act in determining moral responsibility. However, it is not clear in the hypnosis case that Trevor *chooses* to kill Wayne, since his will is not involved; he acts like an automaton (assuming that hypnosis might work in this way). Trevor does not choose to so act. So, though he is causally responsible (or partly thereof) for throttling Wayne, he is not culpable (or not completely, solely culpable), since he did not choose to so act. That is the point. And it is a point about the nature of the action; whether

The Authorship of Sin · 77

it was chosen or not, and therefore whether Trevor is culpable or not. Nor is this example parallel to Edwards' theological determinism. God may implant a desire for Trevor to kill Wayne. But in Edwards' view, God's willing Trevor to so act and Trevor desiring to so act happen at the same time (in fact, God gives Trevor this desire to so act). The same cannot be said for the hypnotist. The whole point of the folk-picture of hypnosis at work in this example is that Trevor acts without consenting to his actions, simply because ordered to do so by the hypnotist, whilst hypnotized.

34 *YE1*: 428.

35 This skates over several important ethical points it is worth pausing to mention. First, it does not account for altruistic action, if there are any such. Even if there are not, it does not account for human actions that are either (a) evil for a greater good (for example, killing Hitler), or (b) of mixed motives (such as so-called crimes of passion). It does not establish that a person is morally culpable for *all* kinds of actions, nor for actions that may be culpable in one respect, but not in another, as with the murder of Hitler (where a person may be culpable for murder, but not for killing a mass murderer). Actions whose moral orientation is unclear, like crimes of passion, are also not accounted for here.

36 Is this a violation of premise (3) of the DDE, outlined earlier? This was that 'a good effect is not produced by an evil effect'. In this context, that translates as 'God violates (3) if he causes my sinful choices and causes them for a greater good end, since this involves producing a good effect via an evil effect (my sin)'. As I mentioned earlier in the context of the Calvinist construal of the DDE, it is not clear that Calvinists, Edwards included, have an adequate response to this problem.

37 See *New Essays in Philosophical Theology*, eds MacIntyre and Flew, ch. VIII, especially pp. 162–4.

38 In the sense of being an action that is informed by a rational decision where that agent was presented with no coercion or obstacle to their choice as opposed to, say, a physical reflex, which is not the result of any voluntary choice on the part of the human agent.

39 Of course, it may be argued that Trevor makes a choice to go to the hypnotist and submits to his ministrations, but only for benign purposes, never with the intention that he be instructed to throttle Wayne. In such instances a person's moral responsibility is diminished, to be sure, but is it negligible? I think not. The case for alcohol and mind-bending drugs is easier to discern, since their unpleasant effects would usually be known in advance of taking them.

40 Namely, the compatibilist account of the liberty of spontaneity over indifference.

41 However, as with the earlier example, this is too simple. My moral responsibility may increase or decrease according to circumstances, just as my causal responsibility may too. For instance, I might be the one who incites the crowd to riot, but that does not absolve the members of the crowd from responsibility for their actions, nor does it mean I am wholly or completely morally responsible for what they do as a result of my inflammatory speech. That is, I might be a necessary, but not sufficient condition of the rioting and subsequent moral culpability. Nevertheless, the point about being morally but not causally responsible for an action, with these qualifications, holds.

42 Flew, 'Divine Omnipotence and Human Freedom', p. 164.

43 This presumes that human and divine justice is, to some degree at least, commensurable. I take it that a constituent of the perfect being tradition to which Edwards belonged was that God was essentially just and that his justice is reflected, albeit incompletely and falteringly, in the notions of justice he has bequeathed to humanity in divine revelation and conscience. In addition, Edwards thought that the punishment of sin furthered the greater glorification of God, the aim behind all God's works. See *End of Creation* in *YE8*. Edwards believed that an essentially just and holy God not only may, but must punish the sin of his creatures. The fact that they have been predestined to do this sin is irrelevant. For it is not the cause but the nature of the will that matters, as we have already established from Edwards.

44 Flew, 'Divine Omnipotence and Human Freedom', p. 164, n. 28. It need hardly be said that this is a controversial reading of Calvin.

45 *End of Creation* in *YE8*: 530.

46 A similar use of a principle of transitivity is deployed by William E. Mann in 'God's Freedom, Human Freedom, and God's Responsibility for Sin', p. 202.

47 The material on this issue is considerable. In addition to Frankfurt's contributions, there have been rejoinders from van Inwagen, Fischer and many others. See, 'Alternate Possibilities and Moral Responsibility', 'Coercion and Moral Responsibility' and 'What We are Morally Responsible for', reprinted in Frankfurt's *The Importance of What We Care About* as chs. 1, 3 and 8 respectively. Van Inwagen's comments can be found in 'Ability and Responsibility'; Fischer's writings on this subject include material in the anthology *Moral Responsibility*.

48 I refer to Keith Lehrer's 'Cans without Ifs'.

49 Poached from William E. Mann in 'God's Freedom, Human Freedom, and God's Responsibility for Sin', pp. 184–5.

50 A crucial constituent of Frankfurt's analysis depends upon how one construes the ignorance of the moral agent involved. Frankfurt thinks that in this kind of example, ignorance of Trevor's threat and prior desire for the same course of action, means that Wayne is still culpable. But van Inwagen takes the opposite view in 'Ability and Responsibility'. He claims that ignorance of factors outside one's control usually diminishes culpability in the case of a person who refrains from doing an action.

51 Frankfurt, 'Alternate Possibilities and Responsibility', pp. 5 and 8–9.

52 'F-style counterexamples' is the term used by van Inwagen to define Frankfurt's counter-examples to PAP.

53 Van Inwagen, 'Ability and Responsibility', p. 204, cited in 'What We are Morally Responsible For', p. 97.

54 Leaving aside the question of whether this could help Edwards at all, since van Inwagen thinks it will only work where incompatibilism obtains.

55 Nor does it matter whether the state of affairs in question involves external acts or internal ones. That is, whether it involves states of mind (or brain states, or whatever), or volitions involving bodily movements. Whether Trevor thinks about a particular action, but discounts it, or whether he thinks of it, and acts upon that making external, bodily movements to achieve it, is immaterial. God is the direct and immediate cause of his mental and physical states on (P1)&(P2).

56 Of course, this is not to say that a species of theological compatibilism might not be able to overcome this problem; only that Edwards' version appears not to be able to.

CHAPTER 4

The Secret and Revealed Will of God

In the previous chapter, we considered the authorship problem. We saw that Edwards is unable to overcome problems besetting the distinction between God being causally but not morally responsible for the action of another moral agent. To re-cap, Edwards adheres to the two following principles:

(P1)   All creaturely volitions are necessary.
(P2)   God determines all events that come to pass.

In addition to these, he also holds to a version of occasionalism, including:

(P3)   God is the sole cause of all events; all mundane 'causes' are merely occasions (one mundane event has no power to cause, or bring about another).[1]

In this chapter, we turn to a related aspect of the AP, namely, the secret and revealed will of God.

The Secret and Revealed Will of God

The Calvinistic distinction between the secret and revealed will of God, has traditionally been used by theologians as a device for preserving the integrity of God's character in the face of the sin of his creatures.[2] Take, for instance, Turretin's explanation of the distinction:

> The former [secret will] has for its object all those things which God wills either to effect or permit (and which he wills to do in particular concerning individuals and are therefore absolute and determined to one thing). The latter [revealed will] relates to those things which belong to our duty and are proposed conditionally. The former always takes place; *the latter is often violated*.[3]

Unlike Arminian theologians, Calvinists have claimed that God determines the actions of his creatures. This aspect of the Calvinist compatibility thesis (that is, the compatibility of human free will and divine determination) is, as we have already seen, particularly problematic if a constituent of that argument is that God determines all events, including the sinful acts of his creatures. Moreover, commanding his creatures to act in a way that is morally good, whilst determining that the same creatures will commit sin, casts aspersions on the divine character, and calls into question divine benevolence. In this chapter we shall concern ourselves with whether Edwards' use of the secret and revealed will distinction can be made to work with respect to the specific question of God commanding his creatures to act morally, whilst determining them to sin.

Divine Commands and Insincerity

In *FOW* IV: 11, Edwards says:

> [T]here is no repugnance in supposing it may be the secret will of God, that his ordination and permission of events should be such that it shall be a certain consequence, that a thing never will come to pass; which yet it is man's duty to do, and so God's preceptive will, that he should do; and this is the same thing as to say, God may sincerely command and require him to do it.[4]

Edwards believes that God secretly wills an agent (say, Judas Iscariot, the example Edwards uses) to do x, where x is to betray Christ. But God's revealed will is that Judas does ~x. This seems insincere, and raises a question regarding God's moral character.

But we need to distinguish between these two kinds of willing in God. The secret or *disposing* will of God is what God wills for the greater good, all things considered. By contrast, the *preceptive* or revealed will of God is what he commands as being agreeable to his moral nature, that is, what is good and what he loves (*FOW*: 415). So the two wills are consistent because they have different objects.[5] In the case of Judas, God may ordain his sin for the greater good – here, the salvation of the elect – whilst decrying the act of betrayal itself, as contrary to his own moral nature. So, the secret, disposing will corresponds to the divine decrees, whilst the revealed, preceptive will corresponds to divine (moral) commands.

The problem seems to devolve upon several moral intuitions. These are:

(S1) There are certain activities, particularly moral activities, that are inherently teleological (that is, aim at a particular outcome), for example, commands, exhortations and counsels. Example: 'I insist that you tell me the truth!'

(S2) Engaging in such moral activities for some other reason than the stated one (such as personal gain, power, and so on) without declaring this to the parties concerned, opens one to a charge of insincerity and deception.

(S3) If a person knows that their moral aim will not be achieved by a certain action, that person cannot sincerely engage in that action towards their stated moral aim.

We can put this in terms of God and Judas:

(1) God has disposed things (secretly) such that his exhortations and commands to Judas (revealed/preceptive will) will be ineffective.

(2) God does not reveal this to Judas.

The Secret and Revealed Will of God 81

(3) God cannot address moral exhortations to Judas in order to initiate penitence and a change of heart (from (S2), (S3) and (1)).
(4) Judas assumes God's moral commands are addressed to him for this purpose (S1).
(5) God is thereby open to the charge of insincerity and deception (from (S3), (1) and (2)).
(6) God *has* addressed certain commands to Judas.[6]

From here, Edwards mounts another *tu quoque*, in order to deflect attention away from the fact that he has no answer to this argument. It is important to bear this in mind: Edwards offers no response to this argument beyond claiming that it is a problem common to Arminians as well as Calvinists.

Wainwright points out that Arminians might respond with the following refinements to our second moral intuition. First, *if a person knows E will not be achieved by doing x, he cannot do x to achieve E.* And second, *if a person knows E cannot be achieved by x, he cannot do x to achieve E.* Edwards' adherence to (P1), (P2) and (P3) means that there is no chance of Judas being penitent. He must do x, he is determined to do x. Therefore (3) obtains.

Not so the Arminians. They are not committed to (3), because they are not committed to Edwards' deterministic premises in (P1)–(P3). They do not believe that Judas *must* do x, only that he *will* do x. How does this contrast between 'must' and 'will' help? Nelson Pike initially introduced this distinction into the modern literature.[7] He differentiates between these two kinds of proposition:

Judas *will* do x.
Judas *must* do x.

On Edwardsian determinism, Judas must do x, because God ordains (according to his secret will) that this be the case, even though God's moral nature commands Judas to do ~x (according to his revealed will).[8] But on Arminian libertarianism, Judas will (but not must) do x, because God foresees x. Judas still has the power to refrain from x, even though, in point of fact, he will not refrain from x. If he were to refrain from x (because he has a libertarian free will), then God would not have foreseen x. Instead, he would have foreseen ~x, because Judas would have done ~x, rather than x. That is, if Judas had chosen to do ~x, rather than x, then God would have believed a different proposition from the one he did believe, because he would have foreseen that Judas would have done ~x rather than x. So, it appears that the Arminian God is not exposed to the charge of insincerity, in the same way that Edwards' God is.

Edwardsian Counter-arguments

However, there are several counter-arguments to this claim that could be brought to bear at this point. To begin with, we shall examine Wainwright's argument against

82   *Jonathan Edwards and the Metaphysics of Sin*

there being parity between the Arminian and Calvinist's God with respect to the charge of insincerity. As it stands, his argument is flawed. Edwards shows that, given a particular understanding of the freedom and foreknowledge debate, the Arminian God is in a similarly problematic situation, since the Arminians cannot maintain this distinction between Judas may do x and Judas must do x. He achieves this by recourse to the notion of accidental necessity.

Having seen this, we will turn once again to the question of whether this gets Edwards off the hook with respect to the insincerity charge. We shall see that, although he does establish that there is parity between Arminian and Calvinist on this charge, Edwards' defence of his own position is not able to get beyond this second line of *tu quoque*, on several counts. Therefore, his argument succumbs to the problem set by the insincerity charge. However, there may be a way forward for an Edwards-style argument that is successful in overcoming these problems.

Foreknowledge and Accidental Necessity

Edwards' argument to this end can be found in *FOW* II: 12. There Edwards endorses a version of what Alvin Plantinga (following William of Ockham) has called accidental necessity, or necessity of the past.[9] Edwards' argument for accidental necessity in *FOW* II: 12 incorporates both 'hard' and 'soft' facts. That is, temporal (or tensed) facts which may be entirely about the past and therefore 'hard', or partially about the past, but with reference to the present or future, and therefore 'soft'.

According to Plantinga, Ockham thought that only hard facts were genuinely and strictly about the past, and therefore necessary *per accidens*. Soft facts, contrary to Edwards and theological determinists, are not necessary in this sense. So Edwards' argument for a species of necessity of the past (particularly with reference to divine foreknowledge) fails.[10] Let us examine Plantinga's contention. If he is correct, then this Edwardsian response to the Arminian argument regarding freedom and foreknowledge fails.

In *FOW* II: 12, Edwards claims that past events are accidentally necessary (though, of course, accidental necessity is not an Edwardsian term). Citing his earlier section of the treatise Edwards says, 'I observed before, in explaining the nature of necessity, that in things which are past, their past existence is now necessary: having already made sure of existence, 'tis too late for any possibility of alteration in that respect: 'tis now impossible, that it should be otherwise than true, that that thing has existed.'

He goes on to enumerate the same kinds of temporal philosophical necessity which he had delineated earlier in *FOW*, namely, temporal ('hard') accidental necessity, and consequential ('soft') necessity, in the context of the divine foreknowledge–human freedom debate:

> If there be any such thing as a divine foreknowledge of the volitions of free agents, that foreknowledge, by the supposition, is a thing which already has, and long ago had existence; and so, now its existence is necessary; it is now utterly impossible to be otherwise than this foreknowledge should be, or should have

The Secret and Revealed Will of God

> been ... 'Tis no less evident, that if there be a full, certain and infallible foreknowledge of the future existence of the volitions of moral agents, then there is a certain infallible and indissoluble connection between those events and that foreknowledge; and that therefore, by the preceding observations, those events are necessary events; being infallibly and indissolubly connected with that whose existence already is, and so is now necessary, and can't but have been.[11]

Plantinga recognizes that this argument relies on two intuitions. The first is that, although the past is not necessary in some broadly logical sense, it is none the less necessary in some sense, in that it is fixed and outside the control of agents to change it after it has happened. Second, whatever is necessarily connected with something which is necessary, is itself necessary as a consequence of this connection. This Edwardsian notion invokes a *transfer of necessity principle*: Where p is accidentally necessary after t1, and p strictly implies q, then after t1, q is also necessary *per accidens*.[12]

With this information, we may now express Edwards' version of accidental necessity as follows:

(N1) A proposition is accidentally necessary if, and only if, the sentence that denotes it refers to,

(N1a) something which has already come to pass, and is therefore a completed, past action (a 'hard' fact),

(N1b) something which has already some to pass and continues to be at the present time, and is therefore a continuing object or action (a 'soft' fact).

And:

(N2) Consequential necessity (using the transfer of necessity principle): Where p entails or is strictly implicated by q, and p is accidentally necessary after t1, then after t1, q is necessary *per accidens*.

So why is Edwards' argument untenable according to Plantinga? In subsuming what I have termed 'consequential' necessity and both 'hard' and 'soft' facts under necessity *per accidens*, Edwards commits himself to the view that all facts about the past are necessary. Furthermore, his view of God's foreknowledge is such that what God knows, has to come to pass, even if it is still future. If God is omniscient, then this means that God knows all future actions, and that these future actions must, of consequential necessity, come to pass. Therefore, no action of any agent is ever free. All actions are determined in advance by the fact that God knows they will occur. This is his deterministic thesis, and he deploys this aspect of that thesis *ad hominem* against Daniel Whitby, one of the antagonists in view in *FOW* II: 12. Whitby distinguished between foreknowledge and predestination, arguing that the former is compatible with libertarianism, whereas the latter is not. Edwards, in stating this aspect of his deterministic thesis, sought to respond by showing that such a distinction between

84   Jonathan Edwards and the Metaphysics of Sin

foreknowledge and predestination is untenable, if all that God knows, he knows in a 'hard' way.

But Ockham and Plantinga claim that there are both hard and soft facts about the past, which Edwards' argument cannot accommodate. For, according to the deterministic strand of the Edwardsian compatibility thesis, all facts are known to God (from eternity past, one presumes), and because all temporal facts known to an omniscient being must come to pass, (that is, they cannot fail to obtain, if an omniscient being knows them), all facts, at whatever temporal index, are hard.

It may be thought that this does not do enough to stave off the criticism that the temporal relation involved between present and past, and present and future, is essentially asymmetrical. The past is determinate in relation to the present, but the future remains essentially indeterminate, and therefore not 'there' to be known by any agent, even God, until and unless it takes place. However, Edwards has two interesting arguments to counter such an approach. The first is this: foreknowledge may *show* a future event is necessary even if it does not *cause* that event to take place, making it necessary. He reasons that it is absurd to say that a future event will certainly and infallibly obtain because it is foreknown, and yet that event turn out not to obtain. So if God foreknows that event x will obtain, there is no way that x may not obtain, even if God is not the direct cause of x obtaining. For instance, God may infallibly foreknow the outcome of the election, and that outcome be necessary, by virtue of his foreknowledge, without causing the outcome of the election. A second argument is this: if God foreknows that a future event will occur, then that future event already has an existing effect, namely God's foreknowledge of that event. If God's prescience of event x is an effect of x that exists prior to x obtaining, then it would be strange indeed to claim that the effect of x obtains but the cause of that effect, x itself, may not obtain, since it is a future event which is still contingent.[13]

In addition, Edwards is committed to an 'A', rather than an 'O' view of foreknowledge. A-foreknowledge is a strong thesis, corresponding to a causal kind of knowing (or of bringing about that a thing takes place at a certain time and place). O-foreknowledge is weaker, describing the more notional idea of knowing a thing. Paul Helm points out that most discussions of this foreknowledge-human freedom problem in the recent literature typically assume O-, rather than A-foreknowledge.[14] Edwards, by contrast, assumes A- rather than O-foreknowledge, in keeping with his theological belief in the absolute sovereignty of God.[15]

But to return to the central issue regarding hard and soft tensed facts, there seems to be considerable problems with the very distinction which Plantinga and Ockham want to make against Edwards. For instance, quite what it means for a proposition to be entirely 'hard' is not clear, as Plantinga himself admits.[16] Propositions which appear to be entirely about the past, and therefore 'hard', on closer examination seem to entail 'soft' facts about the present and the future, some of which are not merely ersatz, or Cambridge notions. So, for example, the proposition, 'Caesar was murdered on the Ides of March, in 44 BC', whilst apparently past and therefore 'hard', and perhaps even accidentally necessary, entails at least the following 'soft' propositions (where

The Secret and Revealed Will of God 85

these propositions are uttered in 2004 AD), 'Caesar will not eat breakfast this morning' and 'Caesar will not cross the Rubicon in 2020 AD'. Thus, propositions entirely about the past appear to entail propositions about the present and future, which lead Helm, in commenting on this distinction, to say:

> [P]erhaps it is true of any action completed in the past that it entails the non-occurrence of some state of affairs at a time future to the action's completion-date. If so, then any completed action is 'soft', since completion implies truths about the future. But if completed actions, the most promising candidates for 'hard' facts, are in fact 'soft' facts, what is the distinction worth?[17]

Plantinga believes that the 'hard' and 'soft' fact distinction made by Ockham in his defence of accidental necessity can be reformulated so that it works, and is a useful concept in the philosophical armoury. Let us allow that Plantinga can refurbish the Ockhamist vocabulary in such a way as to make sense of these terms. Nevertheless, in so doing he makes a number of assumptions which can be successfully challenged by Edwards, or an Edwardsian determinist.

The first of these involves the assertion that if accidental necessity can be explained in terms of the power of agents, then there are some tensed facts that not even a divine agent can make hard, and therefore, candidates for accidental necessity. These include propositions specifying God's past foreknowledge of human actions, and his past beliefs about future human actions. The problem with this is that it assumes that God's foreknowledge is exactly that: *fore*-knowledge. Plantinga maintains that Edwards' takes a temporal view of God's eternity *qua* everlasting, and works on that basis. However, later in the very section which Plantinga cites as the basis of his own attack upon theological determinism, Edwards states in an unequivocal way, his endorsement of a timeless view of God's eternity: 'If, strictly speaking, there is no foreknowledge in God, 'tis because those things which are future to us, are as present to God, as if they already had existence: and that is as much as to say, that future events are always in God's view as evident, clear, sure and necessary, as if they already were.' Moreover, 'Nothing is more impossible than that the immutable God should be changed, by the succession of time; who comprehends all things, from eternity to eternity, in one, most perfect, and unalterable view; so that his whole eternal duration is *vitae interminabilis, tota, simul*, and *perfecta possessio*.'[18]

It would be difficult indeed to find a more definite endorsement of divine timelessness with respect to knowledge. The fact that Edwards speaks of God in a tensed way (which seems to have misled Plantinga), is merely a demonstration of the inadequacy of human language in capturing aspects of divinity, and should be treated anachronistically:[19]

> [W]hen we speak of cause and effect, antecedent and consequent, fundamental and dependent, determining and determined, in the first Being, who is self-existent, independent, of perfect and absolute simplicity and immutability, and the first

86   *Jonathan Edwards and the Metaphysics of Sin*

> cause of all things; doubtless there must be less propriety in such representations, than when we speak of derived dependent beings, who are compounded, and liable to perpetual mutation and succession.[20]

This puts things with respect to accidental necessity in quite a different light. Rather than arguing that God foreknows (in some tensed way) that if it will dawn tomorrow (hard fact, via divine knowledge), then necessarily it will dawn tomorrow (consequential necessity), Edwards is claiming that God's omniscience is complete and immutable precisely because it is atemporal. So all God's knowledge is hard; there can be no soft aspects to God's knowledge because it is timeless. Therefore, all events, past, present and future, are 'accidentally' necessary, because all events are known to the mind of God according to A-'fore'knowledge.

But can this stronger, timeless version of Edwards' temporal necessity work? The answer, under the terms which Plantinga sets out, is that it can. Plantinga's critique of theological determinism relies upon a particular understanding of what a proposition is, which need not be assumed by defenders of a timeless God. In particular:

> Plantinga's argument is only plausible because what God foreknows is relativized to some observer or agent in the present and so the truth of what God foreknows is not a timeless proposition. But what is past (and so accidentally necessary) is God's knowledge of what Paul is doing at a particular date, regardless of whether that date is not past, present or future relative to some moment in time. The propositions which are the objects of God's knowledge do not become true or false, they are timelessly true.[21]

This can be shown as follows:[22] if truth refers to tensed sentences, then those sentences have some of the characteristics of an event, and events happen at a particular time. But Helm shows that a proposition can be true or false without the sentence expressing it being assertable, for example, 'All human life is annihilated.'

Plantinga uses propositions in a tensed way (that is, expressible in tensed sentences). But those who defend a timeless view of God's omniscience need not believe that propositions are tensed. They can hold that propositions are timeless, having precisely the same truth-value at any particular time index. What God knows when he knows proposition p is that p is true irrespective of any temporal index. It is accidentally necessary just because it is true that God knew p yesterday, and the fact that God knew it in the past ensures the accidental necessity of what is known. So the 'hard' and 'soft' facts of Ockham's Way Out have no purchase where propositions are understood in a timeless way, because the Ockhamist view relies on a tensed view of propositions and their sentence tokens.

But, as even the previous paragraph has shown, referring to God in a consistently tenseless way is a difficult exercise to maintain. Edwards (following Aristotle's maxim), thinks with the wise and speaks with the vulgar when he refers to God in this matter. And Helm observes that what God knows tenselessly, is ontologically prior to any recognition of that knowledge by time-bound creatures: 'For God to foreknow that p is not for him to know that p expresses an event that will happen in his future, it is for us to ascribe to God a knowledge of the truth of p which may contain within it the description of some event which is due to occur after the time we ascribe that knowledge to God.'[23]

This leaves us with the problem of the ambiguity in Edwards' exposition of temporal necessity. (N1a) is 'hard' on an Edwardsian timeless model. What of (N1b)? Arguably, it too is hard, given the timeless model, in which case, the parenthetical suffix can be dropped, since it is *not* a soft fact. For if Edwards understands God's omniscience in timeless, A-foreknowledge terms, then this is a necessary and sufficient condition for a particular proposition which God knows being true.

Similarly, (N2) follows on a timeless view of propositional truth and divine omniscience. The transfer of necessity principle provides the required justification for (N2) to obtain given the conjunction of (N1) and timeless propositions.

Aspects of Edwards' formulation of this problem might still be unclear. But it seems that the central thrust of his articulation of temporal necessity as a species of accidental necessity with respect to divine foreknowledge is coherent, contrary to claims by Plantinga via Ockham. And this provides a counter-argument against the Arminian notion that all that foreknowledge implies is that Judas may choose x, not that Judas must choose x. For, according to the Edwardsian argument in *FOW* II: 12, Judas *must* choose x because x is a hard fact, 'fore'known by God.

But this is not all. William Wainwright in his recent article on this issue claims that, although Edwards is right about this in one respect (that is, the Arminian is not much better off than Edwards, since his God is still morally if not causally responsible for sin, a problem we will come to in a moment), he is wrong in another sense. The Arminian God does not *determine* the sin of Judas as the Calvinist's God does.[24] But we have seen in the foregoing argument that Edwards has a response to this criticism, in his use of accidental necessity. Edwards' argument demonstrates that, on his 'A'-foreknowledge view, the Arminian's God *is* as culpable as the Calvinist's God. The Arminian will not accept such a view of divine foreknowledge, to be sure. But the point is this: if the Arminian accepts the substantive issue of Edwards' use of accidental necessity in defence of foreknowledge ((N1)), then she or he is committed to the view, via the transfer of necessity principle of (N2), that apparently 'soft' facts are, on closer inspection, 'hard' facts. And if they are hard facts, then the Arminian appeal to 'O'-foreknowledge folds since, according to Edwards, there is no metaphysical distinction to be made between 'hard' and 'soft' facts, or between foreknowledge *simpliciter* and determinative foreknowledge. If Edwards is right about this, then the metaphysics that underpins the Arminian understanding of freedom and foreknowledge is unstable and the Arminian is far worse off than the Calvinist. This argument is a substantial response to the Arminians, *tu quoque*, and to Wainwright and Plantinga who have defended them in different respects.

Moral Inability and Responsibility

Be that as it may, this does not let Edwards off the hook on the charge of divine insincerity with respect to the distinction between the secret-revealed will distinction.

Edwards may be right that on an accidental necessity-style understanding of the Arminian argument, Judas must do x. But this only reinforces the problem of divine insincerity. For, if it is not the case that Judas may do x, but that he must do x, and that he must do x on an 'A'-foreknowledge view of divine omniscience, then God is responsible for bringing it about that Judas does x, rather than ~x. Edwards has two further arguments to try to diminish this problem of divine insincerity. Though they are not entirely successful, a third argument that has much in common with Edwards' view may have some success where the other two Edwardsian arguments fail.

In *FOW* Edwards makes much of the notion that 'moral' necessity is requisite to praise and blame, contrary to libertarianism.[25] Part of this involves a distinction between moral *in*ability to respond to the commands of God, and natural ability to do so. Take his example of a king and his imprisoned subject. In the first of two scenarios, Edwards says that a common misrepresentation of Calvinism is

> ... that of a man who has offended his prince, and is cast into prison; and after he has lain there a while, the king comes to him, calls him to come for to him; and tells him that if he will do so, and will fall down before him, and humbly beg his pardon, he shall be forgiven, and set at liberty, and also be greatly enriched, and advanced in honor: the prisoner heartily repents of the folly and wickedness of his offence against his prince, is thoroughly disposed to abase himself, and accept the king's offer; but confined by strong walls, with gates of brass, and bars of iron.[26]

Clearly, in such a case, there is no way that the felon can fulfil the commands of the prince; he is literally barred from doing so, even if he wants to do so. Even if he is (in some dim sense) morally aware of his crime and of the need to repent, he is naturally unable to do anything about it, because of his natural state of spiritual torpor.

The second scenario better represents the Calvinist position. A similar situation obtains. A prisoner, rightly convicted and of a 'haughty, ungrateful, willful disposition', 'brought up in traitorous principles', and with a heart, 'possessed with an extreme and inveterate enmity to his lawful sovereign' is confronted by his prince, as in the previous scenario. But unlike the first situation, this prince has the man unchained, and the prison doors thrown wide open. From outside the prison, he exhorts the prisoner to repent and come to freedom. But the prisoner is so full of 'haughty malignity' that he refuses to come out of his cell and accept the offer, preferring instead to remain where he is.

Edwards claims that this illustrates the difference between moral inability to turn to God, because human nature is vitiated as a result of the fall, and a natural ability to do so. There is no natural impediment to the felon leaving his cell and following his prince, but he so hates and despises the king who has rightly convicted him, that he refuses this offer. So it is only this second scenario that adequately captures the difference between the moral inability and natural ability of fallen man to turn towards God for salvation.

We may apply this to the insincerity charge in the following way. Judas is morally, but not naturally vitiated. This means that Judas could naturally choose ~x, but will not do so, because of his morally vitiated nature. But this does not help Edwards to absolve God. The divine secret disposing and ordaining of Judas' moral nature means that Judas must do x. It is not that the imprisoned felon could have walked free; his moral nature, determined by God's disposing will, means that he must remain in his cell. The illusion that Edwards' second scenario creates in favour of the Calvinistic picture in this regard is just that: an illusion. It does no work in getting the Deity off the hook, because all he has done is transfer the problem from the natural to the moral nature. The point is that the felon still must remain in his cell, because he has been caused to have the moral nature he does, which means he will inevitably reject the advances of his prince, however winsome. So Edwards' refinements to the Calvinistic picture of depravity, locating the vitiation in the nature of humanity to the moral, rather than 'natural' faculties, does not present a more promising solution to the insincerity charge.

The Parent–Teenager Analogy

A third counter-argument to the Arminians is articulated by Wainwright, on behalf of Edwards. The question is whether the principle *if a person knows E will not be achieved by doing x, he cannot do x to achieve E* (mentioned earlier in connection with divine commands and insincerity), is false as the Arminians claim it is. Wainwright thinks not. There are circumstances in which I think a person will do y (where y is some undefined, but immoral action), but nevertheless try to persuade them against this. I only try to persuade such a person because I believe there might be a chance that the other person might heed my exhortations and not do y, as a parent might, with a recalcitrant teenager.

But, surely, this will not work in the case of the Deity. He is not in a position of ignorance with respect to the desires and motives of any agent, whether Judas, or a recalcitrant teenager, or whoever. After all, he is omniscient and the determiner of the very dispositions any particular agent might exhibit at any particular time. This means that the analogy between a parent and a teenager will not work in the case of God and some other moral agent. God, unlike the parent, is never in a position where he thinks a person will do y, but nevertheless could try to persuade them otherwise, *believing there might be some chance that this person will heed his exhortation, and refrain from y*. God could only be in such a position if he was not sure that the agent would do y or ~y, or neither y nor ~y. But, Edwards' God is clearly not in this situation, because he has determined that y will obtain. So this defence of Edwards' position will not work either.

Moral Responsibility and the Arminian God

The fourth counter-argument involves the most serious version of the insincerity charge. This is: *God's secret will determines Judas will not respond whilst at the same time, God's preceptive will commands Judas to respond*. This is the position Edwards finds

90 *Jonathan Edwards and the Metaphysics of Sin*

himself in, and from which, I have argued, he has no escape. But, by way of ameliorating the situation, are the Arminians also exposed to problems which, though not exactly the same, have a similar outcome, in being similarly grave for their conception of God's sincerity? The answer is affirmative.

Let us take a simple Arminian model regarding freedom and foreknowledge, to demonstrate this point. It may be that God puts Judas (or whoever) in circumstances where he knows that Judas will not respond to his preceptive will. God has not determined Judas' response (he *will* do x, but might not have done so: it is not that he *must* or *necessarily* will do x, as per Edwards). But God foreknows that given state of affairs S, Judas will not respond to his moral exhortations and commands. (A standard libertarian rejoinder is this: if Judas would have responded, God would have believed differently, because he would have foreknown different actions on the basis of the counterfactuals of freedom that obtained.) So, although the Arminian God is not guilty of insincerity on the same (deterministic) grounds as Edwards' God is, he is still guilty. For the Arminian God is guilty of putting Judas into circumstances where he foreknows that Judas *will* do ~x, rather than x. In this way, God may be morally responsible for the actions of Judas (or whomever), even though he is not causally responsible for their actions, since they arise from a libertarian freedom. (This is another application of our earlier examination, in the previous chapter, of the constituents of the proxy problem, and in particular (PX2). This dealt with whether A can be morally responsible and not causally responsible for y. Clearly, according to Arminianism, the answer is yes.)[27]

Divine Duty and Ineffectual Commands

Wainwright offers one more possible way out for both Edwards and the Arminians. It relies upon God having a duty to offer moral commands and exhortations even when he knows that they will be ineffectual. Parallel cases are not hard to find: a parent and teenager; a counsellor and addict; a platoon leader to a shell-shocked soldier, and so on. The trouble here is that for Edwards, God knows that his commands will be ineffectual because he has ordained this, not because other circumstances have intervened, as is the case with all the other 'parallels' (the addict, the soldier and the teenager). There are no other causal factors to account for, as there are in all these other cases. So, God is still insincere. Although, at least – but for different reasons – the Arminians are in a similarly unenviable situation to Edwards on this particular charge.

The 'Whole Will' Response

There may be one final defence of Edwards on the sincerity issue, which I owe to Paul Helm.[28] It could be that Edwards' use of the 'secret-revealed will' distinction could be taken *in toto*, as a solution to the insincerity charge, rather than as two parts of a whole. On this reading of the distinction, God intends the whole of his secret and revealed will for some greater good (a point Edwards makes so eloquently in his essay, *End of Creation*[29]). If God intends the whole of 'secret-revealed will', it does not follow that the insincerity issue can be raised of each *separate component* of that whole. If we were to ask the question, 'did God expect Judas to heed the commandment, "thou shalt not kill"?', as if an answer to this aspect of God's revealed will can be assessed in isolation from the question of his secret purposes in his eternal decrees, then, on this view, one could rule the question out of court. The reason being, that God does not intend this commandment independently of his whole will (hidden *and* revealed). What he intends is the entire decree which embraces issuing commands to Judas (revealed will) and his use of Judas for the purposes of salvation (hidden will). A homely illustration of this will help to clarify this. If I own a tartan tie, every thread of my tartan tie is not tartan (individual threads may be crimson, or cobalt, or navy blue). But every thread is a thread of my tartan tie (whatever colour they are individually, taken together, and only taken together, they form the weave of the tartan plaid). Thus, there may yet be a way in which a contemporary Edwardsian might be able to defend the secret-revealed will distinction, against its detractors.

Summary of the Counter-arguments

To sum up: Edwards is unable to escape the whole force of the conclusion that God is insincere in some way. His distinction between the hidden and revealed will of God does not do the work he wants it to, in absolving God of the charge as it stands on his deterministic principles. But there may be the beginnings of a response in an Edwardsian spirit, that utilizes this distinction to show that God may be sincere if his purposes are taken together, rather than separately. Whether this works or not, the Arminians have problems of their own, generated by their account of the counterfactuals of freedom. Though Edwards does not see that there is a distinction between his own, and the Arminians' case in this regard, he is right in one central point: their conception of freedom and divine foreknowledge does not present a more feasible solution to the problem of divine insincerity.

Conclusion: Does Edwards Solve the AP?

It should be clear from the arguments of this chapter and those of Chapter 3 that Edwards' argument does not solve the AP. Crucially, he cannot demonstrate a plausible scenario in which God might be causally but not morally responsible for the sin of a particular agent. This means that his distinction between divine permission and positive agency cannot work. If God is causally responsible for every event that takes place, then he is morally responsible too. There are plausible scenarios in which such a distinction may work between two human agents. But such scenarios work because one agent cannot be both the necessary and sufficient cause of another's doing x. Clearly this is exactly what Edwards does affirm about God on the basis of (P1)–(P3).

Hence, when this distinction is applied to God, it fails. This does not mean that there are no such plausible scenarios where a compatibility thesis might be able to work. But it does mean that the compatibilism that Edwards deploys cannot work in this regard. God is still the author of sin, on Edwards' construal of this particular aspect of the problem of evil.[30]

William Mann observes that 'the distinction between passivity and activity does no moral work in the case of God'.[31] That is, an attempt to circumvent problems of moral responsibility via an appeal to God's permission, rather than positive agency in an action, does not yield the required result: God is still responsible. But even if this is the case, Mann thinks that God may be insulated from the charge of wrongdoing if he *brings about*, but does not actually *do* any evil. This might be a promising route to solving the problem. However, it is not a route open to Edwards, on the basis of (P1), (P2) and (P3). That is, there are no circumstances according to (P1)–(P3) where the following claims might all be true:

(1)   A knowingly and willingly brings it about that B knowingly and willingly brings it about that S.
(2)   A knowingly and willingly brings it about that S (from (1)).
(3)   S is a situation that is evil.
(4)   In knowingly and willingly bringing it about that S, B does something that is wrong.
(5)   In knowingly and willingly bringing it about that S, A does nothing that is wrong.[32]

The strength of (P1)–(P3) mean that together, there is no possibility of (5) obtaining, where A is God and B is some other agent. The reason being that Edwards' God does not just bring about certain states of affairs, he directly causes all events to take place. Mann claims that what is important in view of the AP is to justify God's bringing about sin, rather than excusing his doing so. Edwards thinks he has done just this in terms of a greater good argument.[33] But this cannot work where (5) cannot obtain. Edwards cannot claim that God merely brings about a state of affairs in which an agent sins (*qua* Mann), though his argument for divine permission seems to point in that direction. For, given the premises of his argument, God is causally responsible for every event that takes place, not just for a state of affairs that obtains, as might be the case for the libertarian. So Edwards can neither excuse God of sin, nor provide a justification for his permission of sin, since Edwards' God is the necessary and sufficient cause of sin. Clearly, this raises considerable problems for Edwards' concept of God. For if God is the author of sin, then he appears to lack what is usually taken to be a defining characteristic of God in the western tradition, namely, benevolence. At the very least, this raises questions about the theistic acceptability of Edwards' concept of God.

Nevertheless, Edwards is right to point out that some version of the AP is a problem common to Arminianism as well.[34] Indeed, Edwards' use of accidental necessity shows that, *contra* Wainwright and Plantinga, Arminians do have the same problems as

The Secret and Revealed Will of God 93

Calvinists regarding foreknowledge and creaturely freedom. If Edwards is right in this respect, then, although he has not solved the AP, he can at least console himself with the thought that he is not alone in having no feasible solution to it that absolves God of moral responsibility for sin. Having looked at the fall and the AP with respect to the origination of sin, we may now turn to consider another implication of the fall, and one crucial to classical theology: the imputation of Adam's sin.

Notes

1 This is only one constituent of a full-blown occasionalism. The other, the reader will recall, is a continuous creation thesis.
2 Although, of course, this distinction between the hidden and revealed will of God predates Calvin.
3 Turretin, *Institutes of Elenctic Theology Volume I*, p. 225, emphasis added. The scriptural basis for this doctrine includes texts like Deuteronomy 29:29, Psalm 115:3 and Matthew 7:21.
4 *YE1*: 415.
5 However, from this it seems to follow that what is agreeable to God and what is for the greater good are not necessarily consistent, a problem that Edwards does not seem to deal with. (Edwards is not alone in this. Compare Heppe's *Reformed Dogmatics* V: 25, pp. 85 ff. Heppe's compendium of Reformed thought does not appear to turn up any more promising ways of dealing with this problem either.) One possible way of addressing this issue might be to use Frege's distinction between sense and reference. God's secret and revealed will have different senses, but one reference: God. And as with Frege's example of the morning and evening star, the morning star does not have the same sense as the evening star, though both refer to the same object, Venus. In a similar fashion, it may be that the two wills of God are different in sense, but not in reference, and thus not contradictory, though they may appear to be contradictory. However, further elucidation of this point would take us away from Edwards' discussion of it.
6 Taken, with minor adjustments, from Wainwright, 'Theological Determinism and the Problem of Evil', pp. 16–17.
7 I refer to Nelson Pike, 'Divine Omniscience and Voluntary Action'. A useful summary and discussion of this argument, and the distinction between 'will' and 'must' is given in William Lane Craig, *The Only Wise God*, ch. 3ff.
8 Wainwright maintains that it is not necessary on Edwardsian principles that Judas die in mortal sin, that is, a denial of (3). But this is not the case on (P1)–(P3).
9 Accidental necessity, or necessity *per accidens*, is discussed by Alvin Plantinga in 'On Ockham's Way Out' in *The Concept of God*, Morris (ed.).
10 Plantinga claims that Ockham's way of disarming theological determinists like Edwards relies upon a denial of the following premise, 'if p is about the past, then p is necessary'. Therefore, the general claim that all facts about the past are accidentally necessary, is seen to be false (on Ockham's rendering of things) – or, at any rate, there seems to be no reason at all to believe it. And this dissolves any argument for theological determinism which, like Edwards', accepts this premise about accidental necessity in its full generality, ibid., p. 183.
11 *YE1*: 257–8, cited in Plantinga, 'On Ockham's Way Out', pp. 173–4. A detailed analysis of this earlier section of *FOW* would take us outside the bounds of the present discussion. See *FOW* I: 3.
12 See Linda Zagzebski, 'Foreknowledge and Human Freedom'.
13 Both of these arguments are discussed by Hasker in *God, Time, and Knowledge*, pp. 72–3. They occur in *YE1*: II: XII: 263 and 265 respectively. If it is claimed that there are just no facts about the future to be known, because the future is essentially 'open', Edwards would simply have denied this view. He was, after all, a theological determinist.

94   *Jonathan Edwards and the Metaphysics of Sin*

14   This 'A'–'O' distinction comes from Helm, *Eternal God*, pp. 129 ff. If God O-foreknows that event p will happen, then God knows that p, but not as a result of bringing it about that p is true. In this sense O-foreknowledge is 'notional'. As Helm puts it, 'There is a contingent connection between the foreknowledge of p and the making of p true; O-foreknowledge results from possessing evidence which ensures the truth of p, or from some other factor.' God A-foreknows that p as a result of ordaining that p is true. Helm again: 'At the very least [God's] A-foreknowing that p is causally necessary for the truth of p and perhaps it is causally sufficient as well', *Eternal God*, p. 129.

15   See, for example, *Miscellany 490*, in *YE13*: 533–4.

16   'It is extremely difficult, however, to say precisely what it is for a proposition to be strictly about the past, and equally difficult to say what it is for a proposition to be accidentally necessary', Plantinga, 'On Ockham's Way Out', p. 185. Nevertheless, Plantinga does believe that by the end of his essay he has located a form of accidental necessity which depends upon an explanation using the power of agents, ibid., pp. 199–200.

17   Helm, *Eternal God*, p. 134.

18   *YE1*: 267 and 268 respectively, author's emphasis.

19   And one might add, that was the whole point of Edwards' *ad hominem* argument against Whitby, anyway.

20   *YE1*: 376–7.

21   Helm, *Eternal God*, p. 138.

22   What follows is drawn from Helm, ibid.

23   Ibid., p. 140.

24   Wainwright, 'Theological determinism and the problem of evil', p. 92.

25   We shall have to take Edwards at his word on this notion of 'moral' necessity. He distinguishes between several kinds of necessity in *FOW* I: III and IV, but not altogether clearly. An examination of these concepts is not possible here.

26   *YE1*: 362.

27   This is presuming that the libertarian account of freedom and foreknowledge is coherent. That is, I am criticizing the Arminian view on its own terms, not from an Edwardsian perspective. However, it might be that the concept of *foreknowledge* proves a harder nut to crack for contra-causal freedom than libertarians think it is. For instance, how can a person whose choices are contra-causally free make choices which may be foreknown by anyone, even an omniscient agent? If they are truly 'free' choices (free in the libertarian sense, that is) up to the point of choice, then how can anyone know in advance what another agent will choose, until they have chosen it? The point that compatibilists like Edwards make is that the libertarians presume too much when they claim that Judas *will* betray Christ, but that this does not mean he *must* betray Christ. Surely the very notion that he may do x rather than y is precisely what cannot be known before the event, otherwise, in what sense is the action in question an exercise of the liberty of indifference? This skirts big issues on the nature of time (McTaggart's 'A' and 'B' series), the nature of God's relation to time and the propositional expression of truths about time (either 'tensed' or 'tenselessly') about which, I shall say no more here. My central point, the query about the coherence of libertarianism, must, for now at least, remain no more than that: a query.

28   Suggested in private communication.

29   In *YE8*.

30   Even Edwards' recent defender, John Kearney, concedes that 'Edwards's replies to the Arminian "author of sin" charge rely heavily, then, on his use of *tu quoque* arguments, the distinction between causing evil and permitting evil, and the distinction between the revealed and secret will of God', 'Jonathan Edwards and the "Author of Sin" Charge', p. 15. My point is that the *tu quoque* does no work in defending the coherence of Edwards' account. The insincerity charge, utilizing the secret and revealed will distinction turns out to be another *tu quoque*, so fails for the same reasons. And the substance of Edwards' defence, namely, the causing-permitting notions actually do not deliver the required distinction between causation and permission for God to be absolved of responsibility on the AP.

31 See Mann, 'God's Freedom, Human Freedom, and God's Responsibility for Sin', p. 207.
32 Ibid.
33 Mann suggests that another route towards theodicy lies in claiming that God has a unique position as Creator which invests him with peculiar rights, responsibilities, privileges and immunities over us. The analogy he offers in this respect is that of a parent allowing a child to sin to teach them some lesson. Such parental permission would not be extended, he thinks, to others acting *in loco parentis*, ibid., pp. 208–209.
34 And I think that, with modifications, it could be shown to be a problem common to libertarians like Molinists, who try to marry a strong doctrine of divine providence (and omniscience) to a libertarian thesis. But space prevents a fuller elaboration of this. This has been done by Hugh McCann in his 'Edwards on Free Will', in *Jonathan Edwards: Philosophical Theologian*.

CHAPTER 5

Temporal Parts and Imputed Sin

There are three constituent parts to the traditional doctrine of original sin: first, explaining the proneness to sin in humanity as a whole (usually through the fall); second, identifying and dealing with the cause of this proneness to sin (in the person of Adam); and third, defining how the fault accruing to this original sin is passed down the generations in inherited guilt. In *Original Sin*, Edwards attempted to outline and defend the first two of these central strands of a full-orbed doctrine of original sin (namely, explaining the proneness to sin in humanity, and identifying and dealing with the cause of this sin, as he saw it, in Adam). The first he spent the majority of his time defending in *OS* against Arminian adversaries. The second, he dealt with in his peculiar brand of imputation. It was Edwards' concern in *OS* to defend the first, general thesis, and develop a formula by which he might ensure that the second, more particular thesis was rationally defensible. He also sought to address the third aspect of the full-orbed doctrine of original sin, that is, the concept of inherited guilt.

In the opening chapters of this volume we assessed whether Edwards was able to deal with the problem of the primal sin of Adam and its effect upon humanity as a whole. We also dealt with the related problem of the authorship of sin. In this chapter we shall outline and discuss Edwards' doctrine of the imputation of sin. This leaves the notion of inherited guilt, which we shall consider in the next chapter.

Chisholm on Edwards

The classical tradition of Reformed theology maintains that Adam's sin, though grievous, is in principle transferable to his posterity, so that both Adam and his progeny bear the punishment for Adam's sin. The reason being that Adam is the representative of the whole human race, by divine ordination. If the representative of the race sins, then, in virtue of his role as representative, the punishment for his fault devolves upon his posterity, whom he represents.

The problem with this is that it seems monumentally unfair and unjust, and perhaps unreasonable, 'inasmuch as Adam and his posterity are not one and the same'. Edwards' doctrine of the imputation of sin was principally directed towards solving this problem that had dogged Reformed theology and its federal account of imputation. His solution was to develop a more careful, nuanced metaphysical account of the nature of imputation. God dealt with Adam, 'as the head of the whole body, and the root of the whole tree; and in his proceedings with him [Adam], he dealt with all the branches, as if they had been then existing in their root'.[1]

Edwards' theory of the imputation of Adam's sin depended on his views on the metaphysics of persistence through time, and in particular, the doctrine of temporal parts. This view claims that any object that persists through time is made up of numerous successive temporal parts, so that only one part of the persisting object, the current temporal part, is present at any one moment of its existence.[2] Edwards claims that Adam and his progeny are, in fact, one metaphysical entity, not many, made up of temporal parts. The objection to this view

> . . . is founded on a false hypothesis, and wrong notion of what we call sameness or oneness, among created things; and the seeming force of the objection arises from ignorance or inconsideration of the degree, in which created identity or oneness with past existence, in general, depends on the sovereign constitution of the law of the Supreme Author and Disposer of the universe.[3]

Roderick Chisholm, in his book *Person and Object*, defends precisely the view that Edwards repudiates, and claims that Edwards' position makes the divine constitution of things arbitrary:

> God, according to Jonathan Edwards, can contemplate a collection of objects existing at different times and 'treat them as one'. He can take a collection of various individuals existing at different times and think of them as all constituting a single individual. Edwards thus appeals to a doctrine of truth by divine convention; he says that God 'makes truth in affairs of this nature'. God could regard temporally scattered individuals – you this year, me last year, and the vice-president the year before that – as comprising a single individual. And then he could justly punish you this year and me last year for the sins that the vice-president committed the year before that.[4]

Chisholm's argument raises an important question about the precise nature of the unity constituted by God between Adam and his progeny. The question is this: *if God can take Adam and his posterity and treat them as one although they are temporally scattered individuals, then what prevents him from doing so with any group of temporally scattered individuals?* That is, what gives Adam-plus-progeny any greater ontological privilege than, say, the constituting of an object made up of you this year, me last year and the vice-president the year before? Why should Adam's sin be imputed to me rather than, say, those of the vice-president, or someone else? Let us call this the arbitrariness problem for Edwards' account of temporal parts.[5]

Clearly the basic point around which these related issues cluster involves the apparently 'arbitrary' nature of Edwards' temporal parts argument. Paul Helm summarizes this as follows:

(1) The identity of a contingent individual depends entirely upon the arbitrary will of God.
(2) So, there is no 'natural' identity through time of anything.
(3) Therefore, it is possible that God for certain purposes constitute Adam and his posterity a unity.
(4) God has in fact constituted a unity between Adam and his posterity, as shown in Scripture, and by the consent we give to the sin of Adam.

(5) Therefore, the objection that the divinely constituted unity between Adam and his posterity contradicts the true nature of things is invalid.[6]

The apparently 'arbitrary' nature of Edwards' doctrine of temporal parts can be seen in premise (1) above. But even if Chisholm is willing to allow (1) with the proviso that 'arbitrary' is being used to refer to the wise ordering of God according to his divine justice, he can still ask whether this ordering is not merely an ontological fiction (a development out of (2) and (3)). And more broadly, he may ask whether on the Edwardsian scheme, such ordering of personal identity does not lead to personal identity being a similar, grander, ontological fiction, a fiction maintained simply by divine fiat.

All this provides an opportunity to elucidate the Edwardsian argument for imputation, and in the process point out where Chisholm is wrong. We pick up from where Helm left off:

(6) The unity between Adam and his posterity is an expression of the divine will, wisdom and justice.
(7) God may constitute a unity where there are temporally scattered concrete individuals who have communicated to them like properties, relations and circumstances by God.

To this extent, Edwards is following a broadly Lockean scheme, inasmuch as where two things share personal identity:

(8) A in 2003 and B in 2004 have a spatio-temporally continuous history, which links them at their respective time indexes.

(Assuming, for the sake of simplicity that this history is uninterrupted.) But according to (1) and (2) there is no 'natural' identity through time of the sort that Locke would have understood, of either physical or non-physical parts of a person. According to Edwards' doctrine of temporal parts, the spatio-temporal history of any two temporal parts of an object depends immediately and constantly on divine constitution, and nothing else.

Like Locke, Edwards uses the notion of organic unity as a crucial constituent in the identity of a thing, such as a plant, whose identity can be traced through successive stages of its existence and development. Locke states that

> . . . being then one Plant, which has such an Organization of Parts in one coherent Body, partaking of one Common Life, it continues to be the same Plant as long as it partakes of the same Life, though that life be communicated to new Particles of Matter vitally united to the living Plant, in a like continued Organization, conformable to that sort of Plants.[7]

Edwards, using a similarly organic analogy asks,

Temporal Parts and Imputed Sin

> [W]ho can determine, that the Author of nature might not, if it had pleased him, have established such a union between the root and the branches of this complex being, as that all should constitute one moral whole; so that by the law of union, there should be a communion in each moral alteration, and that the heart of every branch should at the same moment participate with the heart in the root, be conformed to it and concurring with it in all its affections and acts, and so jointly partaking of its state, as a part of the same thing? Why might not God, if he had pleased, have fixed such a kind of union as this, an union of the various parts of such a moral whole, as well as many other unions, which he has actually fixed, according to his sovereign pleasure? And if he might, by his sovereign constitution, have established such an union of the various branches of mankind, when existing in different places, I don't see why he might not also do the same, though they exist in different times.[8]

Moving from a temporal parts account of the persisting individual spacetime entity, Edwards claims that as a plant grows but is one individual aggregate of its temporal parts, so Adam and his progeny are an aggregate of temporal parts viewed as such by the ordination of God. There is the same spatial and temporal continuity through a succession of moments from Adam to all his progeny in a sequence of contiguous slices, such that identity can be traced along these lines.[9] But this identity does not involve a diachronic causal nexus. Instead it involves a rather specialized form of what can be traced from Adam's progeny to back to Adam himself. None of these parts cause the existence of the next according to Edwards, since they no longer exist in order to bring the next thing into existence (*OS*: 400). But God takes each temporal slice together with the previous one in a nexus existing in his mind; thereby constituting a new metaphysical unity that is ontologically real. Adam and his progeny are as real a spacetime entity as any other number of gerrymandered metaphysically real constructs.

But this only raises Chisholm's question once again: why should any unity that God establishes have a 'sufficient qualitative identity' for God to treat them as one, and what does such identity consist in? If Adam and his posterity are, according to Edwards' temporal parts account of persistence through time, as real as any other hunk of matter, why should God privilege certain hunks over others?

It is clear from the argument thus far that there are no metaphysical facts to which Edwards can appeal to support some notion of metaphysical truth by (mundane) convention. In other words, the constitution of certain objects as a unity does not *depend* on them sharing certain properties which means God may treat them as one. God *may* treat Adam and his posterity as one because they share certain properties. But he need not. Certain objects may appear more metaphysically viable than other gerrymandered objects without such common properties, such as an entity gerrymandered from a part of a biscuit in 2005, a fossil in 1995 and a locomotive from 1955. But for Edwards, the attribution of these properties is due simply to divine, not mundane, convention: 'For if same consciousness be one thing necessary to personal identity, and this depends on God's sovereign constitution, it will still follow, that personal identity depends on God's sovereign constitution.' Nevertheless:

100   *Jonathan Edwards and the Metaphysics of Sin*

> When I call this an arbitrary constitution, I mean, that it is a constitution which depends on nothing but the *divine will*; which divine will depends on nothing but the *divine wisdom*. In this sense, the whole course of nature, with all that belongs to it, all its laws and methods, and constancy and regularity, continuance and proceeding, is an *arbitrary constitution*.[10]

And this, of course, is Chisholm's point. The fact that God *does* constitute Adam and his posterity a unity is simply arbitrary.

However, Edwards need not subscribe to a view of gerrymandered objects as all deserving the same status. It does not follow that because Edwards espouses a doctrine of temporal parts that he must endorse the view that all hunks of matter, however gerrymandered, are as 'natural' as each other. (The biscuit-fossil-locomotive being as 'natural' as temporal parts of Crisp.) It may be that God deems it more 'natural' or more 'suitable to his purposes' to divide the world in certain ways at the level of objects, and perhaps of properties and parts too. It may also be that the constitution of Adam and his posterity as a unity is one such 'fitting' object, whereas the biscuit-fossil-locomotive is not.[11] This does not mitigate the arbitrary nature of the divine constitution of things. But it does mean that there may be certain ways of carving up matter that are more fitting for divine purposes, and therefore privileged in a way that other, equally arbitrary objects like the biscuit-fossil-locomotive are not. God need not treat every hunk of matter on a metaphysical par.

This needs some further development. But before turning to consider this, we need to dispose of another, related problem. The account thus far still leaves open the question of the kind of relation established by God in the unity instituted between Adam and his posterity for imputation. What sort of relation does Edwards have in mind and how does it work?

Helm, in a recent paper on the subject, has pointed out a helpful category that may be applied at this point *contra* Chisholm.[12] The unity instituted by God between Adam and humanity means that each individual can be described as 'genidentical', that is, made identical with some non-identical part in a chain that goes back to Adam. So Dean at t2 and Wayne at t1 are genidentical with Dean at t1 and Wayne at t-1 going all the way back to Adam. However, the use of genidentity here is peculiar because, as a result of Edwards' doctrine of occasionalism, God is the only causal agent there is; there can be no mundane causation. Consequently, Wayne at t1 is made one with Adam (by God) via Wayne at t-1 and so on. That is, Wayne's temporal parts are made one with Adam via an immediate activity of God who views all of the spacetime entity Wayne and all of Wayne's ancestors going back to Adam as part of an organic whole, just as a plant existing in seed form and at its full flowering across a temporal duration is a spacetime entity all of whose temporal parts make up one plant, and all of whose branches and chloroplasts are parts of a single spacetime entity.

The difference, in Adam and his progeny, are that they are temporally dispersed over a much greater area. But, as Edwards points out, this is merely a quantitative, rather than qualitative distinction.[13] Once the temporal parts ontology has been granted in principle, the whole fits together and Adam and his posterity can be treated as a unity by God precisely because they actually are such a unity in the mind of God. But this notion of being 'made one' that Edwards uses is not mere conventionalism. It really is the way things are, according to Edwards.

A second point made by Helm in his paper, is that the relation which exists between Adam and his posterity is not transitive. He says, 'Adam has been made one with Peter at t1 and Paul at t1, but it does not follow that Peter at t1 and Paul at t1 are identical with each other. Not strictly identical, and not genidentical either, because God has chosen not to communicate "like properties, relations and circumstances" to Paul at t1 and Peter at t1.'[14]

For present purposes, the important point that Helm touches upon here is that in Edwards' argument, Adam and his progeny share a relation, namely, that Adam has been made one with his offspring. But this does not mean that any two or more of Adam's offspring are identical with each other simply because they both happen to share a relation of identity with Adam. That is, though Adam at t-1 has been made identical with Dean at t1 and Wayne at t2, this does not mean that Dean and Wayne at t1 and t2 are therefore themselves identical with each other. The relation at work in the spacetime aggregate that is Adam and his progeny is *unidirectional*. Wayne at t2 and Dean at t1 remain distinct for all other purposes other than the unity specifically constituted by God in imputation. (Of course, the fact that this relation is *uni*directional is due merely to the divine will.)

But all this does not overcome the fundamental question of why God cannot impute the sin of one individual to another, or another group of individuals in a whimsical fashion. For if Edwards' doctrine of temporal parts leaves him entirely at the mercy of the divine ordering of temporal parts into a contiguous whole, and if on this basis God can, and has constituted a unity in Adam and his posterity, then why cannot God do the same with Chisholm's vice-president of yesteryear, me yesterday and you today? There appears to be no reason other than the divine will, since there is no secondary causation and no possibility of existence without the immediacy of divine intervention, given Edwards' occasionalism. And, on a doctrine of temporal parts, there is no metaphysical reason to deny Chisholm any gerrymandered aggregate of temporal slices he wishes to assemble.

The 'Federal' Aspect to Edwards' Doctrine

Edwards does not appear to be embarrassed by this implication of his position. God 'makes truth in affairs of this nature' and constitutes things as they are because they best reflect his glory and his character, which being perfect and ordered, seeks to represent that order in creation.

However, there is another strand to Edwards' argument. Adam and his posterity constitute a unity unlike that offered by Chisholm because of Adam's unique position as the father of the race. And surely this is the point of Edwards' argument: that

Adam and his posterity can be looked upon as such a unity because of Adam's unique position as the first human. Consequently, Adam's sin can be imputed to his posterity in a way that my sin cannot be imputed to, say, Dr Dolittle in the nineteenth century, or Professor Higgins in the twentieth century. At the beginning of *OS* and subsequently at the beginning of his discussion of imputation, Edwards points out Adam's unique position as the father of humanity in a way which can only be construed as broadly 'federalist'.[15] But under the terms of Edwards' discussion of the union established by God in imputation found in his doctrine of temporal parts, this 'federalism' should be construed, not in the traditional Calvinistic nomenclature in which Edwards had been schooled, but under the terms and conditions of the occasionalism that he set forth.[16] This should not be taken to be a denial or modification of the overarching tenor of Edwards' Calvinism. It is simply to say that Edwards reconceived what that meant in terms of imputation, in ways that utilized the Early Enlightenment thinking on these matters (the thinking of philosophers like Locke and Malebranche[17]). It is certainly the case that Edwards' theology had a place for federalism in his doctrine of the covenants.[18] But it is not the case that Edwards was simply reiterating a standard position on federalism. In order to vindicate the inviolability of God's nature in imputing Adam's sin to his posterity, he utilized a perspective that, whilst within traditional Augustinianism, diverged from traditional federalism in his conception of the unity established by God.

So, we return to Chisholm's point with this in mind. The significant difference between Adam and the vice-president, or, indeed any other individual we care to name, is that no other human could take Adam's place in the divinely instituted unity of humanity without taking on his role as *homo primus*, or first human.

Chisholm could seek to respond with the claim that Adam's place as father of the race is purely an arbitrary one, and that any individual could have been that person. And although that is true, and God could have constituted Dean or the vice-president as father of the human race in a counterfactual Garden of Eden, such a state of affairs has not obtained. And if it had, the result would, according to Edwards, have had the same outcome, namely, the fall, and thence the same for the 'arbitrarily' constituted unity of Dean and his posterity. Dean would have fallen just as Adam did (though perhaps not at the same time or place, or even for the same reason), and God would still be able to constitute the conjunction of Dean and his posterity a unity, and 'impute' original sin to his posterity accordingly.

In other words, the problem is not with the 'arbitrary' nature of the divinely constituted unity between the first human and their progeny (whoever that first human actually was). The problem actually lies in the relation that exists in the mind of God between the father of humanity and his progeny. Adam's importance is in the place that he held in the mind of God, as the father of humanity, not in the fact that he happened to be called Adam. God could have constituted that unity differently so that Dean, or anyone else held that position. The net result would have been the same given Edwards' belief that the fall happened as a result of God's withholding confirming grace from Adam.

Temporal Parts and Imputed Sin 103

So whether the federal head is Adam or Dean, or the vice-president, the issue remains the same: that God constitutes the *homo primus* and his progeny a unity for the sake of the imputation of sin. And he treats Adam and his progeny as one unity, privileging it above other, gerrymandered unities, because this unity comports with his design in creation and redemption. This is an arbitrary decision. In that respect, Chisholm is correct. But it is based upon a relationship that God specifically constitutes with regard to humanity, a relation rooted in an ontological link that has been established by divine fiat between Adam and his progeny. Such a link cannot be carried over to Chisholm's argument, since it is peculiar to the theological context for which it was instituted (the imputation of sin). Hence, although Chisholm is right in his accusation of arbitrariness, he is wrong to think this commits Edwards to the belief that just any old conjunction of matter is as fitting for the purpose of imputation, as any other. Chisholm overlooks the importance in Edwards' scheme, of *divine* convention. God privileges certain objects over others, not because they are more 'natural' but because they are more to the divine purpose. And since God has constituted Adam as *homo primus*, it is simply not the case that the sin of any person, at any time, can be imputed to anyone else. That *could* have been the case (the arbitrariness element). God could have constituted matter this way. But he did not do so, because it does not suit the purposes of divine wisdom to order things so.

This is not to say that Edwards endorsed the federalist solution to the problem of imputed sin wholeheartedly. He did not. It appears, rather, that Edwards held back from endorsing the traditional Reformed position as a *complete* explanation of the formal cause of the imputation of original sin. His doctrine of temporal parts is an important qualifier to his federalism. But it is far from clear that he believed that there was *no* sense in which Adam's office as *homo primus* set him apart, so that the fate of his posterity lay in his own behaviour. And in this he could be seen to be developing a strand in Calvinian thinking that later formulations of federalism had not taken seriously enough.[19]

In sum, Edwards embraces the arbitrary nature of the divine constitution of matter. God 'makes truth in affairs of this nature'. This, according to Edwards, means God constitutes Adam as a representative of humanity, and imputes his original sin to his progeny, not the sin of any other, at any other moment than that at which Adam committed his primal sin. But the way this is brought about depends upon a view of Adam and his posterity as one gerrymandered object, comprising numerous temporal parts. God has good reason for making truth in this way, rather than some other way, because this way best suits the divine purpose. The fact that human beings may not be privy to the reasons why this is the best fit for divine purposes does not mean that there is no reason; just that we do not have epistemic access to those reasons. Chisholm is right about the arbitrary nature of all this. But he is wrong in thinking that, simply because God constitutes things according to a doctrine of temporal parts, the sin of any one person could be attributed to anyone else. There appear, on Edwards' argument, to be reasons why God arranges the metaphysics of the matter in the way in which he does. And this does not commit Edwards to the permissive view of temporal parts

Chisholm thinks it does. But is this just, fair and reasonable? These were the issues Edwards sought to answer in his account of imputed sin. It is to these issues that we now come.

Temporal Parts and Perdurantism

Edwards' doctrine of temporal parts seems to be a facet of a larger theory of persistence-through-time, which in the contemporary literature is called perdurantism. Perdurantists claim that it is impossible for a concrete individual to be numerically identical through time. Instead, an individual who exists at different times is an aggregate of discrete, temporal parts that have some qualitative identity. In this way, perdurantists treat time as a fourth dimension alongside the other three dimensions of space.[20] The alternative to this theory, endurantism, claims that a concrete particular can only persist through time if it exists wholly or completely at different times, that is, it is numerically the same through different times. Edwards' doctrine of temporal parts seems to fit with a perdurantist account of temporal persistence, rather than an endurantist one (although, as we shall see, this is problematic). For instance, in the case of the union that exists between Adam and his posterity Edwards says:

> Who can determine, that the Author of nature might not, if it had pleased him, have established such an union between the root and branches of this complex being, as that all should constitute one moral whole; so that by the law of union, there should be a communion in each moral alteration, and that the heart of every branch should at the same moment participate with the heart of the root . . . I know not why succession, or diversity of time, should make any such constituted union more unreasonable, than diversity of place. The only reason, why diversity of time can seem to make it unreasonable, is, that difference of time shews, there is no absolute identity of the things existing in those different times; but it shews this, I think, not at all more than the difference of the place of existence.[21]

Perdurantists believe their theory of temporal persistence offers a rich means of *ontological analysis* and *synthesis*.[22] In other words, there is a two-way traffic in the perdurantist ontology: from familiar common-sense objects to a conception of concrete individuals as a complex of temporal parts. For instance, Dean is a concrete individual who, on the perdurantist ontology, is an object whose parts extend across the length of a temporal continuum that he inhabits. Each temporal part along that continuum represents a part of the whole object, and each part is as ontologically real as any other. So unlike endurantism, there are no ontologically privileged temporal parts that are real because they are present.

The opposite flow of ontological traffic in the perdurantist scheme, ontological synthesis, moves from a disparate conglomeration of temporal parts (including in many cases, parts of existing concrete individuals) to the postulation of objectively real material objects which occupy a certain portion of filled spacetime. Such objects, uncovered through ontological synthesis, are a second kind of metaphysical entity. An example of such a gerrymandered object might be the biscuit-fossil-locomotive, mentioned earlier. The perdurantist position at this point broadens its ontology to take in any number of objectively real material objects that occupy a region of spacetime that is filled with matter. These objects are real, inasmuch as they are parts of spacetime that may be given metaphysical status, because on the perdurantist ontology spatial parts have no more privileged status than temporal parts. Spatial parts are subject to a similar kind of dissection from the perdurantist as temporal parts.[23] Furthermore, the perdurantist is able to cut up the filled region of spacetime in any number of ways to postulate any number of ontologically real, material objects, gerrymandered though they may be.

This application of ontological synthesis to things made up of disparate temporal and spatial parts like the biscuit-fossil-locomotive has an interesting application for Edwards' thinking. There are several different ways it could be used, that reflect different strengths of argument at different points in his discussion of the matter in *OS*: IV: III.[24]

First and foremost, it offers a weak perdurantist underpinning of the kind of Edwardsian argument that has been offered so far in light of the analysis of Edwards' doctrine of temporal parts by Chisholm. On this view, God 'treats' Adam and his posterity as a unity for certain moral purposes. Second, it can be understood in terms of a strong perdurantist reading of Edwards' argument. This means that God constitutes Adam and his posterity a single gerrymandered metaphysical unity. Third, it can be used to draw out Edwards' occasionalism. On this view, God the sole causal agent creates all things *ex nihilo* at each moment, with the appearance of creaturely persistence through time. This third option represents the state of Edwards' final thoughts on his ontology of imputation. The first two applications of ontological synthesis may offer an account of imputation that avoids the problems that Edwards' peculiar brand of occasionalism throws up for his metaphysics. We shall see that there are strong reasons for thinking that if an Edwardsian understanding of imputation is to be endorsed, then a form of the strong or weak perdurantist argument is to be preferred to his occasionalistic development out of these.

For the sake of simplicity of argument, let us assume that when perdurantism is referred to in what follows, this concept includes the following constituent parts,

(D1)   eternalism, comprising:
(D1a) ontological analysis,
(D1b) ontological synthesis, and
(D2)   that all concrete particulars are temporal aggregates who are four-dimensional spacetime entities.

As a consequence of this simplified version of perdurantism, we may assume that any region of spacetime filled with matter can be delimited to pick out a material object (from (D1) and (D1b)). Given this, there are grounds for utilizing perdurantist ontological synthesis to come up with a spatio-temporal aggregate of Adam and his posterity which make up a temporally scattered object that shares certain morally significant properties and can be constituted a complex individual by divine fiat. This individual we shall term '*Perdurantist Humanity*' (hereinafter, PDH). This whole is made up of an aggregate of all and only those parts that constitute Adam and his posterity. Together, they form a new, temporally and spatially scattered whole, which is as ontologically real and objective as Dean, the biscuit-fossil-locomotive, or whatever. This ontological unity is constituted for the specific purpose of imputing original sin. And since this new metaphysical unity is a real object (given (D1), (D1b) and (D2) in conjunction with our adaptation of Helm's rendition of Edwards' argument), not only is God justified in viewing PDH as a whole for certain harmartiological purposes, but his doing so involves the delineation of a new metaphysical entity, PDH (on the basis of perdurantism). This perdurantist version of an Edwardsian imputation argument not only gives metaphysical weight to the previous Edwardsian argument (the weak perdurantist argument), it also takes the Edwardsian agenda a step further, into the stronger version of the Edwardsian argument for persistence through time (strong perdurantist argument). And in so doing, it defends the Edwardsian persistence thesis in a way that constitutes PDH, not as a metaphysical expedient, but as an objectively real, ontological aggregate. This strong perdurantist argument can be expressed more clearly in the following fashion:

(1)   Any region of spacetime filled with matter can be cut up into constituent parts to pick out a material object on the basis of ontological synthesis (following (D1) and (D1b)).
(2)   Such an ontological synthesis comprises:
(2a)   spatially and/or temporally scattered constituent parts, and
(2b)   spatially and/or temporally scattered constituent properties (from (D1)–(D2)).
(3)   God constitutes Adam and his posterity an ontological synthesis, PDH (conjunction of (1) and (2)).
(4)   PDH is an objective, ontologically real metaphysical unit (via ontological synthesis) which is a material object (from (D1), (D1b), (D2) and (3)).

From this argument the following conclusions can be drawn which reflect two strengths to Edwards' position on imputation. The first is weaker, the second, stronger:

(5)   God treats PDH as a unity, privileging them on the basis that they share common moral properties in a circumscribed region of spacetime (weak perdurantist argument).
(6)   God, by constituting PDH, effects a new metaphysical spacetime entity which comprises all and only those parts and properties that constitute PDH (strong perdurantist argument).

Temporal Parts and Imputed Sin 107

(5) is an adapted version of the conclusion reached in the previous weak perdurantist temporal parts argument, whilst (6) encapsulates a strong perdurantist view which uncovers new, and considerably stronger grounds upon which God may justifiably impute sin, since PDH is an objectively real entity which can be treated as such by God. And if it can be treated as an object made up of spatially and temporally scattered parts, then God may still impute sin to the whole object.[25]

This strong perdurantist position represents a more robust argument than that offered against Chisholm. What was said there assumed only conditions similar to (5). That is, God has a metaphysical warrant in constituting PDH a unity for the purposes of imputing original sin, and this sequence of reasoning follows a (perdurantist) doctrine of temporal parts, where Adam is the father of the race. (6) is compatible with this reading of Edwards' perdurantism, but is not entailed by it; the two propositions are distinct. This is the case because (6) is not simply allowing that God may *treat* PDH as a unity for the sake of certain metaphysical transactions. Instead, it is saying that PDH *is* a metaphysical unity. God does not simply create Adam and his posterity and then gerrymander them into some unity for the purposes of imputation. Adam and his posterity are not distinct perduring objects, which God treats as if they were one object for his own purposes in imputation. Instead, Adam and his posterity are themselves perduring objects, which are parts of a larger perduring object, PDH.

Thus (6) provides a strong support to Edwardsian imputation. Edwards himself was assuming some kind of metaphysical unity similar to that postulated by contemporary perdurantism as evidenced in *OS*. There he first appears to put forward a position similar in strength to (5):

> I am persuaded, no solid reason can be given, why God, who constitutes all other created union or oneness, according to his pleasure, and for what purposes, communications, and effects he pleases, may not establish a constitution whereby the natural posterity of Adam, proceeding from him, much as the buds and branches from the stock or root of a tree, should be treated as one with him, for the derivation, either of righteousness and communion in rewards, or of the loss of righteousness and consequent corruption and guilt.[26]

Before adding a footnote (which we have already had cause to note) to the effect that God could have constituted PDH a unit in a way similar to (6):

> [W]ho can determine, that the Author of nature might not, if it had pleased him, have established such a union between the roots and branches of this complex being, as that all should constitute one moral whole; so that by the law of union, there should be a communion in each moral alteration, and that the heart of every branch should at the same moment participate with the heart of the root, be conformed to it and concurring with it in all its affections and acts, and so jointly partaking in its state, as a part of the same thing?[27]

Edwards goes on to underline the fact that he has no qualms about God constituting such a unity from temporally, as well as spatially, scattered objects.[28]

108 *Jonathan Edwards and the Metaphysics of Sin*

So, it appears on the basis of both the temporal parts arguments strengthened by the *homo primus* reading of Edwardsian imputation (where Adam is the father of the race), and on perdurantist grounds independent of, but congruent with Edwardsian imputation, that Edwards is able to make a metaphysical case for his position. In fact, the strong perdurantist argument provides grounds stronger than those Edwards takes his stand upon, which could be defended through an Edwardsian reading of imputation.[29]

Taken on their own, (5) and (6) could be used to defend an Edwardsian understanding of imputation without the occasionalist paraphernalia which Edwards insists upon deploying in his argument. However, it is clear that Edwards believed that occasionalism was important in his overall metaphysical schema. But the addition of this occasionalist strand invokes an argument that is stronger than even (6) is. On the Edwardsian occasionalistic scheme, there is no continuity involved in persistence through time: any object such as Dean is as illusory in its apparent perdurance as a biscuit-fossil-locomotive, since both depend entirely upon God as sole cause of their continued existence. And this causation is based entirely upon God's arbitrary choosing: no part, spatial or temporal, exists for anything more than a moment, so that the constitution of Dean is as arbitrary as that of a biscuit-fossil-locomotive, or PDH.

It appears that, as far as Edwards' occasionalism is concerned, the perdurantist distinction between ontological analysis and synthesis has no metaphysical payload, since analysis and synthesis are both as arbitrary (that is, dependent upon the will of God moment-by-moment, *ex nihilo*) as the other. The concept of ontological analysis has no more purchase in metaphysical reality than ontological synthesis has: both are equally arbitrary (immediately and constantly dependent upon God's will), although the former is apparently more real than the latter to the pre-philosophical mind.

So the constitution of PDH, biscuit-fossil-locomotive, Dean, or whatever, is purely a matter of divine ordering according to God's will, nothing more, since there is no place for secondary causation in occasionalism. The reason for this being that all causes are merely the occasions of God's actions.[30] Consequently, (6) as it stands, is not strong enough as a description of Edwards' occasionalism. The force of the occasionalistic requirement of Edwards' thinking here can be expressed as follows:

(7)   God constitutes PDH according to an occasionalist ontology. This means that,

(7a)   the ontological structures of Edwards' metaphysics are entirely dependent upon God's will (*arbitrium*),

(7b)   consequently, no metaphysical object is any more or less gerrymandered than another since,

(7c)   all metaphysical objects are called into being moment-by-moment *ex nihilo* by the mind of God.

(7d)   Moreover, PDH, biscuit-fossil-locomotive, Dean (or whatever) are thereby causally dependent upon God moment-by-moment, and

(7e) PDH (or whatever) cannot and does not persist or perdure. Its apparent perdurance, and the apparent perdurance of any metaphysical object is (strictly speaking) an illusion.

In this context, the word 'illusion' means only that the perdurance of a particular object is unreal, not that the object itself is unreal. That was certainly not a position that Edwards would have countenanced. The point here is that if all objects are re-created moment by moment in the mind of God, then their perdurance is indeed an illusion which is perpetuated by the ordering by God of all things in a way that reflects his perfection and beauty. This aesthetic strand to Edwards' metaphysics can be found, for example, in his notes on *The Mind*, where he says, 'if the world had been created without any order or design or beauty, indeed all species would be merely arbitrary'. However, in point of fact, God has created the world such that things do agree, 'either as to their outward appearance, manner of acting, the effects they produce or that other things produce on them, the manner of their production, or God's disposal concerning them, or some peculiar perpetual circumstances that they are in'.[31]

But this is not all:

(7f) PDH (or whatever) is constituted, not of numerous temporal parts, but of numerous distinct concrete individual objects, none of which can persist for more than a moment in time.

That is, each moment that God recreates the world *ex nihilo*, he creates a new set of concrete individuals. PDH is made up of such non-enduring individual objects, not of perduring temporal parts of objects. This means that, in endorsing occasionalism, Edwards undercuts his perdurantism, ending up with what seems to be an endurantist theory of temporal persistence instead. As Mark Heller points out:

> [O]ur conventions allow us to act as if there are enduring wholes; they allow us to treat certain momentary objects as if they compose an enduring whole, but the world itself does not contain any enduring objects. This is the sort of view that would be expected from an account of temporal parts that is formed against a background supposition of three-dimensionality. Someone might believe that no object can really exist for more than a moment. If one of these instantaneous objects could exist for longer it would be a three-dimensional enduring object. But there are no such enduring objects. Instead there are collections of these instantaneous objects added together (by convention) to form the objects that we typically talk about. Someone holding such a view would be reasonable to accept the Edwardsian conception of temporal parts. But I do not accept the background supposition of three-dimensionality.[32]

Edwards' occasionalism entails that objects exists wholly and completely at one moment only to be destroyed and replaced by temporally contiguous objects of zero, or miniscule duration, which also exist wholly and completely at that temporal index, only to be destroyed and replaced, and so on. The apparent perdurance of objects

110   *Jonathan Edwards and the Metaphysics of Sin*

across time is merely a matter of divine convention, nothing more. 'Temporal parts' of an object are really nothing more than 'parts by convention'. They are actually numerous distinct individual objects. This raises several problems. First, Edwards' theory of imputation seems to oscillate between a perdurantist doctrine of temporal parts, and an occasionalism that requires endurantism (objects exist wholly and completely at each moment they exist).[33] Edwards' considered view is occasionalism, but he thinks he can hold this alongside a doctrine of temporal (perduring) parts. He cannot. Second, Edwards' occasionalism destroys imputation. If there are no perduring objects, only objects existing wholly and completely for zero duration contiguous with other such objects, then no individual object exists for long enough to perform any action. Adam does not commit a sin; temporally contiguous objects (Adam 1 at t1, Adam 2 at t2, Adam 3 at t3, and so on), are each created and destroyed, with the appearance, but without the reality, of persistence through time.[34]

The net result of this examination of Edwards' position on imputation is that (7) is mutually exclusive of (5) and (6) (assuming (7f) cannot be read along weak or strong perdurantist lines); (6) could subsume (5), but does not necessarily entail (5); but both (5) and (6) seem to work as expressions of an Edwardsian approach to imputation without the need for (7). However, it is precisely the occasionalism of (7) that Edwards insists upon in his discussion of imputation in *OS*. It may be that (7) needs to be discarded as unworkable, whilst (6) and/or (5) can be retained in such a way that the view of imputation which Edwards expresses may be salvaged without the unfortunate repercussions which his occasionalism involves.

Notes

1   *YE3*: 389. A more detailed account of the theological foundations of Edwards' doctrine of imputation is given in Oliver D. Crisp, 'On the theological pedigree of Jonathan Edwards's doctrine of imputation'. Edwards was seeking to rebut criticisms of the Reformed position made by opponents like John Taylor.

2   See E.J. Lowe, *A Survey of Metaphysics*, pp. 49 ff. for an account of temporal parts.

3   *YE3*: 397.

4   Chishom, *Person and Object*, pp. 138–9.

5   In commenting on this use of Edwards by Chisholm, Paul Helm believes Edwards' notion of an 'arbitrary' unity refers to individuals that share significant moral properties: 'Edwards did not hold that just any set of things whatsoever could, by the divine will, be constituted into a unity . . . the phrase "treats them as one" may suggest either whimsy or even mindless tyranny, but Edwards makes clear the sense in which he intends his readers to take this phrase by adding that God can only treat new effects as one "by communicating to them like properties, relations and circumstances"; in the case of Adam and his posterity, the properties include significant moral properties.' But Chisholm's criticism depends on temporally scattered humans, not gerrymandered hunks of matter with no specific genus. Moreover, it is not clear, as we shall see, that Helm's invocation of a conventionalism with respect to temporal parts, will help Edwards, since God '*makes truth*, in affairs of this nature' (*YE3*: 404). See Helm, *Faith and Understanding*, p. 171.

6   Ibid., p. 169.

7   Locke, *Essay*, II: XXVII: 4, p. 331, cited in Helm, *Faith and Understanding*, p. 172.

Temporal Parts and Imputed Sin

111

8   *YE3*: 405–406, n. 6.

9   This could be understood in terms of DNA (as per the plant analogy), but it could also be understood more general in terms of the 'like properties, relations and circumstances' that Helm cites.

10 *YE3*: 399 and 403–404. See also 405, author's emphasis.

11 Discussion of so-called 'natural objects' and whether there are objects that are more 'natural' than others, in a perdurantist world, can be found in Katherine Hawley's *How Things Persist*, pp. 90 ff.

12 Helm, 'A Forensic Dilemma: John Locke and Jonathan Edwards on Personal Identity'.

13 See *YE3*: 405–406, n. 6.

14 Helm, 'A Forensic Dilemma', pp. 56–7.

15 *YE3*: 259, 260 and 389. I refer to the Calvinistic notion of Adam as 'federal' representative of the human race. This point has been argued for in Crisp, 'On the theological pedigree of Jonathan Edwards's doctrine of imputation'.

16 Although, it must be admitted, there are times when Edwards does sound disconcertingly traditional, particularly in his early notebooks. See, for example, *Miscellany 35*, where he says, 'There have never been two covenants [namely, the covenant of works and grace], in strictness of speech, but only two ways constituted of performing this covenant: *the first constituting Adam the representative and federal head, and the second constituting Christ the federal head*; the one a dead way, the other a living way, and an everlasting way', *YE13*: 219, emphasis added.

17 This has been argued for in much of the recent secondary literature on Edwards. See, for example, Norman Fiering, 'The Rationalist Foundations of Jonathan Edwards's Metaphysics', and the editor's introduction to *YE6*.

18 See, for example Harry Stout, 'The Puritans and Edwards'. On p. 143, he says Edwards 'was every bit the federal theologian that his Puritan predecessors were'. And, on p. 157, 'The federal covenant – unlike questions of epistemology, psychology, and moral philosophy – was not a philosophical problem for Edwards, but part of the taken-for-granted reality in which New England society grew and took shape. In fact, no eighteenth century established minister dared to deny the federal covenant and New England's attendant identity as a special people with a messianic destiny.'

19 See David Weddle's article on Edwards, 'Jonathan Edwards on Men and Trees, and the Problem of Solidarity', p. 162, note 15, where he points out that Calvin's rejection of the older, Traducian picture of the transmission of sin led him to espouse a version of transmission which sounds at points quite Edwardsian: 'For the contagion does not take its origin from the substance of the flesh or soul, but because it had been so ordained by God that the first man should at one and the same time have and lose, both for himself and for his descendants, the gifts that God had bestowed upon him.'

20 This is not to suggest that endurantists cannot use a similar four-dimensional notion of spacetime. It is simply that perdurantism requires it. Nor do I mean by this use of time as a fourth dimension that only Einsteinian views of spacetime apply. An 'absolutist' view of space and time, such as that of Newton, could be used here, and presumably would have been used here by Edwards.

21 *YE3*: 405–406, n. 6.

22 For these two notions, see Loux, *Metaphysics*, Chapter 6.

23 This touches on the perdurantist endorsement of eternalism, the view that there are no ontologically privileged parts of an object. Eternalists believe that tensed language referring to temporal parts of an object can be translated, without loss of meaning, into tenseless language that better expresses the logical parity between different times. However, this is controversial, and is not an issue Edwards pursues. So, I shall ignore it here.

24 Paul Helm points this out in greater detail in 'A Forensic Dilemma'.

25 Quite how a gerrymandered object like PDH can have moral properties at all is a question addressed in the following chapter in the context of original guilt.

26 *YE3*: 405.

27 Ibid., pp. 405–406, n. 6.

28 Ibid., where he says, ' I know not why succession, or diversity of time, should make any such constituted union more unreasonable, than diversity of place. The only reason, why diversity of time can seem to

112 *Jonathan Edwards and the Metaphysics of Sin*

make it unreasonable, is, that difference of time shews, there is no absolute identity of the things existing in those different times: but it shews this, I think, not at all more than the difference of the place of existence.'

29 C. Samuel Storms in his *Tragedy in Eden*, concludes his treatment of Edwardsian imputation with this note: 'My conclusion is that there is no commonly communicated "stuff" whereby an individual may be reckoned as one with Adam to which Edwards may appeal. God simply reckons it so . . . There is no "stuff" or substantial basis, be it material or immaterial, which Adam and posterity share by arbitrary divine constitution that would lead us to believe they are one. God simply says that as far as he is concerned he has determined to treat them or look upon them as one', pp. 255–6.

But the notion of some kind of metaphysical 'stuff' of which Adam and his posterity are made, is beside the point once the perdurantist nature of Edwardsian imputation is made plain. Adam and his posterity, on perdurantist ontology, are made of the same stuff as the rest of the universe: matter. What is important is that Edwards is interested in a metaphysical unity, not in any bogus 'substratum' of which Adam and his posterity are made. And once that is clear, the force of Edwards' argument is apparent.

30 See *YE3*: 402–403, cited earlier.

31 *YE6*: 366, entry 47.

32 Mark Heller, *The Ontology of Physical Objects*, p. 22.

33 Note that occasionalism cannot admit a doctrine of temporal parts, because nothing persists for more than a moment. So, nothing perdures long enough to have any temporal parts.

34 Philip Quinn in 'Divine Conservation, Continuous Creation, and Human Action' has raised a similar point. We shall return to this issue in the last chapter.

CHAPTER 6

Inherited Guilt

In this chapter I shall assess the argument put forward by Jonathan Edwards for the concept of inherited guilt in *Original Sin*. In the process, I shall concentrate in particular on William Wainwright's attack on Edwards' defence of this notion. In an essay entitled 'Original Sin', in the symposium *Philosophy and the Christian Faith*,[1] Wainwright argues that Edwards' argument for inherited guilt fails to satisfy. I will show that Wainwright is wrong in several important respects, and that Edwards' argument does represent a coherent and original articulation of the traditional doctrine of inherited guilt. The solution to problems affecting the question of the imputation of guilt may be applied, *mutatis mutandis*, to Edwards' doctrine of imputed sin. The reader is invited to make the relevant changes and apply the findings of the argument here to the question of imputed sin, discussed previously.

The Defensibility of Inherited Guilt

We begin with Edwards' summation of his own position at the beginning of *OS*: IV: III:

> [B]oth guilt, or exposedness to punishment, and also depravity of heart, came upon Adam's posterity just as they came upon him, as much as if he and they had all coexisted, like a tree with many branches; allowing only for the difference necessarily resulting from the place Adam stood in, as head or root of the whole, and being first and most immediately dealt with, and most immediately acting and suffering.[2]

Wainwright claims that Edwards' discussion, which this citation prefaces, does not establish that the doctrine of inherited guilt he defends is scriptural. He does demonstrate that the New Testament concept of redemption presupposes a prior state of sin (*OS*: 361–71). He also shows that the Christian doctrine of salvation presumes that humanity is in need of deliverance because they are trapped in a state of sin (*OS*: 353–9). But according to Wainwright, the texts Edwards advances do not show that Adam's guilt is passed on to his descendants (for example, Romans 5:12–19). Wainwright distinguishes between the following claims, which may be construed from a biblical presentation of original sin:

(1) because of Adam's sin humanity is subject to death
(2) because of Adam's sin human nature has been vitiated
(3) because of Adam's sin humanity is guilty.[3]

114   *Jonathan Edwards and the Metaphysics of Sin*

It appears that (1) is clearly taught in the Bible, whilst (2) and (3) could be extrapolated from Romans 5. However, according to Wainwright, Edwards' examination of the issues does not render a sufficient warrant for (3).[4] I shall not pass judgement on Edwards' exegesis. Instead, the focus of what follows will be on the extent to which Edwards' defence of (3) represents a coherent argument.

Wainwright distinguishes two strands of argument in Edwards' defence of imputation. The first involves the legal and moral bond that exists between Adam and his progeny such that his fault is accounted as the fault of humanity as a whole. Wainwright correctly places this aspect of Edwards' thinking within his appropriation of federalism.[5] The second strand of argument refers to Edwards' doctrine of temporal parts (although Wainwright himself does not use that term). These distinctions inform the argument which Wainwright develops against Edwards' version of inherited guilt.

The Legal and Moral Bond Involved in Inherited Guilt

On the question of the legal and moral bond that exists between Adam and his posterity, a distinction needs to be made between feeling a sense of shame at the actions of another, and being guilty because of the actions of another in which we are somehow implicated, or share responsibility, and as a consequence, blame. Edwards needs to establish this latter sense of guilt for his argument to work. Wainwright takes a considerable amount of care in elucidating five case studies of situations in which people are held responsible for the actions of another. In each case, he finds the emerging concept of guilt to be too ineffectual, or insufficient for effectual transposition onto a doctrine of original sin.[6] I shall not reproduce the detail of these five case studies here. However, it is worth considering Wainwright's five studies in brief, to make the point. In each case it is clear that liability is not the same as guilt, and guilt is non-transferable.

First, sharing (part of) the blame for the actions of another, either an individual or community, may make one blameworthy, but not guilty of the crimes of the other(s) involved. For instance, those Germans who remained silent in the face of the atrocities committed by the National Socialists in 1930s Germany may be blameworthy for not speaking out (they may not, of course). But they are not thereby guilty of the crimes committed by the Nazis who were in power.

Second, there may be situations in which guilt seems to be distributed from one person to another: for instance, where a person fails to intervene to save someone being stabbed at a bus stop. It might be thought that, in such a case, guilt is distributive to all those who failed to stop the stabbing, who were able to do so, and who were standing at the bus stop at the time of the stabbing. However, once again, in this scenario it is not guilt that is distributive, but partial responsibility for allowing the stabbing to take place. It is not the bystander(s) who stab the unfortunate victim. They are not guilty of the crime committed by the perpetrator.

Inherited Guilt 115

A third case involves collective fault, although only one member of a group acts in a way that brings about harm as a result of that fault. So, a group of drunken students driving home one night who hit a pedestrian might be said to be collectively guilty of the fault of being drunk. And the drunken driver is the member of the group whose actions, on the basis of this fault of being drunk, lead to the death of the pedestrian. But here too, the guilt of the drunk driver does not distribute to the other drunken students in the car. They may be guilty of being drunk, and partially responsible for allowing the driver of the car to take them home that night. But they are not guilty of knocking down the pedestrian.

Fourth, there may be cases of vicarious liability, that is, liability where a person acts on behalf of another. Someone may be authorized to act as the agent of another, or under the employ of command of another, or as surety for another. This does track an important theme in Edwards' account of inherited guilt. According to Edwards, Adam acts on behalf of humankind, and God has ordained this.[7] It is a beneficial state of affairs, because Adam is offered future reward (eternal life), for remaining morally upright. In this arrangement, God has gone beyond what simple justice required of him in his offer to Adam and his posterity. And although Adam's posterity did not authorize this arrangement (they did not exist in order to authorize it), it is a reasonable arrangement, because it is beneficial. Or so says Edwards. Nevertheless, this arrangement, and the notion of vicarious liability that underpins it, does not entail vicarious guilt. Adam's posterity may (perhaps) be liable for the arrangement instituted by God, but they are not thereby guilty of Adam's sin.

One final case involves collective liability for a particular sin. Once again, this picks up an important aspect of Edwards' argument. Imagine a medieval feudal society where the serfs share a collective liability to the Lord of the Manor for any crime committed by one of their number. If one serf commits a crime and is not offered up for punishment, the Lord of the Manor may fine the whole group of serfs, who act as surety for the person who has sinned, and may be liable for compensation required of the criminal too. In a similar fashion, Edwards' argument for original sin assumes that each member of humanity is liable for the fault of one of its members, Adam. The punishment he deserves is distributed to the members of the group as a whole. Thus, God institutes a kind of 'collective liability arrangement' between Adam and his progeny. This seems reasonable, and a beneficial community of (mutual) interest is involved between Adam and his posterity. (Interests like the eternal destiny of human beings, for instance.)

However, here, as before, liability for the guilt of another may be distributive, but guilt is not. The serfs may suffer for the sin of one of their members. They may be liable for that sin. But they are not guilty of it. The same can be said of Adam and his posterity: even if they are liable for Adam's sin, the rest of humanity is not guilty of his sin. Wainwright comments:

> [L]iability must be distinguished from guilt. Although it is sometimes reasonable
> to hold a person liable for the deeds of another, our legal and moral practice

116 *Jonathan Edwards and the Metaphysics of Sin*

> provides no situation in which a person can reasonably be judged guilty of another's offence . . . Thus, even though liability can be transferred from one person to another, guilt cannot. Adam's posterity cannot be guilty of Adam's fault unless Adam's act is somehow literally their own.[8]

This contention is pivotal to Wainwright's argument. If guilt is non-transferable, then Edwards' argument for inherited guilt cannot work (and, one presumes, the same goes for any defence of imputation that includes this concept). Furthermore, since the concept is a crucial constituent of Edwards' defence of imputation, this raises a question mark over the whole programme of *OS*.

The Perdurantist Element to Edwardsian Inherited Guilt

Returning to the second strand of Edwards' argument, Wainwright outlines three theses, which form the heart of Edwards' perdurantism as it bears upon inherited guilt:

(W1) God is the author of criteria of identity (through time): 'for it appears, that a divine constitution is the thing which makes truth, in affairs of this nature' (*OS*: 404, cf. *OS*: 399).

(W2) Edwards believes that personal identity depends upon sameness of consciousness (but not wholly on this): ''tis evident, that the communication or continuance of the same consciousness and memory to any subject, through successive parts of duration, depends wholly on divine establishment' (*OS*: 398).

(W3) God constitutes Adam and his posterity a single metaphysical unity, PDH, for the purposes of imputing guilt: 'The first existing of a corrupt disposition in their heart [of humanity] is not to be looked upon as sin belonging to them, distinct from their participation of Adam's first sin: it is as it were the extended pollution of that sin through the whole tree, by virtue of the constituted union of the branches with the root' (*OS*: 391).[9]

These three criteria need some fleshing out: according to Wainwright, (W1) is ambiguous. Edwards appears to mean different things at different times (or perhaps includes different things at different times under the same rubric, but without making this entirely clear). So at certain times he means that God determines what the various criteria of identity will be for different kinds of things. But at other times he seems to want to make the weaker claim that God brings it about that certain things meet these criteria. Wainwright thinks that Edwards needs both of these aspects for his version of imputation. They can be taken together with the strong conservation thesis that Edwards advocates, stipulating that physical laws determine kinds, and kinds determine criteria of identity. The laws are themselves established by God who institutes the criteria of identity through them as his instruments.

This means that God determines the criterion of identity arbitrarily (according to his *arbitrium*, or will). But it does not necessarily mean that God can arbitrarily

Inherited Guilt

determine that the fulfillment of any old criterion of identity entails responsibility or guilt. Whether it does so or not depends upon the *nature* of the criterion in question. The criterion has to be of the right sort, in order that the guilt of the metaphysical entity comprising Adam and his posterity distributes across time to all parts of PDH. Edwards appears to be aware of this issue:

> [T]here is no identity or oneness in the case, but what depends on the *arbitrary* constitution of the Creator; who by his wise sovereign establishment so unites these successive new effects, that he *treats them as one*, by communicating to them like properties, relations and circumstances; and so, leads us to regard and treat them as one. When I call this an arbitrary constitution, I mean, that it is a constitution which depends on nothing but the *divine will*; which divine will depends on nothing but the *divine wisdom*.[10]

In commenting on this passage, Paul Helm remarks, 'as this quotation makes clear Edwards did not hold that just any set of things whatsoever could, by the divine will, be constituted into a unity. For instance, he did not hold that my left shoe today, the Taj Mahal ten years ago, and my favourite cherry tree tomorrow, could be constituted into a unity simply by the divine will.'[11]

In this regard, we might distinguish between two views on the question of gerrymandering matter. There is *conventionalism*, which states that God can only gerrymander matter given certain criteria for identity across time being fulfilled (Edwards' 'like properties, relations and circumstances'). God cannot, on this view, gerrymander any old matter into a metaphysical object, like Helm's 'shoe-Taj Mahal-cherry tree'. Then there is *perdurantism*, which claims that God can gerrymander any hunk of matter he chooses to, since there is only the arbitrary divine fiat that ordains truth in such matters.

It seems at times that Edwards himself does not want to endorse perdurantism, but something more like conventionalism. God 'makes truth in these matters', but does so by 'communicating like properties, relations and circumstances'. So, *qua* Helm, God does not just gerrymander any old matter. In which case, the question is whether Edwards is able to provide relevant criteria of identity through time in order to substantiate his claim about the transfer of guilt from Adam to his posterity. We shall return to this problem presently.[12]

We come to (W2). The Lockean criterion of identity supplied by (W2), coupled with (W1), means God brings about sameness of consciousness according to his sovereign decrees. And if the criteria for personal identity are dependent upon God's ordering, then he can bring it about that Adam and his progeny are constituted a whole such that Adam's guilt is passed on to his descendants. But this too involves a problem: 'That x can inherit y's guilt is not in itself a criterion of identity, but a logical consequence of the fulfillment of certain kinds of criteria of identity.'[13] In a situation where x is culpable for the sins of y this must mean either, x is identical with (or is the same person as) y, or x is part of the same corporate entity as y. And as Wainwright goes on to point out, 'Even if God constitutes these criteria, he does not constitute the

118   *Jonathan Edwards and the Metaphysics of Sin*

fact that if these criteria are fulfilled, and x is therefore the same person or corporation as y, y's sins can be imputed to x. This fact is a logical fact and Edwards nowhere suggests that God constitutes facts of this kind.'[14]

(W3) is the crucial proposition, since if it works, the first two are redundant, and it is this argument that Edwards seeks to outline in defending imputation (see *OS* IV: III). Therefore, it is in terms of this argument that the consistency and intelligibility of Edwards' doctrine of inherited guilt must either stand or fall. Edwards needs to establish that the kind of identity constituted by God in PDH entails inherited guilt. Wainwright's argument against Edwards' position can be expressed thus:

(1)   God constitutes Adam and his posterity PDH along perdurantist lines.
(2)   This means that if Adam sins then the whole of humanity sin, since PDH constitutes a unity for the purposes of imputation (or perhaps *is* a unity).
(3)   Hence, if Adam is guilty of original sin, then his posterity is also guilty by virtue of a similar transference of guilt in imputation (following (2)).

Here is the problem:

(4)   Faults committed by a person do not ordinarily distribute to their parts.

For example, if a man looks lustfully at a woman, it is the man as a whole who has committed the act. That does not mean that every part of him has committed the act or is guilty of it. His eye did not commit the act, nor is it guilty; it was merely instrumental in the action being carried out. So, it is the whole person who is guilty of the act. This has a clear application to Edwards' position: if PDH exists then the fault of Adam is the fault of the whole of humanity. But this does not mean that it is the fault of his descendants (since they are only parts of the whole PDH).

Can Edwards' perdurantism overcome (4)? He could respond along the lines of:

(5)   Given (1)–(3) each member of PDH is literally affected as Adam is affected, consenting to and concurring with his sin and guilt.[15]

But, as Wainwright points out, though God could have so ordered things, is this actually the state of affairs in the world? If it were, then it would mean that each individual making up PDH would be literally affected as Adam was, and would literally consent to and concur in, Adam's act. This line of argument appears to have proved too much. Not even Edwards would agree that every member of PDH is literally affected as Adam was (according to Wainwright).

Moreover, Wainwright claims that Edwards is guilty of conflating corrupt inclinations and guilty choices, thereby obscuring the distinction between the transmission and effects of Adam's sin (inclinations and nature), and the guilt pertaining to Adam's particular first sin (his choice). We may be inclined to act as Adam did because we share a vitiated nature passed on in imputation, but this does not mean that our participation in the effects of his original sin upon our natures is the same as our participating in the guilt belonging to Adam's choice. The two are separate issues. Thus, concurring with Adam's sin is not the same as consenting to it, just as having a tendency to being a kleptomaniac is not the same as consenting to someone else's theft.

Edwards appears to attempt to outflank this line of criticism in the following:

(6)   PDH would have consented to Adam's sin if they had been present with Adam (or had known about it).

But we ordinarily do not condemn someone who would have done a thing were he there to commit the act, though in fact he was not! As Wainwright observes, 'What is needed is an actual consent of concurrence which is given at the moment one comes into being. Nothing less will show that we are born guilty of Adam's fault.'[16] Clearly this is not possible, since from the moment of birth we are not moral agents conscious of Adam's fault. This is underscored by Richard Swinburne who argues that 'no-one can be guilty in a literal sense for the sins of another, unless he had some obligation to deter that person and did not do so. Since none of us today could have had the obligation to deter the first sinner from sinning, we cannot be guilty for his sins.'[17]

So Edwards fails to distinguish the difference between inclination and choice in the transmission of sin and guilt in imputation. Consequently, he fails to show inherited guilt to be part of the equation. At best, in Wainwright's estimation, he manages to show that:

(a)   We can be held liable for Adam's failure (with regard to the legal consequences for human nature).
(b)   Adam's fault is (in some sense) the fault of the whole species (PDH).

But he has not shown that:

(c)   Adam's fault is the fault of each of his descendants.

Therefore, according to Wainwright, he has not shown how Adam's progeny share in his guilt.

Assessing Wainwright's Argument

An initial assessment of Wainwright's argument might lead one to conclude that it has severely damaged the credibility of Edwards' claim to be defender of a full-orbed doctrine of original sin with reference to inherited guilt. However, this is not entirely the case. Much of the force of the criticisms brought by Wainwright against Edwards depend upon a particular understanding of Edwards' doctrine of imputation which is

120   *Jonathan Edwards and the Metaphysics of Sin*

at odds with the picture of Edwards developed thus far in this volume. In particular, Wainwright seems to have underplayed the truly radical nature of Edwards' argument, which has implications for some of the more damaging aspects of his attack upon Edwards.

In the foregoing argument, Wainwright made four central assertions that need to be dealt with:

(1)   that Edwards' position on inherited guilt is not biblically substantiated;
(2)   that liability must be distinguished from guilt. Liability is transferable; guilt is not;
(3)   that faults committed by a person do not distribute to their parts; and
(4)   that Edwards conflates (corrupt) inclinations with (guilty) choices.

We shall argue that (2) and (3) do not refer to the actual position Edwards holds, and that (3) on a perdurantist ontology, is false; (1) is moot, and as a consequence we shall pass over in silence; and (4) points out a real problem with Edwards' conception of volitions (picked up in more detail in his treatise, *FOW*).

First, Edwards' argument for imputation in *OS*.[18] He begins his discussion of imputation by rejecting one conception of inherited guilt, and embracing another. The notion that people are born with a double guilt, pertaining to the guilt of Adam's sin and the corruption of their own hearts is, according to Edwards, misconceived. The two are in fact one and the same. (Although in what sense they are one and the same he does not specify. Presumably it is to do with the notion that they share all and only the same properties, namely, arising from and being sustained by participation in the sin of Adam.) However, there is a sense in which inherited guilt is in two parts. For Edwards, there is a guilt accruing to the first inclination to sin with which all humanity is born post-Adam, as an effect of sharing in Adam's vitiated nature. It is a consequence of the 'extended pollution of that sin'.[19] But there are further grounds for guilt in it becoming a confirmed principle in the lives of humanity after birth. Edwards believes that this was the case with Adam in his first sin and is the case for all his posterity after his fall. It is at this point that Edwards begins to bring to bear his view on inclination and act, which Wainwright makes the substance of criticism (4). According to Edwards, the act of sinning is not distinct from the disposition to sin formed in Adam's heart. Inclination and choice are parts of a single whole in volition. (We shall return to this point in due course.)

Inherited guilt, then, accumulates because of the extended pollution in spacetime as a result of humanity being somehow identified with Adam's sin. As branches of a tree or members of a body participate in the whole, so humanity participates in the guilt of its head, Adam, in full 'consent and concurrence' with Adam's first sinful act. This means that the sinner has a disposition to approve of Adam's sin 'as fully as he himself approved of it when he committed it'. Edwards goes on to explain that this depraved disposition is not a consequence of imputation, any more than Adam's inclination was the consequence of his first sin. It is prior to it in the order of nature: 'The first depravity of heart, and the imputation of that sin, are both the

Inherited Guilt

121

consequences of that established union: but yet in such order, that the evil disposition is first, and the charge of guilt consequent; as it was in the case of Adam himself.'[20] Thus far, Wainwright's exposition appears secure.

However, if we turn to Edwards' perdurantist arguments, it becomes clear that there may be grounds upon which Wainwright's reading of Edwards may be challenged. Let us begin with the difference between a *weak* perdurantist reading of Edwards and a *strong* perdurantist reading developed in the previous chapter (not to be confused with conventionalism and perdurantism, mentioned earlier). If Edwards is understood to be defending a weak perdurantist thesis, then he is not claiming that Adam's sin is *literally* mine. He is only claiming that Adam's sin might be imputed to me through a metaphysical arrangement whereby the whole of humanity is treated as one unit for certain metaphysical purposes in the divine plan. This understanding of Edwards, though not precisely that expressed by Wainwright, comports with the substance of his argument, outlined thus far. However, it does not appear to take sufficient account of what Edwards says about the 'consent and concurrence' of PDH with Adam in his sin that we have just cited.[21]

On the other hand, if Edwards is defending a strong perdurantist thesis, then this is not the case. A strong perdurantist reading of Edwards seems to agree with what he says at the outset of his defence of imputation about this issue of 'consent and concurrence'. For instance, Edwards maintains, 'the sin of apostacy is not theirs [that of Adam's posterity], merely because God *imputes* it to them; but it is *truly* and *properly* theirs, and on that ground, God imputes it to them'.[22] Wainwright's reading of Edwards' perdurantism seems to involve the weak perdurantist option only. As a result he seems to have overlooked the truly radical implications of Edwards' perdurantism (especially when coupled with his occasionalism). For on a strong perdurantist reading of Edwards, he is saying that Adam and his posterity are one metaphysical unity in the mind of God, which is why he can 'impute' Adam's sin and guilt to the whole of humanity. They form one corporate spacetime entity, such that Adam's guilt is transmitted to his posterity immediately, though consequent to the imputation of his sin. (Of course, if this is the case, then the notion of 'imputation' seems rather empty. There can be no imputation – as that notion has been traditionally understood in Christian theology – on this view, since there is no duration from the time of Adam's first sin to the time at which God constitutes PDH.)

If this is an important aspect of the position that Edwards is defending (and it seems that it is), then the second and third criticism levelled by Wainwright can be met and defeated. The second criticism states that liability is transferable, whereas guilt is not. But if Edwards is defending a strong perdurantism, then there is no transference of guilt from one person to another – as with all the examples cited by Wainwright, since on the strong perdurantist model, the spacetime worm PDH is one concrete particular. It is not that God treats the whole of PDH *as if they were one thing* for certain metaphysical purposes. Rather, PDH *is actually one entity*, such that God can reasonably 'impute' the sin of Adam to the rest of PDH without violating the principle of the non-transferability of guilt outlined by Wainwright.

The third thesis can also be met in principle once the second is dealt with. In the third thesis Wainwright claims that faults are not distributed to the parts of a concrete particular. (As with the analogy drawn earlier between a man lusting after a woman and his eye lusting after her: the man may be said to lust and incur guilt, the eye cannot. It is simply instrumental in the act of lusting.) But if Edwards is defending a strong perdurantist argument, then he is not claiming that the guilt of the person of Adam distributes to his parts in his posterity, since both are one metaphysical whole in PDH.[23]

However, this is not without its problems. If Edwards is claiming that the primal sin is committed by Adam alone (not PDH as a whole), but the guilt of that sin accrues to PDH as a whole (not Adam alone), then he seems only to have reconstituted a species of the problem that Wainwright raises, in perdurantist language. But this difficulty can be overcome, once it is recognized that Wainwright's third criticism appears to be guilty of committing the fallacy of equivocation. That is, Wainwright is guilty of assuming that the parts that he refers to are the same as the parts that Edwards has in mind. They are not. A distinction needs to be made between the physical parts of a person-stage at a particular time index, and temporal parts of a concrete particular *in toto*. Consider the example of Trevor. At t1 Trevor has all his bodily parts. That is, he has suffered no loss of or defect to any of his bodily parts. At t2 Trevor stabs Dean with a kitchen knife over luncheon. At t3 Trevor loses his right (stabbing) hand in a farming accident. Who is guilty of the crime at t2? Surely it is Trevor (not his right hand). Trevor is the concrete particular involved here; his hand is a spatial part of Trevor, and one which is not mereologically essential to him (we know this because, at t3, he loses his hand, but remains Trevor).

But if it is Trevor who is guilty at t2, is Trevor still guilty at t3? And was he the same Trevor who was going to be guilty at t1 of the crime committed at t2? The answer to this question, for Wainwright, appears to be in the affirmative. The individual, Trevor, is guilty, not any physical part which he has at an earlier but not later time index (such as his right hand at t2 and stump at t3). The same is true for the perdurantist. According to perdurantism, the spacetime entity Trevor is the concrete particular who is guilty of the crime at t2. It is not Trevor's hand that is guilty of the crime according to the perdurantist, any more than it is for Wainwright. Though Trevor commits the act at a particular time slice, t2, it is Trevor as the spacetime worm who is guilty, not any physical part of Trevor at that particular index.

Let us assume in this thought experiment, that the perdurantist in question is an eternalist/detenser (although Edwards does not explicitly defend this view). If the Trevor-part at t2 is guilty of the crime at t2, then Trevor the spacetime worm is guilty, was and will be the one guilty of the act of that Trevor-part at t2 at all times. Expressed tenselessly,

Trevor is guilty of stabbing Dean during luncheon at t2.

If this is timelessly true, then all temporal parts of Trevor participate in this truth. To put it another way, the proposition stating Trevor's guilt at t2 is always true at all times, for all moments of Trevor's existence. That is not the same as saying that the above proposition states a timeless truth about the physical parts of Trevor at all temporal indexes. That would be patently absurd. To illustrate: if I was always going to fail my exam, then that truth of this failure, expressed propositionally, will always be true of me, whenever it is articulated in this particular world. But the fact that my right hand wrote the wrong answer does not mean that it was the guilty part of me, and that it was not my fault that I failed, but the fault of that particular physical part of me instead. Were I to maintain this, I would be a laughing-stock.

So, temporal and spatial parts, though equally important on perdurantist ontology, have different properties that describe different ontological roles. Temporal parts, being parts or person stages of one whole person are different from spatial parts. Thus, to return to Trevor, he is still the same spacetime worm, through all the changes that take place between t1–t3, even though he has different spatial parts (especially after t3), as well as different temporal parts at each time index. But Trevor is guilty as a spacetime worm of actions in a way that his spatial parts are not. Why? Because if that were not the case, we should have peculiar situations arising where Trevor at t1 was not guilty of the crime; Trevor at t2 was; and Trevor at t3 was not either (on the principle which Wainwright sets forth, that the guilt of a person does not distribute to his parts). So Wainwright's criticism of Edwards must be referring to spatial not temporal parts, whereas Edwards himself, in his version of imputation, is actually referring to temporal not spatial parts. Once that is established, the idea that Adam commits original sin at t1, and is guilty of it, and that that guilt is 'imputed' to PDH at all subsequent time indexes is perfectly reasonable, providing that both Adam and his posterity are together temporal parts of the whole aggregate object, PDH, which, on strong perdurantism, is the position Edwards appears to be defending. Hence, Wainwright's third criticism of Edwards is sidestepped. Once that is clear, then original sin *is* committed by Adam alone (not PDH as a whole), but the guilt accrues to PDH as a whole (not Adam alone), since both Adam and his posterity are temporal stages of the one object, PDH. And guilt *does* distribute to temporal parts in a way that it cannot do with spatial parts. To put it another way, Adam sins at one time index, but he is only one part of the whole object PDH which extends through spacetime. Just as the Trevor at t2 who commits the crime is only one temporal part of the whole Trevor as he extends through time, so Adam is one temporal part of the whole PDH.

However, in light of this line of argument, it might be thought that Edwards commits the fallacy of composition. The fact that a part of a thing is blue does not mean that the whole thing is blue. If a book has a blue part – its cover, say – it does not follow from this that the whole book is blue. The pages between the covers are not blue. Similarly, if Adam has original guilt, it does not follow from this that the rest of PDH has original guilt. What is more, the fact that PDH is a gerrymandered object means it is very difficult to see how it can have moral properties ascribed to it, such as 'having original guilt'. However, such an argument fails to take into account the radical way in which Edwards conceives of the metaphysics involved in persistence through time. For Edwards, there can be no appeal to something metaphysically primitive apart from

124 *Jonathan Edwards and the Metaphysics of Sin*

the divine ordination of things. As long as this divine constitution of things is both in harmony with the way God has arranged the constitution of other things in the creation, and has good ends or useful consequences, Edwards is satisfied that he has no grounds for judging God's action unreasonable or unjust.[24] This may seem rather extreme, but it is consistent with what we have already seen of Edwards' views on these matters. And in any case, as Edwards believed, there is nothing more metaphysically fundamental than the divine ordering of things moment by moment.

On the related question of how it is that PDH can have the property of original guilt, Edwards could respond with something like the following (Edwards himself does not address this problem, but this response is in keeping with the tenor of his argument). Perhaps PDH does not have the property of original guilt (or, for that matter, original sin) *per se*, but has a complex property including having temporal parts, all of which after Adam's primal sin possess original guilt. This would mean that original guilt cannot be ascribed to the whole entity PDH as such, but only to all the parts that make up PDH post-primal sin. The whole PDH merely has the property that describes the fact that all its parts have original guilt, post-fall. Once again, this is the case because of a divine constitution: '[I]t appears, particularly, from what has been said, that all oneness by virtue whereof pollution and guilt from past wickedness are derived, depends entirely on a divine establishment.'[25]

This avoids the problem of ascribing moral properties to an abstract object like PDH. In any case, on Edwards' argument, the whole of PDH cannot have the property of original guilt, since some parts of PDH do not possess this property (the temporal parts of Adam prior to the fall, for instance). Of course, it is possible that a whole object has properties its parts do not possess (a globe is spherical; its hemisphere-parts are not). But in this instance, it cannot be the case that PDH has original guilt and its parts do not, since some of the parts of PDH do not have original guilt, and (in this particular instance), this means that the whole PDH cannot have the property of original guilt. Recall the case of Trevor and Dean. At t2 Trevor kills Dean. All of Trevor's temporal parts thereafter are guilty of that crime at t2. One could say that, it is eternally true that Trevor murders Dean at t2. Nevertheless, it is not true that Trevor is guilty of the murder of Dean prior to t2. Only those temporal parts of Trevor after t2 are guilty of Trevor's crime at t2. It seems that the whole spacetime entity Trevor has the property of being guilty for Dean's death at all those temporal parts after the murder of Dean. But one could not say, surely, that the whole spacetime entity, Trevor, is guilty as a whole, of Dean's death. For there are temporal parts of Trevor that this is not true of. So the whole Trevor cannot possess a property that would entail that all the temporal parts of Trevor would have that particular property. Hence, Trevor as a whole cannot have the property 'possessing temporal parts all of which are guilty of killing Dean'. Nor, strictly speaking, could he have the property, 'being guilty of Dean's death' *simpliciter*. He has the properties, 'being guilty of Dean's death at t1' and 'having temporal parts after t2 all of which are guilty of killing Dean at t2'. But neither of these properties entails 'being guilty of Dean's death' *simpliciter*. In a similar way, Edwards could argue that PDH does not have the property of original guilt *simpliciter.* But it does have the property 'possessing temporal parts after Adam's primal sin, all of which are guilty of Adam's primal sin'. This can be expressed tenselessly, such that 'temporal parts of PDH after Adam's primal sin are guilty for that primal sin' is eternally true. But this does not entail the property 'PDH has original guilt', since this does not ascribe a property to the whole PDH, only to certain temporal parts of the whole. Nor does this mean that the whole PDH has a moral property that is distributed to all its parts. Rather, the whole PDH has a property in virtue of those temporal parts that do have original guilt. This means that it is not the whole that is guilty of original guilt. It is those parts of the whole after Adam's primal sin that are guilty of Adam's sin. The relevant property of the whole PDH refers to these temporal parts, not to the temporally extended whole. So Edwards' argument is not necessarily guilty of conflating properties of wholes with properties of parts of wholes.[26]

Still, it might be thought strange that God constitutes PDH such that original guilt only obtains forwards, through time, from Adam to his posterity, and only from *Adam* to his posterity. Why not from Seth to his posterity too, or from Abraham to his posterity? In fact, why not say that, for every new member of the entity PDH, that member has 'imputed' to them the guilt of all preceding members of PDH, including the sin of Adam? Once again, according to Edwards, God 'makes truth' in these matters. Perhaps there is something about imputation working forwards across time in this way, not backwards, and not cumulatively across time, in the way just mentioned, that is in harmony with other things God has constituted, such that this way of 'imputing' guilt is 'a beautiful analogy and harmony' and involves a 'useful consequence' and/or 'good ends'. And perhaps, as we saw in Chapter 5, God constitutes a genidentical relation between Adam and his posterity that is unidirectional. Even if Edwards were willing to concede that God could have arranged things differently in this respect, it seems reasonable that God act in *this* way, rather than some other way.[27]

There is one further way in which problems with person-stages could scupper Edwards' argument.[28] This has to do with Edwards' partial endorsement of Locke's emphasis on 'same consciousness' as a criterion of identity through time. Edwards says, 'And if we come even to the *personal identity* of created intelligent beings, though this be not allowed to consist wholly in that which Mr. Locke places it in, i.e. *same consciousness*; yet I think it can't be denied, that this is one thing essential to it.' But he continues, ''tis evident, that the communication or continuance of the same consciousness and memory to any subject, through successive parts of duration, depends wholly on a divine establishment . . . an arbitrary constitution of the Creator'.[29]

Although Edwards does not wholly endorse Locke's position on 'same consciousness', it is clear from this passage that he does believe that sameness of consciousness is an 'essential' component to personal identity. This raises the following problem: suppose Trevor at t3 suffers total and irrevocable amnesia. Would it be just or appropriate to punish or even blame Trevor at t3 for what earlier person-stages of

126   *Jonathan Edwards and the Metaphysics of Sin*

Trevor did at t1 and t2? If not, then the argument from hard perdurantism in defence of Edwards' doctrine of original guilt appears to be in jeopardy. For then, it seems, a temporal part of PDH could suffer amnesia and not be guilty of Adam's sin.

But this need not prove problematic for Edwards. First, we should distinguish between *feeling* guilt and *being* guilty. Trevor could have a false guilt at t3, believing himself to have committed a crime at some earlier time, though he is innocent. Or Trevor could feel no guilt for a crime committed at an earlier time. Is he therefore not guilty of the crime committed at an earlier time by an earlier person-stage? Not obviously. Whether I *feel* guilty about something or not is no reliable indicator of whether *I am* guilty of something or not. What then of amnesiac Trevor at t3? Is he guilty of Adam's sin or not? Once more, whether Trevor is *aware* of his guilt or not does not seem relevant to the question of whether he *is* guilty or not (although it is morally relevant to the question of responsibility and culpability for his actions). If Trevor at t3 has no memory of the earlier stabbing incident, would it be just to absolve Trevor at t3 of any guilt of the earlier crime? This touches on important considerations in moral philosophy about which we cannot enter into here. But, at face value, it does not seem obvious that it would be unjust to punish Trevor at t3, whether he recalled committing the earlier crime or not.

In any case, as Edwards sees it, sameness of consciousness and, presumably, imputed sin and guilt, are down to a 'divine establishment' that is 'arbitrary'. God communicates sin and guilt immediately to all parts of PDH however temporally and spatially scattered they are. Whether parts of that metaphysical object are suffering from amnesia or not is also down to God. Presumably, Edwards' God would have no problem communicating both properties to the same temporal part of a concrete individual. And the reason is not hard to find. Whether or not Trevor has knowledge of Adam's crime, he is part of the entity, PDH, and may be treated similarly for the purposes of imputation.[30]

This leaves the last criticism of Edwardsian original guilt: that Edwards conflates (corrupt) inclinations with (guilty) choices. Once it is recognized that Edwards saw guilt as 'imputed' but not inherited, along perdurantist lines, this line of criticism dissolves too. Wainwright claims:

> Once one assimilates inclination and choice [which Edwards clearly does, *OS*: 390–91], it is easy to assimilate sinful (corrupt) inclinations and sinful (guilty) choices. It is then easy to suppose that since the first can be inherited, so can the second . . . His [Edwards'] assimilation of corrupt inclinations and guilty choices would make it difficult for him to see that the transmission of guilt involves a different issue, and that this issue has not been satisfactorily resolved.[31]

It may be that Edwards did not see clearly enough that original guilt is a different issue from the assimilation of inclination and choice in volition, but whether he did so or not, his position works on the grounds that Wainwright sets out. He does conflate inclination and choice as two aspects of original guilt, but he does not use that to establish the separate argument from imputation to original guilt. The former supplies

Inherited Guilt 127

the content of original guilt as it is imputed to PDH, whereas the latter details the mechanism by which God carries out the action of imputing original guilt. Wainwright seems to think that Edwards believed that guilt was *inherited* in some way. Unfortunately, this ends up misrepresenting Edwards' position.

As previously noted, Edwards begins his discussion of the subject by pointing out that Adam and his progeny share this dual aspect to their guilt before God, since a depraved disposition and the subsequent corruption which confirms the initial disposition to evil attract double guilt. However, they are not imputed separately to Adam or his posterity.[32] As Adam is the root of the tree, so the rest of the tree is infected with his guilt as well as his sin. He then moves on to deal with how this can be the case, and arrives at the conclusion that original guilt, like original sin, is imputed (not inherited, and it is important to note that, although Edwards himself does not make much of this distinction, for such a distinction does helpfully highlight the perdurantism Edwards defends). Hence, Adam is an earlier temporal part of the whole PDH to whom guilt is imputed as a whole. In the nomenclature of perdurantist eternalism, Adam's sin and guilt are a temporal part of PDH such that,

Adam's sin and guilt are judicially 'imputed' to PDH

is timelessly true, since Adam is simply a part of the whole that is PDH, scattered throughout spacetime. God views all the parts of PDH taken together, and as a whole metaphysical entity attributes the action of one part to the whole.

One further point arises here. For this to work for Edwards, does the action of the one part that is attributed to the whole have to be the first part? For instance, suppose that Zechariah is the last human being, the race having been faultless up to Zechariah's arrival. Then suppose Zechariah sins. Could Zechariah's sin be attributed to his faultless ancestors? The answer on Edwards' theory would appear to be that it could not. Zechariah's sin could not be imputed backwards to his ancestors as, conversely, Adam's sin is imputed fowards to his posterity, because Zechariah is not in the peculiar position that Adam is in, namely, that he is the first individual specimen of humanity. Adam, unlike Zechariah, has progeny but no ancestors. And this is an important constituent of Edwards' theory of imputation. Adam is the father of the race, and thereby occupies a special place in the divine plan as *homo primus*, that Trevor, Wayne or Zechariah cannot occupy, by virtue of being created at times later than the *homo primus*. Thus Edwards: 'By reason of the established union between Adam and his posterity, the case is far otherwise between him and them, that it is between distinct parts of individuals of Adam's race; betwixt whom is not such constituted union: as between children and ancestors.'[33]

Thus, Wainwright's critique of Edwardsian guilt appears to have failed to give a comprehensive account of how Edwards viewed original guilt, and as a result, his detailed criticisms fall wide of the mark. Edwards' version of original guilt (and, with the relevant changes, original sin), taken as an aspect of the metaphysics that underpin his discussion of imputation in *OS*, is not incoherent if he defends a version of strong perdurantism. It is unfortunate that Edwards goes beyond this to endorse occasionalism.

Notes

1 Wainwright, 'Original Sin', pp. 31–60.
2 *OS*: 389.
3 Wainwright, 'Original Sin', p. 58, note 21.
4 However, Philip Quinn has recently pronounced Edwards' argument for (3) sound. See 'Disputing the Augustinian Legacy: John Locke and Jonathan Edwards on Romans 5: 12–19', p. 246.
5 Wainwright, 'Original Sin', p. 42.
6 Wainwright's analysis of these five case studies is indebted to Joel Feinberg's article, 'Collective Responsibility'.
7 *OS*: 395–7.
8 Wainwright, 'Original Sin', p. 47.
9 These propositions have been altered slightly. As per the previous chapter, I take it that perdurantism is the notion that all objects exist across time in temporal parts (usually, though not necessarily, understood to have zero duration). Perdurantists maintain that hunks of 4-D matter can be carved up into real, albeit gerrymandered, physical objects.
10 *OS*: 402 ff.
11 Helm, *Faith and Understanding*, p. 171.
12 I do not intend to discuss the relevant contemporary problems concerning what I have dubbed conventionalism and perdurantism, since this would take us beyond the purview of this chapter. An example of such a discussion can be found in Mark Heller's *The Ontology of Physical Objects*, pp. 49–51, where he discusses the fusion principle and its relation to the Sorites paradox.
13 Wainwright, 'Original Sin', p. 51.
14 Ibid.
15 This is precisely what Edwards does argue in *OS*: 391.
16 Wainwright, 'Original Sin', p. 53.
17 Swinburne, *Responsibility and Atonement*, pp. 144–5.
18 What follows draws on *OS*: 390–91.
19 *OS*: 391.
20 Ibid.
21 It is certainly true that there is evidence of both a soft- and hard-perdurantism in Edwards' discussion of this issue in *OS*. But it seems to me that it is the hard-perdurantist view that Edwards needs to sustain his overall apologetic aim here. This point has also been noted by Helm in *Faith and Understanding*, p. 168.
22 *OS*: 408.
23 C. Samuel Storms deals with the issue of Edwards' defence of inherited guilt at some length, and in a fashion not inimical to the present chapter, but he fails to draw out the problems that Wainwright's account manages to unearth. See *Tragedy in Eden*, pp. 228 ff.
24 *OS*: 405–406.
25 *OS*: 405.
26 The same reasoning applies, the relevant changes having been made, to imputed sin.
27 If time moves forwards only, by divine fiat, it might be that Adam's primal sin may affect his posterity in a way that subsequent sin, even his own subsequent sin, cannot. A first sin by the first human could be imputed to all subsequent humans in a way that subsequent sin could not. For instance, Abraham's sin cannot affect Adam, if time is forwardsly unidirectional. And Adam's subsequent sins cannot affect earlier temporal parts of himself or Eve.

28 Suggested to me in private correspondence by William Wainwright.
29 *OS*: 398–9.
30 This does not address problems with intention. If a person does not intend to commit a crime, their culpability, and, perhaps, guilt, may be ameliorated as a result. But intention does not seem directly relevant in the case of imputed guilt (certainly, Edwards does not seem to think so).
31 Wainwright, 'Original Sin', p. 53.
32 *OS*: 390–91.
33 *OS*: 408. Of course, God could have made Zechariah, Trevor or Wayne *homo primus* instead of Adam. Then their primal sin would have affected PDH as Adam's did. But nothing in Edwards' argument denies this point.

CHAPTER 7

The Problem with Occasionalism

It should be clear by now that Edwards' theory of occasionalism is the single greatest flaw in his doctrine of sin. It is largely as a result of his endorsement of occasionalism that his contribution to the metaphysics of sin has been overlooked. In this concluding chapter, I shall briefly sketch why Edwards' endorsement of occasionalism is fatal to his hamartiology, before drawing out what I take to be Edwards' contribution to the metaphysics of sin.[1]

Occasionalism: The Fatal Flaw

As has already been mentioned in the context of imputed sin and guilt, the central problem for Edwards' use of occasionalism is that it undermines his defence of original sin (the very doctrine Edwards deployed his occasionalism to defend). Edwards uses occasionalism as a means to ensure the absolute sovereignty of God in creation and conservation. However, in so doing, he destroys the argument he has set out via his doctrine of temporal parts, in favour of the imputation of Adam's sin. According to Edwards, God re-creates all things at each moment of their existence, *ex nihilo*. So there is no persistence through time, strictly speaking, and there is no mundane causation either. God is the sole cause of all events that take place. It is clear from what Edwards says in *OS* that he believes in a doctrine of continuous creation: 'God's *preserving* created things in being is perfectly equivalent to a *continued creation*, or to his creating those things out of nothing at *each moment* of their existence' (*OS*: 401, Edwards' emphases).

Moreover, in a passage we have had cause to note previously, Edwards says:

> If the existence of created substance, in each successive moment, be wholly the effect of God's immediate power, in that moment, without any dependence on prior existence, as much as the first creation out of nothing, then what exists at this moment, by this power, is a *new effect*; and simply and absolutely considered, not the same with any past existence, though it be like it, and follows it according to a certain established method. And there is no identity or oneness in the case, but what depends on the *arbitrary* constitution of the Creator; who by his wise sovereign establishment so unites these successive new effects, that he *treats them as one*, by communicating to them like properties, relations, and circumstances; and so, leads us to regard and treat them as one. (*OS*: 402–403)

He says far less on the nature of causation. However, in *FOW* he states, 'Therefore I sometimes use the word "cause", in this inquiry, to signify . . . any antecedent with which a consequent event is so connected, that it truly belongs to the reason why the proposition which affirms that event is true.'

The Problem with Occasionalism
131

But the relation that exists between the antecedent and its consequent, '[i]s perhaps rather an occasion than a cause, most properly speaking' (*FOW*: 180–81). The problem with this is that it means no individual thing persists long enough to bring about any acts whatsoever. And this in turn destroys any hope of human moral responsibility. Not only is God an absolute sovereign. He is also directly responsible for all sin that takes place.

To make this clear, consider the following characterization of occasionalism. I take it that occasionalism involves the following claims: first, the denial of the temporal persistence of created objects. That is, God creates all things out of nothing (*ex nihilo*). Additionally, God creates all things anew, *ex nihilo*, at each moment of their existence subsequent to that first moment of creation. Futhermore, no created thing persists through time for more than a moment (leaving to one side whether a moment has duration or not). This is tantamount to a doctrine of continuous creation. In other words, occasionalism means that God does not create and conserve the world in two distinct phases of activity. Such a two-phase creation and conservation of the world would mean that after the first moment of creation, God conserves the creation in being, rather than re-creating it out of nothing, at all subsequent moments of its existence. Instead of this, the continuous creation aspect to occasionalism means that God continuously creates the world, *ex nihilo*, at every moment of its (apparent) persistence after the initial moment of creation.

The second tenet of occasionalism is the notion that there are no mundane causes, that is, God is the sole causal agent in the world. All mundane, or secondary, causes, such as my striking a match and this action (alongside other causal factors like the presence of an oxygen-rich atmosphere, dry conditions and so forth) causing the combustion of the match, are merely the 'occasions' of divine action. God creates each moment *ex nihilo* and brings about the lighting of the match as a consequence of (among other things) the striking of it against the abrasive strip on the matchbox, and so forth. The subjective 'feel' of continuous activity and of my being one among a number of other necessary causal factors that are jointly sufficient for the match being lit, are no more than an illusion, according to occasionalism. God is the sole cause of each moment, and at each moment, is the sole causal agent of all those things that take place at that moment. Rather like the 'stills' of a motion picture, each 'frame' or temporal slice of the world is a discrete, contiguous moment that has no causal bearing on the 'frame' that follows it, or precedes it. God creates each moment *ex nihilo*. These 'stills' are then run together by God to form what appears to be a continuous, uninterrupted sequence of action, just as a motion picture is a sequence of photographic stills that are projected in contiguous sequence to give the appearance of continuous action on the screen. But in reality, like the 'sense' of continuity in the showing of a motion picture, this 'sense' of persistence through time is an illusion. There is no action across time, and there is no causation apart from God. God is the sole causal agent, and God brings about the appearance of continuous action across time.

The problem with this version of occasionalism should be obvious: it means that God is also the sole moral agent. In which case, no creature is morally responsible for their actions. If this is indeed a consequence of occasionalism, or at least, of the version of that doctrine defended by Edwards,[2] then Edwards has no way out of the conclusion that God is morally responsible for all creaturely actions, since nothing persists long enough to act, and even if it did, any such creaturely action would only be 'occasional'. It would not constitute the action of a moral agent.

Consider the following theological scenario. God creates Adam in a counterfactual garden of Eden. Just as in the Genesis narrative, Adam is given a companion, Eve, and together they eat of the tree that is forbidden to them. As a result of this sinful action Adam and Eve are cursed. Next, let us say that Adam at t1 is the Adam who is created by God from the dust of the earth, Adam at t2 is the Adam who takes the forbidden fruit from Eve, and Adam at t3 is the Adam who eats of the fruit. Here is the problem for Edwards' occasionalism: the Adam who is created at t1 is not the same Adam as the Adam at t2, nor the same as the Adam at t3. Neither is the Adam of t2 the same as the Adam of t3. For all these Adams are not just different person stages of the same temporally extended entity, Adam, as per a conventional doctrine of temporal parts. That is, Adam at t1 and Adam at t2 are not just different parts of one four-dimensional hunk of matter. Rather, these different Adams are different concrete individuals. The reason being that God creates each of these Adams *ex nihilo* at each moment. Nothing persists from one moment to the next. At every new moment, a new Adam is created out of nothing.[3] But if each Adam is a numerically distinct individual, albeit an individual who is a duplicate of the previous Adam in almost all respects, then Edwards has undermined the very doctrine of sin he set out to defend. For on this view, there is no persisting individual whose action results in the fall and the curse upon the rest of humanity. There are only different duplicate Adams at different time indexes, created to appear to be part of a coordinated action. But this seems to mean that the Adam of one moment does not persist long enough to exercise any moral agency, with respect to his own actions, or those of later Adams. Thus, on Edwards' occasionalism, Adam is not responsible for his own primal sin, nor is anyone else. God is. And nothing persists through time. Rather, God populates the world with numerous instantaneous (or near-instantaneous) duplicates of each individual at one moment, only to obliterate these individuals and create almost exact duplicates in their place for the next moment of time, in contiguous sequence. So no created thing persists long enough to bring about any action whatsoever.

Philip Quinn has made a similar point to this one, with greater technical detail, in an article on the nature of occasionalism.[4] He claims that there may be versions of occasionalism that do not fall foul, as Edwards does, of the two problems of denying temporal persistence and denying mundane causation. But, since Edwards does endorse both these things, this is no help to Edwards' version of the doctrine. But it is, as Quinn points out, a 'charming irony' that the very metaphysical notion Edwards deploys to defend his doctrine of imputation, ends up undercutting it. For without a theory of temporal persistence there are no persisting persons to impute sin to. Rather, there are an infinite number of momentary entities existing at contiguous moments in a temporal sequence. And there is no creaturely responsibility for sin, because there is

The Problem with Occasionalism   133

no mundane causation. God is directly responsible for all that takes place in Edwards' occasionalism. Hence, were Adam at t4 to be cursed by God for what Adam at t3 had done in eating the forbidden fruit, this would be unjust, because Adam at t3 has been annihilated, and Adam at t4 is a different, though (almost) identical duplicate of Adam at t3. Adam at t4 is quite literally not guilty of the sin of Adam at t3. Quinn comments:

> God has arbitrarily decided to treat a number of diverse instantaneous persons as one by endowing them with similar properties and relations and to create the illusion that some one person ate the forbidden fruit. But in sober truth no one of these instantaneous persons ate the forbidden fruit, for no one of them existed long enough to do so. Each one of them existed only long enough to perform an instantaneous part of that momentary action. Hence, no one actually ate the forbidden fruit, and the great Christian doctrine of original sin is not defended but dissolved.[5]

Unfortunately, this is fatal to Edwards' occasionalist theory of the doctrine of original sin.

A Chastened Edwardsian Metaphysics

However, this need not mean that Edwards has nothing to say to contemporary philosophical theologians about the nature of sin. On the basis of the preceding chapters, it should be clear that the argument that Edwards develops is a subtle and carefully nuanced defence of original sin, understood from within the Augustinian tradition, but along lines peculiar to Edwards in several important respects. These idiosyncratic arguments devolve upon the question of Adam's fall, the AP and the notion of imputation that Edwards deploys in defence of his doctrine in Part IV of *OS*.

On the question of the fall, we have seen that Edwards' argument, spread across notebooks and various treatises, appears, with certain qualifications, to be internally coherent. Adam could have committed a primal sin on Edwards' rendering of the problem. However, this presentation is at odds with Edwards' occasionalism, which undercuts any moral responsibility Adam might have for committing the first sin. In any case, according to Edwardsian occasionalism, Adam does not persist long enough to commit any actions whatsoever, let alone moral actions.

Edwards' solution to the AP is less successful; it appears that Edwards' God is the author of sin. Edwards is unable to sustain the distinction between moral and causal responsibility for particular actions, one of the central premises of his account. And, although he has some interesting things to say on the nature of the hidden and revealed will of God, things to do with accidental necessity and the freedom and foreknowledge dilemma, an examination of this aspect of his theodicy does not yield a way around the AP.

What Edwards has to say about the nature of imputed sin and guilt involves two sorts of data in Edwards' work: those aspects which can be shown to be supportive of

Edwards' position, and those whose metaphysical ramifications end up undermining central aspects of Edwards' thought (such as his occasionalism).

In the first group is his careful tracing of problems in the doctrine of imputation to problems with the way it has traditionally been conceived under the aegis of the theological realism-federalism distinction. Edwards' reformulation of the theological structure of the doctrine is insightful and useful for the metaphysics of imputation that he goes on to develop. Alongside this are difficulties with Edwards' notion of the ontology of imputation, which have been raised by Chisholm and Helm. Chisholm's problems with the ontology of Edwardsian imputation can be overcome through a more federalist understanding of the theological ontology, which informs his metaphysics. Edwards' doctrine of temporal parts, coupled with his federalism, offer a way out of Chisholm's critique. There are also apparent difficulties with the notion of inherited guilt that Edwards defends, outlined by Wainwright in the previous chapter. Wainwright believes that Edwards does not provide either a sufficient biblical warrant for his view, nor a metaphysical argument that is sound. However, Wainwright's understanding of the nature of Edwards' doctrine seems to be at fault regarding the perdurantist flavour to his notion of inherited guilt.

In the second group of arguments are those aspects of his metaphysics that undermine Edwards' defence of imputation. This involves those issues associated with the radical nature of Edwards' occasionalism, and in particular, how a person's actions can be truly their own, that we have just outlined. One possible way of retaining Edwards' central insight into the metaphysics of imputation without resorting to the use of occasionalism, involves a reconstruction of Edwardsian thinking along more mainstream perdurantist lines. This could be achieved with an argument similar in tone to either the weak or hard versions of perdurantism offered in Chapter 5. Either of these arguments could be used to retain Edwards' insight regarding the nature of imputed sin and guilt, without the problems associated with his occasionalism. This presents a partial solution to Quinn's 'charming irony'. It is partial because, although it avoids the difficulties raised by Quinn, it does so at the cost of rejecting occasionalism *tout court*.

Edwards appears to have considered occasionalism crucial to the substance of his metaphysics. From the reconstruction of his argument for imputation along perdurantist lines suggested here, it appears that he was mistaken in this regard. His argument could have been developed in such a way as to avoid the extremes of his occasionalism, whilst delineating a perdurantism that maintained the defining aspects of his doctrine of sin. Thus the metaphysics of imputation that Edwards seeks to develop in the fourth part of *OS* fail to adequately account for the kind of problems regarding identity-through-time and human action that Edwards sought to overcome. However, where the occasionalism of his developed position fails, a perdurantism *sans* occasionalistic paraphernalia could still provide a broadly Edwardsian account of sin, which is in sympathy with the intentions which lie behind the main structures of his argument for imputation, and which, it seems to me, provides an intriguing response to this traditional theological conundrum.

Notes

1 On the related question of whether Edwards did, in fact, endorse occasionalism at all, see Oliver D. Crisp, 'How occasional was Edwards's occasionalism?' in *Jonathan Edwards: Philosophical Theologian*, Helm and Crisp, eds.

2 This is an important qualification since, in the recent literature, there have been several attempts to make sense of occasionalism in a non-Edwardsian fashion. See, for instance, Jonathan Kvanvig and Hugh McCann, 'Divine Conservation and the Persistence of the World' in *The Metaphysics of Theism*, Morris, ed., and McCann and Kvanvig, 'The Occasionalist Proselytiser: A Modified Catechism' in *Philosophical Perspectives*, 5, Tomberlin, ed..

3 This presumes that time is dense, of course. But even if time is discrete, and Edwards' occasionalism is a 'lumpy' occasionalism, the problem remains. For on such an occasionalism, at each chunk of time (a second say, or a minute) God creates a new Adam *ex nihilo*. So there are still different 'Adams', and the problem of moral responsibility that this denial of temporal persistence entails still obtains, albeit in a slightly modified form.

4 Philip L. Quinn, 'Divine Conservation, Continuous Creation, and Human Action' in *The Existence and Nature of God*, Freddoso, ed.

5 Ibid., p. 66.

Appendix: The Imputation of Christ's Righteousness

In the process of answering questions about the imputation of Adam's sin, a related question arises regarding the imputation of Christ's righteousness. Edwards did not write about this at any length in his published writings.[1] However, in the context of his account of the authorship of sin question, he does make reference to it.[2] There, he deals with what a 'course of nature' means in the context of the will of God in imputing sin to Adam, and righteousness to the elect in Christ. His point is that Adam's sin passes to his posterity as much because God institutes a certain course of nature, as because there is a continued corrupt disposition imputed to Adam + PDH as a result of original sin: 'For Adam's posterity are from him, and as it were in him, and belonging to him, according to an established course of nature, from the tree, in the tree, and belonging to the tree; or . . . "just as the acorn is derived from the oak".' To make clear what he means by a 'course of nature', he goes on, '[w]here the name "nature" is allowed without dispute, no more is meant than an established method and order of events, settled and limited by divine wisdom'.[3] This is a matter, not of conventionalism *per se*, but of divine convention; of God's constituting matter in this way, rather than that, according to his wise ordering.

However, such a construal of the course of nature ordained by God poses problems regarding the asymmetrical nature of imputation. An asymmetry in the ordering of the 'course of nature' arises where the lack of original righteousness (and thereby a vitiated nature), *is* communicated to PDH, whilst 'principles of holiness' are not. Adam's sin passes to his posterity, but Christ's righteousness cannot be passed on in the same way. It involves only the individual to whom Christ's righteousness is imputed, not to that individual's offspring, relatives or descendents. It may be asked whether this construal of the metaphysics of imputation is actually to the point. The relationship between the Christian and Christ is not a natural one, being metaphysically constituted by the will of God. If this is the case, then *a fortiori*, neither should it be presumed that the Christians' relatives and descendents will have a relationship to Christ that is a natural one either. Hence, the problem folds. However, a similar case can be made out for the imputation of sin. Edwards believes that God carves up all those temporal parts that incorporate PDH and constitutes them a single metaphysical entity, as we have already seen. This is not a 'natural' relationship. Adam + PDH have in common those moral properties pertaining to original sin that are attributed to all their parts across spacetime. That, on Edwards' view, is what it means to impute sin to Adam's posterity. So the imputation of the lack of original righteousness that is imputed to Adam + PDH is as metaphysically non-natural as the non-imputation of Christ's righteousness to the whole of Adam + PDH. If this is the case, then the asymmetry that exists between the imputation of the vitiated nature to Adam + PDH, and the non-imputation of Christ's righteousness to the whole of Adam + PDH in a similar manner (either along perdurantist, or occasionalistic lines), needs *prima facie*, some explanation.

Edwards' initial reply is that this is simply the way that the divine mind is pleased to dispose the metaphysics of the matter. However, in the course of this explanation, he hints at another, more satisfactory response:

> Grace is introduced among the race of mankind by a new establishment; not on the foot of the original establishment of God, as the Head of the natural world, and Author of the first creation; but by a constitution of a vastly higher kind; wherein Christ is made the root of the tree, whose branches are his spiritual seed and he is the head of the new creation; of which I need not stand now to speak particularly.[4]

Though he does not elaborate on this, the continuity with the previous organic analogy with respect to Adam and his posterity is not accidental. I suggest that an Edwards*ian* argument can be reconstructed on this basis that explains why there is an asymmetrical relation between the imputation of Adamic sin and Christ's righteousness, utilizing the tools of perdurantism deployed in previous chapters. God treats PDH for the purposes of the imputation of sin, as one hunk of matter (on the basis of ontological synthesis). The 'imputation' of Adam's sin to his posterity is really the treating of Adam as *homo primus* and the rest of PDH as a scattered spacetime entity whose parts (temporal and spatial) comprise one unity for the purposes of sin. That is, Adam + PDH are one unity as far as the imputation of sin is concerned. They are not – for this gerrymandered metaphysical purpose – discrete individuals to whom the sin of one man, and the guilt thereof passes. And God may do this, since, on a perdurantist metaphysics this simply is the way things are: God can cut matter up any which way he chooses.

Now, with respect to the imputation of Christ's righteousness, an analogous model applies, but with important qualifications (qualifications that will solve the asymmetrical problem Edwards poses himself in the passages cited above). God treats the elect according to his eternal decree, just as he treats the reprobate according to the second fork of the same decree of election, to reprobation and damnation. But this means that for the purposes of imputing Christ's righteousness, God treats the elect as one metaphysical unit with Christ as a second *homo primus* (as per Romans 5:12–19).[5] The righteousness of Christ is 'imputed' to Perdurantist Elect Humanity (or PEH). That is, God gerrymanders a certain hunk of matter, which includes all and only those persons who are to make up PEH according to his divine decree. Like PDH, they are treated by God as one metaphysical unity for the purposes of imputation. So, though they are scattered through spacetime, as PDH are, as with PDH, this makes no difference to the metaphysics of the situation: God is able to gerrymander any hunk of matter to form a particular spacetime worm, with particular properties and parts (for the detail of this perdurantist argument, I refer the reader to the discussion in Chapters 5, 6 and 7).[6]

Appendix: The Imputation of Christ's Righteousness 139

To put it another way, if Adam + PDH is one domain, Christ + PEH is another, such that members of the domain comprising Christ + PEH overlap with Adam + PDH just in those areas where members of PDH are also members of PEH. That is, where members of Adamic posterity are at-one-and-the-same-time members of the elect. So members of PEH are also members of PDH, but not conversely. The relation involved here is soteriologically asymmetrical. God imputes original sin to all humanity in PDH, *infra lapsus* (temporally, though not, perhaps logically).[7] But only those persons who make up the number of the elect are simultaneously members of PEH and PDH.

This has the happy consequence of enabling Edwards (or, in this case, the 'Edwardsian') to rebut the criticism with which we began. God establishes the asymmetrical relation between the elect and the reprobate in imputation according to consistent metaphysical principles, which we have elaborated using perdurantist terms in keeping with the foregoing discussion. The reason that God does not allow the established 'course of nature' to communicate the 'principles of holiness' to PEH as he appears to do with PDH, is because he does so in neither case. Contrary to appearances, PDH does not have Adamic sin imputed to it through some realist method, nor strictly, through a simple federalist method. Instead, both PDH and PEH are metaphysical constructs, hunks of matter that God has gerrymandered (in the perdurantist sense of that word) for his own divine purposes, and to which he 'imputes' those properties that are the peculiar preserve of PHD and PEH (and for those members of both groups, PDH and PEH simultaneously).[8] And if we press Edwards for some reason why God gerrymanders matter in this way, rather than another, his response is that this is the most fitting way that God could pursue his end in all his works, namely, his own glory:

> The great and last end of God's works which is so variously expressed in Scripture, is indeed but one; and this one end is most properly and comprehensively called, 'the glory of God'; by which name it is most commonly called in Scripture . . . those things, which are spoken of in Scripture as ultimate ends of God's works, though they may seem at first view to be distinct, all are plainly to be reduced to this one thing, viz. God's internal glory or fullness extant externally, or existing in its emanation. And though God in seeking this end seeks the creatures wellbeing; yet therein appears his supreme regard to himself.[9]

Notes

1 That is, works published in his lifetime. The Yale edition of the *Miscellanies* will soon put into the public domain two entries that do address this issue, Nos. 1185 and 1237. However, neither of these *Miscellanies* affect the present argument in detail, since both are largely references and excerpts from other writers (Drs Williams and Skelton), something that Edwards was doing a lot of in the later *Miscellanies*. For instance, *Miscellany 1185* reads 'Concerning the reasonableness of the doctrine of the IMPUTATION OF CHRIST'S RIGHTEOUSNESS, see Dr Williams fourth volume of sermons, pp. 88–94.' In this reference, Dr Daniel Williams defends a Calvinistic understanding of forensic imputation. I am grateful to Prof. Kenneth Minkema at Yale University for his help with references and

transcripts of these two important *Miscellanies*.

2 *YE3*: 385–6.

3 Ibid.

4 Ibid., p. 386.

5 In his exegesis of Romans 5:12–19, Edwards is very much within the federal tradition, as Philip Quinn has recently shown in 'Disputing the Augustinian Legacy'. We have seen that this adherence to federalism is qualified by Edwards' idiosyncrasies with respect to imputation. Nevertheless, he is unquestionably a defender of a version of federal theology.

6 Although, strictly speaking, on Edwards' occasionalist argument PEH will not be a perduring spacetime entity, since the individuals who make up the body of Christ in PEH are actually composed of numerous non-enduring, distinct concrete individuals in a contiguous sequence, divinely ordained.

7 By that I mean, God may impute sin or righteousness post-fall, at a particular time index – say, at all those moments after the initial time slice in which Adam commits the first sin (leaving aside *when* that actually is, whether when he picks the fruit, or when the desire to rebel takes hold of his heart). But it may be that God has already ordained the sin of Adam and subsequent imputation of original sin and/ or righteousness, 'from eternity past' as theologians say. That is, before the creation of the world. This *could* mean God ordains the sin of Adam and subsequent imputation *supra lapsus*, but imputes sin to Adam and PDH *infra lapsus*. The point being made here is twofold: the index at which sin is imputed is distinct from the question of the logic of the divine decree that ordains that act. God could do so according to infralapsarian theology (after the fall), or *supralapsus* (before the fall). But second, the fact that God imputes sin *infra lapsus*, at a particular temporal index says nothing about whether the decree to do so is itself *infra* or *supra lapsus*, though I am inclined to think that supralapsarianism is the simpler, though perhaps initially less appealing, of the two.

8 The group comprising all and only those members of PEH who are not also members of PDH is probably an empty set. Although, had Adam and Eve had a child that was stillborn, or died in infancy before the first sin, then presumably such a person would be a member of such a group. Children who die in similar circumstances *infra lapsus* do not enjoy the same privileges, at least, not according to classical theology. It may be that such persons are joint members of PDH&PEH. They are not, on a realist, federalist or Edwardsian ontology, only members of PEH exclusive of PDH.

9 *End of Creation* in *YE8*: 530.

Bibliography

Works by Edwards

Edwards, Jonathan (1834), ed. E. Hickman, *The Works of Jonathan Edwards, Volumes I and II*, Edinburgh: Banner of Truth Trust.

——— (1957), *Freedom of the Will, The Works of Jonathan Edwards Volume 1*, ed. P. Ramsey, New Haven, CT: Yale University Press.

——— (1970), *Original Sin, The Works of Jonathan Edwards Volume 3*, ed. Clyde A. Holbrook, New Haven, CT: Yale University Press.

——— (1980), *Scientific and Philosophical Writings, The Works of Jonathan Edwards Volume 6*, ed. Wallace E. Anderson, New Haven, CT: Yale University Press.

——— (1989), *Ethical Writings, The Works of Jonathan Edwards Volume 8*, ed. Paul Ramsey, New Haven, CT: Yale University Press.

——— (1994), *The 'Miscellanies' (Entry Nos. a–z, aa–zz, 1–500), The Works of Jonathan Edwards Volume 13*, ed. Thomas A. Schafer, New Haven, CT: Yale University Press.

——— (1997), *Sermons and Discourses 1723–1729, The Works of Jonathan Edwards Volume 14*, ed. Kenneth P. Minkema, New Haven, CT: Yale University Press.

——— (2000), *The 'Miscellanies' 501–832, The Works of Jonathan Edwards Volume 18*, ed. Ava Chamberlain, New Haven, CT: Yale University Press.

Secondary Literature

Adams, Robert (1987), 'Must God Create the Best?' in T.V. Morris (ed.), *The Concept of God*, Oxford: Oxford University Press.

Aristotle (1955), *The Ethics of Aristotle*, trans. J.A.K. Thomson, Harmondsworth: Penguin Books.

Augustine, Aurelius (1972), *City of God*, trans. H. Bettenson, Harmondsworth: Penguin Books.

Berkhof, Louis (1939), *Systematic Theology*, Edinburgh: Banner of Truth Trust.

Bogue, Carl (1975), *Jonathan Edwards and the Covenant of Grace*, New Jersey: Mack.

Chisholm, Roderick (1971), 'Problems of Identity' in Milton K. Munitz (ed.), *Identity and Individuation*, New York: New York University Press.

——— (1976), *Person and Object*, London: George Allen and Unwin.

——— (1990), 'The Defeat of Good and Evil' in Marilyn McCord Adams and Robert Adams (eds), *The Problem of Evil*, Oxford: Oxford University Press.

Craig, William Lane (1987), *The Only Wise God*, Grand Rapids: Baker Books.

Crisp, Oliver D. (2002),'Review of Gerald R. McDermott's Jonathan Edwards Confronts the Gods', *International Journal of Systematic Theology* **4**: 82–3.

――― (2003) 'How Occasional was Edwards's Occasionalism?' in Paul Helm and Oliver D. Crisp (eds), *Jonathan Edwards: Philosophical Theologian*, Aldershot: Ashgate.

――― (2003), 'Jonathan Edwards and Divine Simplicity' in *Religious Studies* **39**: 23–41.

――― (2003), 'On the Theological Pedigree of Jonathan Edwards' Theology of Imputation' in *Scottish Journal of Theology* **56**: 308–27.

Daniel, Stephen H. (1994), *The Philosophy of Jonathan Edwards*, Bloomington: Indiana University Press.

Feinberg, Joel (1970), 'Collective Responsibility' in *Doing and Deserving: Essays in The Theory of Responsibility*, Princeton, NJ: Princeton University Press.

Fiering, Norman (1988), 'The Rationalist Foundation of Jonathan Edwards's Metaphysics' in Nathan O. Hatch and Harry S. Stout (eds), *Jonathan Edwards and the American Experience*, Oxford: Oxford University Press.

Fischer, John Martin (ed.) (1986), *Moral Responsibility*, Ithaca, NY: Cornell University Press.

Flew, Antony (1955), 'Divine Omnipotence and Human Freedom' in Antony Flew and Alasdair MacIntyre (eds), *New Essays in Philosophical Theology*, London: SCM Press.

Foot, Phillipa (1978), 'The Problem of Abortion and the Doctrine of Double Effect' in *Virtues and Vices and Other Essays*, Berkeley: University of California Press.

Frankfurt, Harry (1988), *The Importance of What We Care About*, Cambridge: Cambridge University Press.

Gerstner, John H. (1991–93), *The Rational Biblical Theology of Jonathan Edwards, Volumes I–III*, Powhatan, VA: Berea Publications/Ligonier Ministries.

Guttenplan, Samuel (ed.) (1994), *A Companion to Philosophy of Mind*, Oxford: Blackwell.

Hasker, William (1989), *God, Time, and Knowledge*, Ithaca: Cornell University Press.

Hatch, Nathan O. and Stout, Harry S. (eds) (1988), *Jonathan Edwards and The American Experience*, New York: Oxford University Press.

Hawley, Katherine (2001), *How Things Persist*, Oxford: Oxford University Press.

Held, Virginia (1970), 'Can a Random Collection of Individuals be Morally Responsible?' in *Journal of Philosophy* **67**: 471–81.

Heller, Mark (1990), *The Ontology of Physical Objects*, Cambridge: Cambridge University Press.

Helm, Paul (1988), *Eternal God*, Oxford: Oxford University Press.

――― (1993), *The Providence of God*, Leicester: IVP.

――― (1997), *Faith and Understanding*, Edinburgh: Edinburgh University Press.

――― (2003), 'A Forensic Dilemma: John Locke and Jonathan Edwards on Personal Identity', in Paul Helm and Oliver D. Crisp (eds), *Jonathan Edwards: Philosophical Theologian*, Aldershot: Ashgate.

Bibliography

Heppe, Heinrich (n.d.), *Reformed Dogmatics*, trans. G.T. Thompson, London: Wakeman Trust.

Holmes, Stephen R. (2000), *God of Grace and God of Glory*, Edinburgh: T&T Clark.

Hoopes, James (1988), 'Calvinism and Consciousness from Edwards to Beecher' in Nathan O. Hatch and Harry S. Stout (eds), *Jonathan Edwards and The American Experience*, New York: Oxford University Press.

Jenson, Robert (1988), *America's Theologian*, New York: Oxford University Press.

Kearney, John (1997), 'Jonathan Edwards' Account of Adam's First Sin' in *Scottish Bulletin of Evangelical Theology* **15**: 135–6.

———— (1998), 'Jonathan Edwards and the "Author of Sin" Charge' in *The Princeton Theological Review* **5**: 10–16.

Kvanvig, Jonathan L. (1993), *The Problem of Hell*, New York: Oxford University Press.

———— and McCann, Hugh (1988), 'Divine Conservation and the Persistence of the World' in Thomas V. Morris (ed.), *Divine and Human Action: Essays in The Metaphysics of Theism*, Ithaca, NY: Cornell University Press.

Lehrer, Keith (1982), 'Cans without Ifs' reprinted in Gary Watson (ed.), *Free Will*, Oxford: Oxford University Press.

Locke, John (1975), *An Essay concerning Human Understanding*, ed. P.H. Nidditch, Oxford: Oxford University Press.

Loux, Michael (1998), *Metaphysics, A Contemporary Introduction*, London: Routledge.

Lowe, E.J. (1995), *Locke on The Human Understanding*, London: Routledge.

———— (2002), *A Survey of Metaphysics*, Oxford: Oxford University Press.

MacDonald, Scott (1999), 'Primal Sin' in Gareth B. Matthews (ed.), *The Augustinian Tradition*, Los Angeles: University of California Press.

Mann, William E. (1988), 'God's Freedom, Human Freedom, and God's Responsibility for Sin' in Thomas V. Morris (ed.), *Divine and Human Action*, Ithaca, NY: Cornell University Press.

Matthews, Gareth B. (ed.) (1999), *The Augustinian Tradition*, Los Angeles: University of California Press.

McCann, Hugh J. (2003), 'Edwards on Free Will', in Paul Helm and Oliver D. Crisp (eds), *Jonathan Edwards: Philosophical Theologian*, Aldershot: Ashgate.

———— and Kvanvig, Jonathan L. (1991), 'The Occasionalist Proselytizer: A Modified Catechism' in James E. Tomberlin (ed.), *Philosophical Perspectives, 5: Philosophy of Religion*, California: Ridgeview.

McDermott, Gerald R. (2000), *Jonathan Edwards Confronts The Gods*, New York: Oxford University Press.

Morris, Thomas (1986), *The Logic of God Incarnate*, Ithaca, NY: Cornell University Press.

Peterson, Michael, Hasker, William, Reichenbach, Bruce and Basinger, Bruce (1998), *Reason and Religious Belief*, New York: Oxford University Press.

Pike, Nelson (1965), 'Divine Omniscience and Voluntary Action' in *Philosophical Review* **74**: 27–46.

Plantinga, Alvin (1974), *The Nature of Necessity*, Oxford: Oxford University Press.

———— (1987), 'On Ockham's Way Out' in Thomas V. Morris (ed.), *The Concept of God*, Oxford: Oxford University Press.

———— (2000), *Warranted Christian Belief*, New York: Oxford University Press.

Quine, Willard van Orman (1953), *From a Logical Point of View*, Cambridge, MA: Harvard University Press.

Quinn, Philip L. (1999), 'Disputing the Augustinian Legacy: John Locke and Jonathan Edwards on Romans 5:12–19' in Gareth B. Matthews (ed.), *The Augustinian Tradition*, Los Angeles: University of California Press.

———— (1983), 'Divine Conservation, Continuous Creation, and Human Action' in Alfred J. Freddoso (ed.), *The Existence and Nature of God*, Notre Dame, IN: University of Notre Dame Press.

Smith, John E. (1992), *Jonathan Edwards, Puritan, Preacher, Philosopher*, London: Geoffrey Chapman.

Storms, C. Samuel (1985), *Tragedy in Eden: Original Sin in the Theology of Jonathan Edwards*, Lanham, MD: University Press of America.

Stout, Harry (1988), 'The Puritans and Edwards' in Nathan O. Hatch and Harry S. Stout (eds), *Jonathan Edwards and the American Experience*, Oxford: Oxford University Press.

Stump, Eleonore (1985), 'The Problem of Evil' in *Faith and Philosophy* **2**: 398–9.

Suter, Rufus (1934), 'The Problem of Evil in the Philosophy of Jonathan Edwards' in *The Monist* **44**: 280–95.

Swinburne, Richard (1989), *Responsibility and Atonement*, Oxford: Oxford University Press.

Turretin, Francis (1992), *Institutes of Elenctic Theology, Volume I*, trans. G.M. Giger, ed. J.T. Dennison, New Jersey: Presbyterian and Reformed Publishing.

van Inwagen, Peter (1995), *God, Knowledge and Mystery*, Ithaca, NY: Cornell University Press.

———— (1978), 'Ability and Responsibility' in *Philosophical Review* **LXXXVII**: 201–24.

Wainwright, William (1996), 'Jonathan Edwards, William Rowe, and the Necessity of Creation' in Jeff Jordan and Daniel Howard-Snyder (eds), *Faith, Freedom and Rationality*, Maryland: Rowman and Littlefield.

———— (1988), 'Original Sin' in Thomas V. Morris (ed.), *Philosophy and the Christian Faith*, Notre Dame, IN: University of Notre Dame Press.

———— (2001), 'Theological Determinism and the Problem of Evil: Are Arminians any better off?' in *International Journal for Philosophy of Religion* **50**: 81–96.

Weddle, David (1974), 'Jonathan Edwards on Men and Trees, and the Problem of Solidarity' in *Harvard Theological Review* **67**: 155–75.

Zagzebski, Linda (1999), 'Foreknowledge and Human Freedom' in Philip L. Quinn and Charles Taliaferro (eds), *A Companion to Philosophy of Religion*, Oxford: Blackwell.

Index

accidental necessity 82–8
Adam 26, 28, 30, 37, 39, 40, 46, 97ff., 107, 113, 128 n.27, 132, 140 n.8
Adams, Robert 47–8
Arminianism 4 n.7, 19, 26, 57–9, 79, 87, 89–90, 96
  see also free will
author of sin 22, 50, 54ff., 61–2, 64ff., 68, 74, 75 n.3, 91–2, 93, 133

Berkhof, Louis 23 n.3

Calvin, John 56, 68, 87–8
  Calvinist 59–60, 61, 102
Chisholm, Roderick 96ff., 100, 103, 105, 107, 110 n.4, 134
Crisp, Oliver 3 n.3, 110 n.1, 135 n.1

divine decree 1 ff., 12, 15, 19, 20, 137ff.
divine self-glorification 7, 11, 14, 17–18, 22, 69, 139
Dolittle, Dr 102
double dutch *see* Plantinga, Alvin
double effect, doctrine of 58–61, 77 n.35

Edwards, Jonathan
  Contribution to doctrine of sin 1–2, 3, 27, 96, 134
  doctrine of double guilt 120
  strange new Edwards 1
  view of historical Adam 2, 25–6
election 7, 12, 15, 23 n.9, 77 n.44, 138ff.
End of Creation, Dissertation on the 7, 9, 10, 17, 21, 69, 91, 139, 140 n.9
endurantism 104, 110

Fall, The 2, 25 ff., 28, 39, 40–42, 43, 45ff., 50 n.1
fallacy of composition 121–4
fallacy of division 8, 9
federalism 30, 101ff.
Flew, Antony 66–8, 77 n.43
foreknowledge 83–6, 87
Frankfurt, Harry 52 n.40, 74
  see also principle of alternate possibilities

free will 31, 33–9, 40, 49, 88–9
  libertarian free will 13, 54, 55, 59, 61, 81, 88, 90
  (theological) determinism 13–14, 21, 27, 55, 57, 61, 64, 68, 73, 81, 85
Freedom of the Will, Treatise on ix, 21, 26, 34, 37, 57, 61, 64, 65, 68, 75 n.8, 80, 82, 83, 87–8, 120, 130–31

Gerstner, John 4 n.6, 16, 18, 22, 46–8, 75 n.1
grace
  confirming 26, 28, 31, 46, 102
  sufficient 26, 28, 39, 40, 46
Great Suprendo, The 65, 76 n.32
  disappearing act of 250

Hawley, Katherine 111 n.11
Heller, Mark 109, 112 n.32, 128 n.12
Helm, Paul vii, 76 n.24, 84–6, 90, 94 n.14, 97ff., 111 n.11, 117, 128 n.21, 134
Higgins, Prof. Henry 102
Holbrook, Clyde 46, 48–9, 53 n.58, 75 n.1
Holmes, Stephen 16ff., 22, 23 n.32

idealism 1, 7
imputation of Christ's righteousness 137–40
imputation of sin, *see* original sin
infralapsarianism 5ff., 15, 22

Jenson, Robert 24 n.35, 75 n.1

Kearney, John 46, 48–9, 54, 64, 76 n.27, 94 n.30

Locke, John 33, 35–9, 41, 52 n.34, 98, 102, 117, 125
Lowe, E.J. 52 n.45, 110 n.2

MacDonald, Scott 25, 51 n.4
McCann, Hugh 95 n.34, 135 n.2
Malebranche, Nicholas 102
Mann, William 71, 78 n.48, 92, 95 n.33
Mind, The 38, 109
Minkema, Kenneth vii, 140 n.1

Miscellanies, The 7, 9, 14, 16, 17, 23 n.5, 30, 31, 39, 41, 42, 51 n.5, 94, 111 n.16, 139 n.1
moral agency 26ff., 28, 34, 62ff., 67, 68, 74–5, 87ff., 131
  moral inability 88–9, 91
  moral nature 29, 42
  moral responsibility 67, 71, 75, 77 n.40, 87, 89, 131–2

occasionalism 1, 3 n.4, 50, 53 n.73, 56, 74, 93 n.1, 101, 105, 108–10, 112 n.33, 128, 130–35, 138
Ockham, William 82–6
original righteousness, doctrine of 27–33, 36
Original Sin, Treatise on ix, 2, 27, 32, 96, 99, 105, 113, 116, 120, 127, 130
original sin, doctrine of 1, 25, 96, 103, 107, 115, 127
  imputed sin 96, 98, 101, 116, 119–20, 133–4, 137, 138
  imputed and/or inherited guilt 113 ff., 120, 121, 125, 126

perdurantism 104–7, 108–9, 116ff., 121, 127, 128, 134, 137–8, 139
Plantinga, Alvin 82–7, 92, 93 n.10
  see also double dutch
predestination 22
primal sin 25, 26, 29, 44, 45, 122

principle of alternate possibilities 70, 72

Quinn, Philip 112 n.34, 128 n.4, 132–3, 135 n.4, 140 n.5

Ramsey, Paul 4 n.7, 35
redemption, doctrine of 18–19, 20
reprobation 12, 15, 20, 21

secret and revealed will 79ff., 90, 91
self-deception 43–5
Smith, John E. 39
Storms, Samuel 3 n.5, 75 n.1, 76 n.28, 112 n.29, 128 n.23
supralapsarianism 5ff., 15, 20, 21, 22, 140
Swinburne, Richard 44, 45, 50 n.1, 119, 128 n.17

temporal parts, doctrine of 96–7, 99, 100, 103, 104, 110, 123
temptation 32
theodicy 22, 25
Turretin, Francis 22 n.1, 24 n.33, 79, 93 n.3

van Inwagen, Peter 50 n.3, 73, 78 n.52

Wainwright, William vii, 49, 53 n.72, 54, 57–8, 62, 63, 69, 75 n.1, 76 n.14, 81, 87, 89, 92, 113ff., 119, 126, 129 n.28, 134
Whitby, Daniel 83, 94 n.19